The RFP Process

THE RFP PROCESS

Effective Management of the Acquisition of Library Materials

Frances C. Wilkinson

Connie Capers Thorson

1998
Libraries Unlimited, Inc.
Englewood, Colorado

Portions of the article "The RFP Process: Rational, Educational, Necessary" appear throughout this work. Reprinted from *Library Acquistions: Practice & Theory*, 19, Frances C. Wilkinson and Connie Capers Thorson, "The RFP Process: Rational, Educational, Necessary," 251-268, 1995, with permission from Elsevier Science Ltd., The Boulevard, Langford Lane, Kidlington, Oxford OX5 1GB, United Kingdom.

Libraries Unlimited, Inc.
P.O. Box 6633
Englewood, CO 80155-6633
1-800-237-6124
www.lu.com

Production Editor: Kevin W. Perizzolo
Copy Editor: Jan Krygier
Proofreader: Felicity Tucker
Indexer: Linda Running Bentley
Typesetter: Michael Florman

Library of Congress Cataloging-in-Publication Data

Wilkinson, Frances C.
    The RFP process : effective management of the acquisition of
library materials / Frances C. Wilkinson, Connie Capers Thorson.
    xix, 199 p. 19x26 cm.
    Includes bibliographical references and index.
    ISBN 1-56308-481-3
    1. Acquisitions (Libraries)--United States. 2. Books--United
States--Purchasing. 3. Library fittings and supplies--United
States--Purchasing. 4. Requests for proposals (Public contracts)--
United States. I. Thorson, Connie Capers, 1940-   . II. Title.
Z689.5.U6W55 1998
025.2'3--dc21   98-19280
                                        CIP

To my mother, who was a librarian;
to my daughter, who is not one;
and to all my friends and colleagues who have
helped me to be a better one.
—Fran

To Jim Thorson.
—Connie

Contents

Part I: Preliminary Considerations

Part II: Writing the RFP

Part III: Writing the Subject-Specific RFP

Part IV: Evaluation, Implementation, and Follow-Up

Part V: The Vendor Perspective

Preface

The tenets put forth in this book were tested during actual Request for Proposal (RFP) cycles at the University of New Mexico General Library (UNMGL) in Albuquerque. Consequently, much of the information presented relies on the experience of UNMGL librarians. UNM is a Research I institution, and the General Library is a member of the Association of Research Libraries (ARL), a national organization of more than 100 of the largest research libraries in the United States and Canada. The budgets for library materials at UNM are substantial, and with the current staffing levels, buying all materials directly from the publishers would be impossible. However, many of the recommendations for using the RFP process made herein are equally valuable for libraries with smaller budgets as libraries are always trying to make the best use of their funds. Using vendors for both book and serial acquisitions makes the best use of staff time and gives the library the opportunity to take advantage of various discounts that vendors offer.

The authors and contributors of this book rely on examples and experiences gained from the UNMGL's participation in several RFP cycles. This is especially evident in chapter 6, which is a case study of the RFP for the Brazilian approval plan at the UNMGL.

The UNMGL purchases materials in a large number of subjects to support the University's many master's degree and doctoral programs as well as to uphold its status as a Research I institution. Determining exactly what RFPs were going to be written became, consequently, another significant part of the RFP process. These determinations are equally significant for smaller libraries with more limited budgets because these groupings can make a difference in discount rates and service charges. Often vendors require a certain level of spending to secure their best discounts or lowest service charges. Those with modest budgets might need to consider putting all their dollars with one vendor to get the most for their money.

Libraries have traditionally grouped materials with like format (e.g., books, serials, and music scores) or materials produced in particular places (e.g., Mexico, Europe, and Africa), but these can also be combined. For the UNMGL's purposes, it seemed best to divide the RFPs into foreign and domestic, then, in most cases, by material. Thus, RFPs were developed for United States and Canadian approval plans with specific questions about university press plans and coupled with United States and Canadian standing orders; for United Kingdom approval plans; for United States and Canadian periodicals and serials; for Continental European serials and standing orders; for United Kingdom serials and standing orders; for art exhibition catalogs; for Mexican materials; and for Brazilian materials. There were, of course, similarities in some sections of the RFP, but the questions were tailored to the specific needs of each request.

The UNMGL decision is but one possible option for grouping materials. Although the following chapters generally use this method, each library will have to consider its unique situation carefully when determining the best combination for its RFP(s).

Acknowledgments

The authors wish to acknowledge their colleagues in the Acquisitions, Serials, Collection Development, and Systems Departments at the University of New Mexico General Library (UNMGL). Their impressive team spirit and support of the RFP process at the UNMGL made the process a resounding success! It was the RFP process at the UNMGL that inspired the authors to write this book, which will, it is hoped, assist others with the process. We also wish to acknowledge the contributing authors for their willingness to share their expertise; also the vendors, of course, without whom there would be no RFP process.

In addition, Fran wishes to acknowledge several people in particular for their exceptional contributions: Carol Renfro, for her unwavering assistance and support in all aspects of acquisitions work; Gail Lane, not only for her editorial assistance, but for years of helpful suggestions on how to write in a clearer, stronger fashion; Darhla Gilson, for being the best office assistant anyone could ever have . . . from research to final production, her patience is legendary; Linda Lewis, for her continual support, good humor, and miraculous eleventh-hour assistance; Sever Bordeainu, who is finished writing a book, for structural and formatting tips as well as editorial suggestions; Nina Stephenson, for her exceptional reference and database searching skills; and Dave Baldwin, another library author, for his encouragement and "quotable quotes."

Connie wishes to acknowledge her new colleagues at Pelletier Library, Allegheny College, Meadville, Pennsylvania, as well as her many friends and associates in the Acquisitions Department in the UNMGL.

Introduction

This book has two specific aims. The first is to encourage libraries of any size and focus to go through the RFP process. The second is to help librarians and staff make reasonable choices in how to plan the process, write the RFPs, and evaluate and choose the vendor final selection. Although this book contains many specific examples of what a large academic library can choose to do, all of the examples can be easily and effectively modified by public, special, or small academic libraries.

Throughout the book, the term *vendor* denotes the seller or provider of materials to libraries, regardless of format. It should be considered synonymous with *agent*, *dealer*, *jobber*, *wholesaler*, *bookseller*, or whatever term one prefers.

The book contains five sections that deal with all aspects of the RFP process for materials in a variety of formats and languages: Writing the RFP for approval plans, serials, and electronic services; writing the subject-specific RFP; evaluating vendor proposals; implementing the decisions; and following up. The final section of the book presents the perspective of the vendors. The bibliography provides suggestions for further reading, while the appendixes provide a sample timeline, a sample cover letter, sample RFP questions, sample questions for vendor references, and a sample evaluation and recommendation form. Note that a sample letter to the Purchasing Officer and a sample award letter to the vendor(s) are not included because the institution-specific information required in these documents cannot be adequately conveyed in a generic sample.

Several chapters are written by recognized experts in their respective fields. Their collective experience represents many years of working with the acquisition of library materials and brings significant authority to their recommendations and analysis of issues. Joan Griffith is the manager of Electronic Products for the highly esteemed European firm Harrassowitz Booksellers & Subscription Agents in Wiesbaden, Germany. She was previously the director of Library Technology and Development (Systems) at the University of New Mexico General Library. Russ Davidson has been the curator of Latin American and Iberian Collections at the University of New Mexico General Library for many years and is an internationally respected scholar. Nancy Pistorius is the associate director of the Fine Arts Library at the University of New Mexico and selects materials for the fine arts and humanities. Linda Lewis has a long tenure as the collection development officer at the University of New Mexico General Library, and Johann van Reenen is the director of the Centennial Science and Engineering Library at the University of New Mexico. Ruth Haest is the paying team leader for the Acquisitions and Serials Department at the University of New Mexico General Library.

Part I: Preliminary Considerations

Chapter 1 presents an introductory overview of the RFP as it relates to the competitive procurement process and a discussion of its advantages and disadvantages. Chapter 2, "Planning the RFP," explains how careful planning can provide a timeline for the library to use to guide it through all stages of the RFP process, keeping it on track and on time. This chapter provides specific detail on what to consider when choosing the RFP committee, how to plan the timeline, and how to deal with the purchasing officers a given institution may have to work with. The chapter also considers the important step of contacting vendors who may want to respond to the RFP and arranging their demonstrations on-site. Writing the RFP, deciding how the vendors' proposals will be evaluated and contracts awarded, and planning for the follow-up process are all considered.

Part II: Writing the RFP

Chapter 3, "Domestic Approval Plans and Standing Orders," discusses writing an RFP for approval plans. It provides historical background on the evolution of approval plans and includes suggestions for handling the decision of whether or not to split a contract, as well as some questions to ask about additional outsourcing. The chapter also discusses the feasibility of having standing orders with the approval vendor. Chapter 4, "Domestic and Foreign Serials," discusses not only every facet of the RFP for serials but includes valuable insight about additional outsourcing and about splitting a contract. Chapter 5, "Library System Interfaces and Electronic Services from Book and Serials Vendors," offers up-to-date information and recommendations about what libraries should look for when assessing the electronic services they require or want. In a clear, comprehensive fashion, it discusses library systems interfaces, customized electronic services, security issues, RFP test transmissions, and emerging trends.

Part III: Writing the Subject-Specific RFP

Chapter 6, "Latin American Approval Plans: A Case Study," opens the section by offering a case-study approach, taking the reader step-by-step through an actual RFP process for Brazilian approval plan materials; the chapter also provides general information appropriate to acquiring area studies imprints. Chapter 7, "Fine Arts Approval Plans," includes recommendations on identifying and meeting collection needs for the visual and performing arts as well as writing the Fine Arts RFP to select a vendor to supply needed specialty materials such as art exhibition catalogs and music scores. Chapter 8, "Science, Technology, and Engineering Approval Plans," discusses the difficulties of finding approval plans for science, technology, and engineering and concludes that approval plans for these areas are possible and that libraries can benefit from the RFP approach.

Part IV: Evaluation, Implementation, and Follow-Up

Chapter 9, "Evaluating Vendor Proposals," discusses not only evaluation criteria but the importance of contacting references. Splitting contracts, negotiating, and making recommendations for the awards are also covered. Chapter 10, "The Vendor Transfer Process," discusses in detail how to deal with the process of transferring from one approval plan to another or one serials vendor to another, as well as comments regarding transfer-

standing orders. It includes information on planning the process, obtaining vendor assistance, executing transfers, and following up after the transfer. Chapter 11, "The Vendor Evaluation Process," takes into consideration why vendors should be evaluated and what factors should be considered after the new contracts have been in place for a while.

Part V: The Vendor Perspective

Chapter 12, "Vendor Interviews," considers library–vendor relationships and outlines the RFP process in depth from the vendor's perspective. It is written as if the vendors were together being interviewed on a panel and includes comments from Basch Subscriptions, Blackwell's Information Services, EBSCO Information Services, The Faxon Co., Harrassowitz Booksellers & Subscription Agents, Swets & Zeitlinger, and Yankee Book Peddler, Inc. The vendors share their insights and points of view regarding such important issues as the elements of a good RFP, information or questions vendors would like to see on more RFPs, the biggest mistakes librarians make when compiling the RFP, the advantages and disadvantages of RFPs, what makes vendors respond or not respond to an RFP, and other timely issues.

PART I

Preliminary Considerations

Chapter 1

An Overview

Frances C. Wilkinson
> Director of the Acquisitions and Serials Department and Associate Professor of Librarianship at the University of New Mexico, Albuquerque, New Mexico.

Connie Capers Thorson
> Director of the Library and Professor of Library Science at Allegheny College, Meadville, Pennsylvania.

Whether you consider [an] RFP to be a panacea or a plague, participating in the RFP process, either as a librarian or a vendor, need not be a painful experience.[1]

> —Bob Schatz and Diane Graves

In the late 1970s and 1980s, a number of states amended their procurement codes to include activities engaged in by state agencies not historically subject to such oversight. This was done in an attempt to make competition more honest and fair, and to offer more opportunity for local businesses, particularly those designated as "minority" businesses, to compete. Libraries, both academic and public, were suddenly subject to provisions that had always been confined to the purchase of dump trucks, pencils, and rebars. Acquisition librarians were abruptly faced with having to go through the same competitive procurement process that any state agency must for large contracts, usually those judged to be in excess of $10,000. Libraries often have such contracts with book and serial vendors. These codes generally allow for the purchase of any item from its publisher or copyright holder regardless of the purchase price, but, of course, since the early 1970s libraries have not been known for buying directly from the publisher unless it is the sole source or offers a significant pre-publication or standing order discount.

The Competitive Procurement Process

The competitive procurement process is most often accomplished via the Request for Proposal (RFP), Request for Quotation (RFQ), Request for Information (RFI), or bid process. This process affords all interested vendors an equal opportunity to submit a proposal or bid stating their ability to supply a good or service, for example, books and serials. In this process the rules and requirements are the same for all vendors; no vendor is given special advantage.

The Request for Proposal (RFP) "represents a formalized process for documenting, justifying, and authorizing a procurement; allows for evaluating different solutions; and provides a means for establishing, monitoring, and controlling the performance of the winning vendor."[2] The RFP should be viewed as a process as well as a document. As a process, it provides a clear, impartial method for a library to state its needs, evaluate vendor proposals, justify its vendor selection and contract award, and monitor vendor compliance and performance based on objective decisions regarding those proposals rather than solely on emotional reactions either for or against a particular vendor. In the document, the library's requirements and desired elements for vendor services are clearly articulated, as are the steps that vendors who wish to submit proposals to handle the library's account(s) must follow.

Fortunately, many states allow libraries to use the RFP process, which is generally done in consultation with the purchasing department of the library's parent institution. A less appealing alternative sometimes required is the Request for Quote, also referred to as the Request for Quotation (RFQ) process, in which awards are based on the lowest price bid:

> A request for bid or a request for quotation usually has a very specific role within accepted purchasing practices. A bid rather than a proposal process is generally followed when the precise specifications for a particular product may be met in virtually identical fashion by several vendors (for example, typewriter ribbons or photocopy paper).[3]

When a library contracts with a vendor, however, "what librarians are purchasing is a service, not a good."[4] The RFQ, therefore, is not a viable option for libraries, although it takes much less time to prepare and to evaluate because, in a true RFQ, it makes every aspect of purchasing library materials contingent on only one factor—the lowest price. All the other important factors that librarians look for in vendors are ignored, so services to libraries can be and often are very nearly nonexistent. Librarians working in states or institutions in which the contract for library materials is awarded as the result of an RFQ find such a method absurdly hostile to the best interests of the libraries and their patrons.

The RFP also differs from the Request for Information (RFI), in that the RFP clearly sets forth the library's requirements of the vendor and provides the criteria by which the vendor's responses will be evaluated. An RFI simply asks for general information from the vendor regarding its available services. RFIs are often valuable tools for a library that is trying to determine what it requires, prior to writing the RFP: "The less formal nature of the RFI allows vendors to present information about themselves without investing an inordinate amount of time in the preparation of the document."[5] An RFI can be used during the planning phase,[6] and can be especially useful if the library does not plan to include on-site vendor visits as part of the RFP process. The more general RFP questions located in appendix B of this book may be useful in writing the RFI as well.

The RFP is clearly the preferred method of finding the right vendor for library materials. Whether selectors or acquisitions personnel, those librarians responsible for purchasing materials need the reassurance that they are spending wisely. The RFP process can provide that reassurance. It gives the library the flexibility to determine which services it requires and values most highly. It allows librarians to consider all aspects of the vendor's service operation and organization, not just the discount or service charge. When the financial consequences are the only ones being considered, the possibility that a vendor might promise much and deliver little becomes real. The RFP makes the likelihood that a vendor can renege on the signed contract very slight.

This book provides a variety of questions for the library to consider when planning and writing the RFP. The process allows all vendors to compete for the library's business equally and fairly by providing each of them with the same operating rules. It "allows the library to evaluate competing firms against identical criteria."[7] Its purpose is to state clearly the minimum requirements of the library and to question the vendor regarding points that are open to consideration. The library must take care to limit its actual requirements to the points that it considers non-negotiable. Including "requirements" that are not mandatory may unfairly eliminate vendors and make the evaluation process more difficult.

Advantages and Disadvantages of the RFP

Proponents and opponents of the RFP process abound. Regardless of its many benefits, the RFP process is undeniably labor intensive and time-consuming. Numerous authors have pointed out its pitfalls: "Unless the library has the patience and pocketbook of the Defense Department and the stomach to put up with expense . . . the Request for Proposal process is a wicked waste of time and money."[8] "Another disadvantage is that the law is inconsistently interpreted . . ." and librarians are advised to lobby against the imposition of the process in their libraries.[9] Yet other authors caution that RFPs can be "badly conceived, constructed, and applied, resulting in few responses by vendors, and disappointments, lost time, and wasted resources for the library."[10]

Falling into a book-buying rut is easy. Having the same vendor supply the same kinds of materials in the same ways in response to some easily ignored profile not revised for years releases the librarians for other (but not necessarily more important) work. In addition, using the same vendors requires very little yearly adjustment by acquisitions and serials staff.

Although climbing out of the self-imposed rut requires Sisyphean dedication, proponents of the RFP process argue that the effort is worth it. It takes months to complete and more months to evaluate the results and changes made, but the collections are ultimately better for the effort, and that is what buying materials for libraries is all about. Rather than a process to be avoided or postponed, the RFP is one that every academic library, and many public, special, and other types of libraries, should consider even when not required to do so. "Choose competitive procurement by the spirit of the law, if not by the letter of the law, by making it a part of your own agenda before it is imposed on you from outside."[11]

Librarians need the opportunity to fine-tune and evaluate what they are buying and how they are buying it. They must ensure that they are receiving the maximum value possible for each dollar they are expending. They need a chance to learn what vendors have to offer, and there is no better way than through a controlled process such as the RFP.

Once the realization that the RFP process will be used sinks in, it becomes immediately obvious that the process will be extremely educational, supplying the library with broad on-the-job-training possibilities that rarely occur. In addition to the educational aspects, the RFP committee will have the opportunity to participate in vendor selection in ways that only technical services librarians usually have. Each section of the RFP can clear up what to some are mysteries or vagaries not to be disturbed or approached.

The single most educational element of the multiple-month quest for the right vendors may well be the presentation by each vendor who is interested in responding to the RFP. Having the vendors on site to demonstrate their products and services gives those doing the evaluating an opportunity to see what is available. More important, it gives the RFP committee members the time to ask questions and to really delve into how some feature works or how something could be done. The on-site visit allows for the follow-up questions that one cannot ask when reading a piece of paper. With the ability to dial into online systems now readily available, the vendor can reach a level of specificity that merely describing something with handouts or overhead projections can never approach. The visits by approval plan and serials vendors provide seminars on all aspects of book and serial purchasing for an audience that has a vested interest in attending the seminars and listening. The vendor visits also give people ideas for questions or issues that should be addressed in the RFP.

There are many other useful educational advantages of the RFP experience. One is giving the people involved the opportunity to write a long document to which other people must respond. Honing writing skills such as clarity of phrase and precision of language is important. Developing a long document that must be well written if it is to communicate the priorities of the library is an opportunity not often available to librarians and staff. Such a document differs markedly from a strategic plan or a collection development policy statement because it must reach a high level of realistic specificity, it must be about what is rather than what might be, and it must look to the future while being firmly anchored in the present.

Librarians are always evaluating something—computer systems capabilities, instructional programs, collections, job performance, to name just a few—but these evaluations are of themselves and the services they offer. Libraries do not often have the chance to develop an instrument that is used to evaluate a document describing an array of future services to be provided by some other entity. Having to develop such an evaluation instrument forces librarians and staff to articulate in very specific terms just exactly what criteria are important to them and to the library.

To read and to understand vendors' responses are also good educational experiences. Much concern today centers on teaching critical thinking skills in schools and colleges. Reading the responses from vendors forces the evaluators to consider each answer with an objectivity that is not often required. Fair evaluation requires critical thinking of the most exacting kind. After all, much hangs in the balance for both parties: The vendor needs the success of securing a large contract for selling library materials, while the library needs to spend its money wisely and get the materials it needs at the most reasonable cost.

Notes

1. Bob Schatz and Diane J. Graves, "Request for Proposal or Run for Protection? Some Thoughts on RFPs from a Librarian and a Bookseller," *Library Acquisitions: Practice & Theory* 20, no. 4 (1996): 428.

2. Bud Porter-Roth, "How to Write a Request for Proposal: A Step-by-Step Outline for Analyzing Your Needs and Soliciting Bids," *Inform* 5, no. 4 (1991): 26.

3. Joseph R. Matthews, Stephen R. Salmon, and Joan Frye Williams, "The RFP—Request for Punishment: Or a Tool for Selecting an Automated Library System," *Library Hi Tech* 5, no. 1 (1987): 16.

4. Barbara A. Winters, "Bids and Contracts: The State Environment," *Library Acquisitions: Practice & Theory* 15, no. 2 (1991): 233.

5. Frances C. Wilkinson and Sever Bordeianu, "In Search of the Perfect Cover: Using the RFP Process to Select a Commercial Binder," *Serials Review* 23, no. 3 (Fall 1997): 38.

6. Rob McGee, "RFIs, RFPs, RFQs, Bid Analysis and Contracts Part 1," in *Second National Conference on Integrated Online Library Systems Proceedings*, ed. David C. Genaway (Canfield, OH: Genaway and Associates, 1984), 254.

7. Schatz and Graves, 424.

8. Patricia Dwyer Wanninger, "The Sound and Fury of RFP," *Library Journal* 115, no. 21 (1990): 87.

9. Stephen D. Clark and Barbara A. Winters, "Bidness as Usual: The Responsible Procurement of Library Materials," *Library Acquisitions: Practice & Theory* 14, no. 3 (1990): 272.

10. Matthews, Salmon, and Williams, 15.

11. Winters, 232.

Chapter 2

Planning the RFP

Frances C. Wilkinson / Connie Capers Thorson

A man who does not plan long ahead will find trouble right at his door.

—Confucius

A well-organized and carefully thought-out plan is crucial to the success of the RFP process. Formal planning of all types has gained popularity in the last several decades. It has become an integral part of most library management processes and is especially embraced by academic libraries. Whether the RFP process is mandated by a governing body or is voluntary on the part of the library, a plan will keep the process clearly delineated and on track. The method by which planning takes place will vary by type of library. The planning recommendations contained in this chapter are directed primarily toward academic and research libraries; however, they can be adapted in part to fit the needs of many public, school, special, and governmental libraries as well.

The purpose of planning for the RFP is to provide a clear, realistic timeline that delineates the steps to be taken to write and evaluate a solid proposal that will lead to a contract award with a vendor whose services will be of greatest benefit to the library. The major stages of the RFP planning process include selecting a well-balanced committee, constructing a preliminary timeline, meeting with the purchasing officer for the library or institution, selecting vendors and arranging site visits with them, writing the cover letter, writing the RFP, evaluating vendor responses, awarding the contract, and following up after the award.

Planning requires one to step back from normal daily tasks to consider the purchasing process in its entirety. Busy librarians find it increasingly difficult to keep up with the latest vendor features, systems, customized report capabilities, and other services. Even with frequent visits from current and potential vendors, frequent monitoring of electronic listservs, attendance at conferences, and reading of current library literature, the librarian is still challenged to keep up with the latest information. With the exploding rate of current technology, last year's cutting edge may be this user's dull blade. A well-organized and well-executed RFP process, though time-consuming to complete, provides the librarian with the opportunity to gain increased knowledge of current options in the marketplace and to pinpoint improved vendor services for the library operation.

Selecting the RFP Committee

Planning is hard work, takes time, and requires competent, well-considered input from those who are involved in the process. Although planning may seem daunting, it lays the foundation for a successful RFP process; once complete, this will prove not only beneficial but often highly rewarding for everyone involved. The RFP process can be conducted by one person (and this may be appropriate in very small libraries); however, selecting a committee can provide a balance of ideas that is not otherwise possible. Therefore, a committee structure, if at all possible, is strongly recommended.

Selecting the optimal group of people to comprise the RFP committee is paramount to the RFP's success. The members of the committee will not only need to be prepared for its rigors, but, for them to provide balanced input to the process, must represent various library departments.

Depending on the type of RFP(s), the committee should include experienced personnel from appropriate departments or units. "[T]he library has to decide who should, or must, contribute to it."[1] Obviously, personnel from Acquisitions, Serials, and Collection Development should be involved in the process and form the core of the committee. These are generally the people who work most closely with selecting, reviewing, ordering, receiving, and processing payment for the books, serials, and other materials acquired by the library. In all likelihood, someone from one of these departments or units will be appointed chair of the committee, as these individuals and their departments will be affected most directly by the contract award. Systems personnel should also be involved because of evolving technologies and formats. Depending on the type and structure of the library and its management style, the library's director, assistant director, or designate may also want to serve actively on the committee as opposed to merely receiving reports on the committee's progress and recommendations. Finally, someone from Administrative Services may be useful in providing input on fiscal requirements of the library and the parent institution, which pays the bills.

The creation of alliances and consortia of libraries is becoming increasingly popular for a number of reasons. "There is a decline in purchasing power resulting from the fluctuating strength or weakness of the U.S. dollar, inflation of costs per title, and the increase in the sheer amount of information published."[2] Consequently, libraries are struggling to maintain a collection of the holdings a library's patrons may require. Cooperative collection development arrangements are not only increasingly attractive, but often necessary. In addition, larger accounts may allow for reduced service charges for serials or deeper discounts for approval plans and general monographic purchases. If the RFP is to cover an alliance or a consortium, personnel from all libraries involved will want to participate. Care should be taken, however, that the committee not become so large that it is unmanageable. "In general, the smaller the working group, the more efficient the process will be."[3]

If the committee is to prepare specialized RFPs, such as for Latin American or other area studies; Fine Arts; or Science, Technology, and Engineering approval plans, subject specialists or bibliographers in those areas are necessary and ideal members. It must be stressed that persons appointed to the committee should have or be willing to make the time necessary to serve effectively. Ideally, they should be knowledgeable in at least one area of the process, willing to learn about new services or technologies, open-minded, and able to work well together.

The committee will need to define the planning role of each member. Then the committee will have to make decisions regarding which members are responsible for executing which parts of the process. At the very beginning, the library must determine who will make the RFP award.[4] Will the library director or the purchasing department make the award based on the RFP committee's recommendation? Will the committee chair be authorized to work directly with the purchasing department to make the award, or will some other method be used? It is imperative that committee members understand clearly why they were appointed to the committee, what their role is within the committee, what the committee's role is in the award process, and the time frame in which they are expected to accomplish the tasks associated with that role.

The Timeline

One of the most important parts of the planning phase is the development of a detailed timeline that will allow enough time to complete each phase of the RFP process. (See appendix A for a sample timeline.) Adequate time must be allotted for each step to ensure the RFP's outcome. Allowing adequate time is not only critical to the success of the RFP but to the sanity of the committee as well. Generally, it is wise for the RFP committee to begin the RFP process nine months, or even a year, prior to the anticipated contract start date. This generous time frame will provide a bit of a cushion in case of unavoidable delays with some aspect of the process.

The timeline should be a dynamic document, open to frequent modification, especially during initial meetings with the purchasing department and the RFP committee. A particular phase may require additional time, forcing other phases of the timeline to be adjusted accordingly. Flexibility and adaptability on the part of the committee are crucial to the success of the process.

Phase 1 of the Timeline

Phase 1 is the preparation of the RFP to send to the vendor(s). This phase should include five key elements with established dates for each: (1) meeting with the purchasing officer, (2) selecting vendors and arranging site visits, (3) writing the RFP, (4) sending the RFP out for library review, and (5) sending the RFP out for purchasing department review. It is imperative to consider each element thoroughly and to allow enough time to complete each element. If any part of the process is rushed, mistakes may be made that could cause serious problems later. For example, the library could be forced to select a vendor that it feels is a bad "fit" for its needs because the RFP was written in a way that did not reflect its actual requirements. In cases where state or other regulations are involved, the regulations must be met or the entire RFP could be invalidated. Thus, for many reasons, the committee must pay attention to each step of the process.

Meeting with the Purchasing Officer

The first step is to meet with the purchasing officer assigned to the RFP, especially if the RFP process is required by state or other law. Generally, it is not necessary for the entire committee to meet with the purchasing officer; normally, the committee chair and one or two others is sufficient. If the RFP is being done by an alliance or consortium, it may be necessary to meet with more than one purchasing officer if members of the alliance or consortium comprise different types of libraries or are governed by different groups or bodies.

A preliminary meeting with the purchasing officer(s) is an opportunity to begin building a positive rapport with your contact person, which will be invaluable throughout the process. Present your tentative timeline and ask if it seems reasonable and what changes, if any, need to be made to accommodate the purchasing officer's needs.

Inquire about requirements that the purchasing department has for the RFP document and for the cover letter, which is sometimes referred to as the "boilerplate."[5,6,7] Typical requirements include a description of the library and its parent organization, the type of materials the contract covers, the dollar amount per annum of expenditure with a vendor for which a contract is required, the terms for shipping, the beginning and end dates for the contract, the number of years the contract will cover, and the evaluation criteria. Contact names, addresses, telephone numbers, e-mail addresses, and fax number, if available, should be included for the purchasing officer, library contact (usually the RFP committee chair), and the library systems contact, if appropriate. In addition, most contracts should carry a disclaimer regarding the dollar amount per annum, for example, "This amount shall not be considered a commitment to purchase but is intended to provide the vendor with an estimated contract value; the library reserves the right to increase or decrease the amount as actual needs determine."

The evaluation criteria must clearly state the percentage amounts that will be awarded for each category, based on the library's requirements and vendor responses to its questions.

> Usually there must be some amount of negotiation between the library and the purchasing department regarding criteria for evaluating bid responses and making contract awards. The purchasing department will be chiefly concerned about lowest cost, but it is critical that the library define the set of minimum acceptable standards which must be met before any consideration of lowest cost can take place. Only the library is qualified to do this.[8]

Once this is agreed to by the purchasing department, the library will set the criteria so that the most important areas carry the greatest weights. From the weights it should be clear to the vendor that the award will not be made on the basis of low bid; however, it is advisable to include a statement to that effect in the cover letter (e.g., "the library is not obligated to award the contract based on the lowest cost proposal submitted").

Finally, always keep your purchasing department contact person apprised of developments at each phase of the process and ask for advice as needed.

Selecting Vendors and Arranging Site Visits

The second element of the process is to select vendors to receive the RFP and, if the library desires, to arrange for vendor presentation visits. To ensure a fair RFP process, all vendors appropriate to your type of RFP should be invited to participate in the process. In addition to the issue of fairness, the entire RFP process may be invalidated if any vendor wishing to receive an RFP is not included for consideration. Thus, "for the competitive aspects of the RFP to be beyond reproach (and possible future legal action), the library will almost assuredly want to distribute the proposal to firms outside those with whom they currently do business."[9]

A list of potential vendors can come from a variety of sources. You should begin the vendor identification process by asking your purchasing officer for the names and addresses of all vendors registered with the purchasing department or the state to receive RFPs for your type of account. All those vendors must be included in the process. The purchasing officer can also provide you with information regarding required special consideration for in-state or minority vendors.

Another method of identifying potential vendors is to take a spin through your Rolodex or (if available) cruise your automated vendor file. This albeit nonscientific method may retrieve names of vendors you currently use and those who have visited your library, called, or written asking for business. Checking with colleagues in your library and at other comparable institutions or placing a notice on ACQNET or SERIALIST (or any other listserv that you prefer) through the Internet may also prove useful. In addition, you could perform a search for appropriate vendor Web sites and peruse various paper directories of vendors.

Once potential vendors have been identified, the library may wish to invite all of them to visit the library and make a presentation. If this is the case, allow them time to make arrangements for the visit. Depending on the library's time frame, a vendor may be able to arrange a visit to the library while it is visiting other libraries in the area, thus reducing the vendor's travel costs (costs that are indirectly passed on to the libraries it serves). Be sure to allow plenty of time for your questions regarding their services and for their questions regarding your needs. Also, be sure to allow plenty of time in the timeline for this stage of the process. Depending on the number of vendors making presentations and the number of presentations per week the committee can absorb, this process may take a month or more. The library may wish to consider inviting noncommittee members to vendor presentations for the education benefit provided, depending on the individual library's preferences and space availability.

Ask each vendor for the name, company address, phone number, and e-mail address for the person(s) who will be making the presentation. Outline briefly the type of presentation the library expects and the amount of time the vendor has for the presentation. Also ask what, if any, audiovisual equipment will be required. Follow up by contacting the presenter to confirm the date, time, location, and audiovisual needs for the visit.

At the conclusion of the vendor visit, inform the vendor representative of the types or categories of RFPs your institution is preparing, for example, an RFP for an all-inclusive approval plan or for just the University Press portion of the plan, or for all serials or just for domestic periodicals, et cetera. Ask that a letter be sent to the RFP committee chair stating which RFP the vendor wishes to receive, if the library is preparing more than one. This step will ensure that vendors have the opportunity to send a proposal for all contracts to which they wish to respond. The library will save time and paper by not sending vendors RFPs in which they have no interest. Also saved are costly errors and potential contract invalidation if vendors do not receive an RFP to which they wish to respond.

Vendor visits provide many advantages to the library. They allow the committee to meet with vendor representatives and, through personal contact, get a sense of the vendor's way of doing business. Also, information gleaned from these visits and their accompanying documentation may generate additional ideas for the final RFP document. These on-site visits provide advantages to the vendors as well. This "is the rep's best chance to make personal contact and pursue answers to questions that will help the company decide if responding to the forthcoming RFP is worth investing its time and resources."[10]

Obviously, the type of on-site visits discussed above are pre-RFP visits. Some libraries may prefer to receive the vendor RFP responses before the site visit, inviting only the finalists to the library. This post-RFP visit saves time for the library and cost for the vendor because only those vendors under serious consideration present. The post-RFP on-site visit is an opportunity for the library to further explore written responses it received from the vendor. This approach can also be used in combination with the pre-RFP site visit to clarify key contract points with the finalists; however, it is often best to do this via a conference call, e-mail, or some other less costly method.

Writing the RFP

The third element of the process, the actual writing of the RFP document, is the most significant exercise in the entire project. Because this document provides vendors with the only input that they will receive from which to construct their proposals, great care must be taken to write as clear and thorough a document as possible. When deliberating about what the library will require in the RFP and the questions it will ask of the vendors regarding the desired elements, the committee should always consider these points: What do we want today? What will we want tomorrow? and What do we want to avoid from yesterday?

The RFP itself will consist of several parts. The first part is the standard information added by the purchasing officer (described in greater detail in "Sending the RFP out for Purchasing Department Review," below). This statement precedes several sections written by the library. The library will prepare the cover letter and evaluation criteria as well as its specific requirements and the actual questions posed to the vendors (see part II, "Writing the RFP" for a detailed description of these sections).

Sending the RFP out for Library Review

Depending on time constraints and the size, type, and organizational culture of the library, the committee may wish to make the RFP draft available to the other library staff for review and comment. The committee will want to keep in mind that the content of the document is generally considered confidential until the purchasing officer reviews it, gives it final approval, and mails it to prospective vendors. Therefore, the committee may wish to make the document available only to a selected group of staff. Despite this caveat, the committee will find value in having others review the RFP. Committee members can easily get bogged down in various details of the document, making overall assessment for clarity and completeness difficult. Having other library staff, with a fresh perspective, review the RFP draft often generates ideas and suggestions that are invaluable to the success of the final document.

Sending the RFP out for Purchasing Department Review

The final element in phase 1 of the RFP is to send it to the purchasing department for review. Clarify with the purchasing officer the form in which the document needs to be prepared. Often, the purchasing officer will wish to receive one or more paper copies, and a copy of the cover letter and RFP document on diskette. If a diskette is requested, ask which word processing software is desired and which edition of that software is to be used. Most recent word processing software allows documents to be saved as other programs, including ASCII.

The purchasing officer will review the RFP for completeness and adherence to regulations. If the committee has worked closely with the purchasing officer, the document should pass muster without major revisions. In the event that some revisions are needed, you have already built flexibility into the timeline for discussing these revisions with the purchasing officer, negotiating and clarifying points if needed, and revising the RFP document. The purchasing officer will attach additional sheets to the RFP and assign a proposal number to it. A due date and time by which vendors must respond to RFP, a purchasing contact name and phone number, and the number and format of required submittal copies will be specified. Depending on the size of the RFP committee and the length of time planned for evaluation of the proposals, you may want to request two or more identical copies of each vendor proposal for the committee's use. Stipulations for submitting a proposal may include such conditions as the following: All information must be word-processed, typed, or entered in ink; corrections must be initialed by the authorized individual signing the proposal; and a sealed bid sticker must be attached to the sealed proposal envelope.

General terms and conditions may include information regarding acceptance and rejection of goods and services, addresses for notices, assignment of the contract, multiple awards, cancellation, changes and alterations after the award, conflict of interest clauses, discounts, requirement of financial statement, references required, governing law, indemnification and insurance, inspections, patent and copyright indemnity, penalties, proposed negotiation rules, termination and delays, warranties, and equal opportunity and affirmative action statements. If these areas are unclear to the library or vendor, the purchasing officer will explain them in detail.

The purchasing officer also provides detailed instructions to vendors responding to the RFP. These may include acknowledgment of addenda, alternative offers, cancellation, clarifications, copies of offer, failure to respond, late submissions, modifications, period of offer acceptance, public information, rejection of offers, telegraphic offers, taxes (materials vs. services), and withdrawal of offers. The instructions usually include a detailed statement of conflict of interest and debarment.

Once all documents are in order, the RFP and attachments are mailed to each identified vendor. The timeline must include sufficient time to allow the vendor to prepare a response to the RFP, usually 45 to 60 days. In addition to allowing enough time for the vendor to respond, the time of the year when the RFP is sent and the proposal is due is also significant. Generally, it is best to avoid setting proposal due dates either shortly before or after the end of the fiscal year or shortly after the December holiday season. These are usually the busiest times for vendors.[11] (See chapter 12 for vendor perspectives.)

Phase 2 of the Timeline

Phase 2 of the timeline is for reviewing and evaluating vendor responses to the RFPs, as well as negotiating and awarding the final contract. This phase includes four key elements with established dates for each. These are (1) receipt of the vendor proposals, (2) evaluation of the vendor proposals, (3) recommendation by the RFP committee, and (4) awarding of the contract(s). As in phase 1, each element must be thoroughly considered and enough time allowed for each. In phase 2, the reward for your efforts in phase 1 will be realized. The vendor responses that you receive should directly reflect the care with which instructions were written and questions developed. In phase 2, the library will select the best vendor to provide services to match the library's particular needs. Here again, for many reasons, each step requires careful attention.

Receipt of the Vendor Proposals

For a vendor to be considered, its proposal must be received by the purchasing department on or before the deadline specified on the RFP. The purchasing officer collects all vendor proposals, certifies date and time of receipt, officially opens them, checks them for completeness, retains one copy at the purchasing department, and prepares the other copy(ies) for the library RFP committee chair. They are then either delivered to or picked up by the committee chair or a designate and brought to the library for evaluation.

The committee chair makes a preliminary review of the vendor proposals, checking each copy again for completeness. Such supporting documents as sample forms, invoices, credits, claim forms, customized reports, financial statements, and other papers can easily be overlooked in a cursory check by the purchasing officer, especially if he or she is not familiar with library-specific documents.

The RFP committee then takes care to secure a quiet location where evaluation of the vendor proposals will take place. In most states where the RFP process is required by law, these documents are considered confidential until the award has been made. At that time, they generally become a matter of public record. Your purchasing officer will specify requirements in this area during phase 1 of your RFP preparation.

Evaluation of the Vendor Proposals

Once the library has received the vendor proposals from the purchasing department, the second most time-consuming part of the process begins. Adequate time must be allotted for each committee member to read and review all proposals carefully. Depending on the number of RFP types and the number and depth of vendor proposals, a thorough evaluation may require several weeks. The committee will complete, in painstaking detail, a vendor proposal evaluation form for each vendor and each type of RFP, with detailed statements to back up these evaluations.

Another potentially time-consuming task is that of calling references, usually three for each vendor submitting a proposal for each RFP type. Although this task is generally divided among committee members, it will normally take several days or even a week or more to complete. (See chapter 9 for a detailed discussion on evaluating the vendor proposals.)

Recommendation by the RFP Committee

After thorough evaluation of all vendor proposals, the committee must tabulate the evaluations from each member and discuss the reference responses. At this point, the committee arrives at a final recommendation for the contract award. If information about the proposals has been carefully and concisely documented on the evaluation forms, this element of the process will progress quickly.

The RFP committee's recommendation to the purchasing officer, written in nonprejudicial language, clearly states why one vendor was selected over the others. It is impossible to avoid some level of subjectivity in an RFP process as opposed to a straight bid; however, the criteria used to make the award must be clearly understood by all parties from the outset of the process and applied as fairly and objectively as possible to all vendors.

Awarding of the Contract

The purchasing officer reviews the RFP committee's recommendations regarding which vendor should receive the contract award. This review is done with an eye toward ensuring that all rules were followed and evaluation criteria were applied evenly and fairly to all vendors submitting a proposal. Once this is established, the purchasing officer notifies all vendors by mail of the award decision. The RFP committee should ask to review the award letters and contracts made to the successful vendors for accuracy prior to sending them out. Areas of the award letters to which the committee should pay special attention include the type of award, the contract start and ending dates, and the estimated annual value of the award.

After the purchasing officer notifies the vendors, the library may follow up with all vendors, including those not receiving a contract. Although a particular vendor may not have submitted a successful proposal during this cycle, it may be an attractive alternative in the future. A wise chair will treat possible future associates with respect and courtesy.

Timeline for the RFP Follow-Up Process

The final aspect of planning the timeline is plotting the activities that will occur after the contract award has been made. The committee will need to take into consideration the time needed to conduct a transfer process if the library changes vendors. The time frame for this process needs to be mutually agreed upon by the library and the new vendor. In addition, some flexible dates for an initial vendor evaluation project should be set. Ideally, this evaluation takes place months, or perhaps a year, after completion of the vendor transfer process. Although it is possible to make an initial judgment earlier, a truer picture of vendor performance data will develop over time. (See part IV, "Evaluation, Implementation, and Follow-Up" for detailed information regarding the vendor transfer process and vendor performance evaluation.)

Notes

1. Bob Schatz and Diane J. Graves, "Request for Proposal or Run for Protection? Some Thoughts on RFPs from a Librarian and a Bookseller," *Library Acquisitions: Practice & Theory* 20, no. 4 (1996): 422.

2. Suzanne Freeman and Barbara A. Winters, "Journeymen of the Printing Office," in *Legal and Ethical Issues in Acquisitions*, ed. Katina Strauch and Bruce Strauch (Binghamton, NY: The Haworth Press, 1990), 87.

3. Joseph R. Matthews, Stephen R. Salmon, and Joan Frye Williams, "The RFP—Request for Punishment: Or a Tool for Selecting an Automated Library System," *Library Hi Tech* 5, no. 1 (1987): 17.

4. Schatz and Graves, 422.

5. Rob McGee, "RFIs, RFPs, RFQs, Bid Analysis and Contracts Part 1," in *Second National Conference on Integrated Online Library Systems Proceedings*, ed. David C. Genaway (Canfield, OH: Genaway and Associates, 1984), 256.

6. Michael L. Thomas, "You Only Get What You Ask For? Tips on Writing the RFP," *Inform* 5, no. 3 (1991): 30.

7. Arnold Hirshon and Barbara A. Winters, *Outsourcing Library Technical Services: A How-to-Do-It Manual for Librarians* (New York: Neal-Schuman, 1996), 59–67.

8. Frank Dowd, "Awarding Acquisitions Contracts by Bid or the Perils and Rewards of Shopping by Mail," *Acquisitions Librarian* 5 (1991): 66.

9. Schatz and Graves, 423.

10. Stuart Glogoff, "Reflections on Dealing with Vendors," *American Libraries* 25, no. 4 (1994): 313.

11. Matthews, Salmon, and Williams, 18.

PART II

Writing the RFP

Chapter 3

Domestic Approval Plans and Standing Orders

Frances C. Wilkinson / Connie Capers Thorson

Can anybody remember when the times were not hard and money not scarce?

—Ralph Waldo Emerson

Many libraries reserve the largest portion of their book budget for approval plans, quite probably because of the erosion of library funding in the last decade—there simply are not enough librarians available to select materials. "Approval plans have grown, amongst other reasons, because they are perceived as largely consistent ways of guaranteeing the growth of a core collection."[1] An approval plan also provides a reasonable way to spend the large part of a book budget that is reserved for new publications in a wide range of subject areas. Having these materials arrive in the library with minimal fuss allows librarians to exert their collection development efforts on other tasks such as locating regional and local ephemera; reading rare or out-of-print dealers' catalogs; chasing down esoteric foreign publications comparing, for example, the agrarian revolts in the Caucasus in 1458 and 1543; and suffering over which periodicals to cancel next.

This chapter discusses the RFP process to select vendors for purchasing books—domestic (United States) approval plans and standing orders. In addition to standing orders, which can be included in the RFP for either books or serials, a library can write monographic RFPs for the purchase of firm orders (books ordered on a title-by-title basis) as well as approval plans. Many libraries choose to combine firm order purchasing with approval plans[2] in one RFP. The firm order RFP may be viewed as a subset of the approval plan RFP, because the approval plan RFP is clearly more complicated due to such factors as subject parameters and profile construction. Although it is the approval plan RFP that is discussed in this chapter, librarians can easily modify these specifications to fit firm order RFPs as needed.

The level of specificity that a library can reach with an approval plan is an equally important reason for relying on them.[3] The specificity can occur in several places: publishers, subjects, and nonsubject parameters. The approval plan that is designed for all kinds of materials published by all kinds of publishers is perhaps the hardest one to maintain. However, the more money a library has, the more useful this kind of plan can be. For libraries that are in straitened financial circumstances, a university press plan coupled with a science/technology plan or a trade publisher plan might be the most easily developed and provide the greatest benefits. These plans give the library the opportunity to expand the subject parameters while excluding some publishers or titles distributed by publishers for other entities. Other monograph plans might include those for everything a publisher or a group of publishers releases on particular topics. These would not be quite blanket order plans, as some latitude for returns is usually possible. The point worth remembering is that the RFP must focus on exactly what the library has in mind, even if the end result is not decided until vendors have responded. Probably the best course of action is to exclude nothing at the beginning. For example, if a university press plan, coupled with a science/technology plan, is a real possibility, the RFP should make this option clear. Conversely, however, if the library is only going to consider large comprehensive plans, the RFP needs to state this as well.

The use of an approval plan is a convenient way to bring new and relevant materials into the library with relative ease, but it will work only if the RFP committee has taken the time and effort to customize it to the library's specific needs. Thus, writing the RFP for approval plans demands significant effort.[4] Sections to consider for the RFP range from invoicing and discount rates to profiling and title selection. First, however, those on the RFP committee who have no experience with approval plans should receive a brief history of them. Following this historical perspective, the entire committee should discuss whether to opt for a consolidated plan or several plans. Then it must develop specific language for the cover letter.

The Evolution of Approval Plans

Approval plans have a relatively short history, emerging in the latter half of the 20th century. An "approval plan provides a group of books that have been prescreened and gathered together for a library so that selection can be made with the book in hand."[5] Approval plans work in two ways. They provide both physical books for consideration and bibliographic forms, which the library completes and returns to the vendor when selecting a title.

Approval plans did not develop, however, until after blanket order plans, first used by the military for purchasing supplies.[6] Blanket orders imply a less malleable acquisitions program as by definition they are designed to encompass numerous, broad subject areas or geographic areas (more common among European vendors) or everything issued by a given publisher (more common among U.S. vendors), and generally do not allow libraries the option of rejecting titles. Although the term *blanket order* means different things to different vendors, blanket order plans are basically considered the opposite of title-by-title ordering:

> The concept of "blanket" procurement reflected the act of literally throwing a blanket over the books and tying off the ends to make a big bundle that is then sent across the ocean. Its success still depends on the ability of the agent or vendor to differentiate between titles of interest to an academic audience and the rest.[7]

Other ways of collecting materials soon followed,[8] but not until Richard Abel (whom many librarians consider to be the father of the approval plan) appeared on the scene did approval plans really come into their own. The early 1960s was a prosperous time for academic and research libraries. They were flooded with both federal and local funding to purchase large numbers of books but, unfortunately, did not have the support staff to handle the workload. Richard Abel offered an approval plan to these libraries, whereby all currently published books from trade and university presses, tailored to fit the profile of needs of each library, were sent to them for one month on approval. The library returned the books it did not want and paid for the rest on one invoice. Services were gradually expanded to include the publications of societies, small institutions, and conference proceedings, as well as titles from the United Kingdom and even standing order programs.

In the 1970s, the outpouring of federal monies slowed, and other factors came into play, leading to the demise of the Richard Abel Company.[9] Librarians became skeptical of approval plans because of the negative consequences resulting from the demise of the company. At the same time, many had grown dependent on approval plans and did not have the staff to return to an entirely title-by-title selection operation even if they wanted to. Fortunately, there were existing vendors to turn to for approval plans, and many new ones sprung up, often staffed by former Abel employees. Although approval plans were both scorned and praised by librarians during this period[10] (and since!), by the late 1970s and early 1980s it became clear that the approval plan was regarded as a reliable and efficient tool to assist librarians with collection development.[11]

As librarianship moves into the next century, approval plans seem to have a secure future. Many libraries avail themselves of the services—everything from books and financial reports to cataloging records and binding—because of cuts in personnel. They also need to spend their library materials budgets as wisely and responsibly as possible. One very important component in the success of any approval plan is the role automation plays. "Through creative applications of automated processes, the potential of the approval plan can be realized: gathering together all materials that could interest the customer, the vendor allows the customer to make collection decisions based on the actual book."[12]

Vendor Consolidation Versus Splitting the Contract

Before writing the RFP, the RFP committee must consider the advantages and disadvantages of consolidating approval plans with one vendor versus splitting awards among several vendors. The advantages for consolidating all approval plans with one vendor are obvious. There is only one profile to create, one set of vendor procedures to follow and systems configurations to consider, and one customer service and one sales representative with whom to deal. In addition, the discount offered is generally greater for larger accounts. The decision to split the award will require greater consideration.

Possibly one of the best reasons for splitting the award is to obtain selection expertise in a specific subject or geographic area. For example, because Latin American materials are very difficult to acquire in any comprehensive way, the library may decide that using a vendor with proven experience in supplying materials from one or more Latin American countries is essential. This expertise should be obvious from the responses to the RFP. Designing an approval plan for specific subjects in this limited geographic area would be worthwhile (see chapter 6). Acquiring materials for the fine arts, such as art exhibition catalogs or music scores, may also lend itself to using an approval plan vendor with the capability to supply these materials in a comprehensive fashion (see chapter 7). Science/technology and engineering plans are available through publishers and even through major vendors or specialty vendors, although they take a lot of monitoring and careful development[13] (see chapter 8).

In deciding whether to split an award, the RFP committee must weigh several additional factors. It is possible that, among interdisciplinary materials, items might be missed or duplicated; for example, would a catalog of an exhibition of Greek archaeological artifacts be included in an art exhibition catalog plan? Carefully constructed profiles will reduce, but not eliminate, this problem. Vendors may offer different discounts for various types of materials; libraries must estimate the impact of the discounts on their individual budgets. It goes without saying that a split award means dealing with two or more vendors, each having specific methods of handling invoices, returns, problems, and profiling, which may create more work for acquisitions staff.[14]

The split most likely to reap benefits for the library wanting broad, subject-based approval plans is that between university press and trade publisher. The choice may not be the same for all subjects: Most areas of the humanities will want university press materials first, while the sciences may prefer trade publications; the social sciences may need both consistently. All of these considerations need to be discussed so that those writing the RFPs can adjust their vendor requirements and questions accordingly, while considering everything and holding decisions in abeyance until later in the process.

In some cases, a library may decide to split a contract that had been held by a single vendor for many years. It is never easy for the library or the vendor to make such a transition; close relationships can grow over time. The purpose of the RFP process is to allow a library to evaluate vendors equitably and fairly and make objective decisions based on the proposals rather than solely on an emotional reaction either for or against a current vendor (see chapter 9 for information on evaluating the vendor proposals).

The Cover Letter

The cover letter (or "boilerplate") must include a description of what the RFP covers. The library must clearly state what services the RFP seeks from the vendor, for example, an approval plan (specify the type [e.g. domestic—trade and/or University Press, Latin American], countries, subjects [e.g., fine arts, science, or engineering]); firm order books, and standing orders. The cover letter must state the estimated dollar value of the contract along with the duration of the contract. It should also state the time frame within which the vendor must respond, along with the format in which it should respond; a description of the library and its parent organization or a description of the consortium; both the size and strength of the library collections as well as the state of library automation; and contact names, addresses, phone numbers, and e-mail addresses and fax numbers if appropriate, for the library contact (generally the RFP committee chair), the purchasing officer, and a library systems contact (if appropriate).

In addition, the RFP should specify the criteria to be used to evaluate the vendor's proposal. Obviously, the vendor has the right to know how the response will be judged and what the library considers the most important elements of the RFP. Being open about the weights and factors will impress the vendors with the seriousness of the exercise and encourage them to respond. Also, having the RFP committee members focus on the factors and weights assigned to them forces them to reflect on what is truly most important to the library.

For an approval plan, profiling and title selection and customer service are the two factors requiring the greatest weight, with computer-based services coming in third. These three factors might consume as much as 55 percent of the weights. The overall cost considerations should be no more than 10 percent, unless otherwise mandated by the institution's purchasing department, because vendors must realize that the bottom line is not the discount rate but the service factor. (The RFP should state explicitly that the library is not obligated to award the contract based on the lowest cost proposal submitted.) The remaining 35 percent can be divided among background and reputation of the vendor (company data), coverage provided, financial procedures, and bibliographic data provided by the vendor. (A sample cover letter with weights and factors for approval plans appears in appendix B.)

The attachment to the cover letter asks the vendor for preliminary information so that the library will know whom to contact with questions or information. The attachment also asks the vendor to be very specific in indicating which kind of plan the vendor is proposing, such as a university press, science and technology, or trade plan; it may well be all of them.

Without this information, the committee may find responses mysterious, or they may find that no vendor will entertain a trade publisher plan.

Writing the Approval Plan RFP

The first step when writing the RFP is to identify clearly what the library's actual requirements are; for example, the vendor's ability to interface with the library's Integrated Library System would likely be a required element. Any requirement made by the library must be clearly stated and fully defined. If a vendor cannot meet all of the required elements, it should not respond to the RFP. If an element is not mandatory, it should not be included by the RFP committee in the requirements section. Instead, the library may wish to have a section for desired elements. The questions asked may even reveal some elements or service components that the library desires and could genuinely benefit from that which it was not aware of when writing the RFP. Always consider how each question asked of the vendor will be evaluated later.

A variety of subjects are covered in the RFP. Each is discussed, in turn, below. Please note that the order in which the subjects are discussed is but one of a variety of organizational arrangements the committee may want to follow when creating the RFP. (Sample RFP questions for approval plans and standing orders appear in appendix B.)

Company Data

Any library considering contracting with a vendor for an approval plan should include questions on the RFP about the company itself. The answers the committee is looking for should provide specific data about the longevity of the company, where it is located, and the number of employees. When issuing an RFP for an approval plan, legitimate questions deal with how long the company has offered approval plans to libraries. A follow-up question might deal with the kinds of libraries for whom the company has provided approval plans and what kinds of plans have been developed. Asking for a list of libraries similar to your own, with accompanying names and telephone numbers, that the library may contact for reference purposes is also a good idea. Although those libraries provided as references presumably will provide a positive reference, it is worth the time to speak to librarians who have worked with the vendor. If for no other reason, the person can provide information about how things are really done!

Because selecting books and profiling them are such important activities for an approval plan, ask a question or two about the qualifications of the people responsible for doing this work. It is also important to ask how many people are involved: It takes both time and people to select and profile titles; too few people can make the process untimely.

Ask the vendor to include a statement regarding the financial condition of the company. This statement could be a financial investment prospectus, a statement of financial solvency from the company's major lender, or an internal auditor's report. A letter of credit from a financial institution also has relevance.

Profiling and Title Selection

The very nature of approval plans makes the section on profiling and title selection extremely important. "No library can maintain a successful plan without an adequate profile that reflects its current information needs and is continuously open to modification as budgetary or curricular changes dictate."[15] A profile that does not adequately reflect the specific subject needs of a library's collection is a profile that will cause dissension among the selectors or bibliographers, the acquisitions personnel, and the vendor. Selectors will see an inadequate profile as adding to their work because they will continually have to check up on it. The acquisitions staff will be irritated because they will be contacting the vendor too frequently, asking about some seemingly obvious title and why it has not shown up yet. The vendor will not have a chance to give its best service because it will be spending all its time putting out brush fires. A profile that is less than 98 percent perfect will be troublesome.

Developing questions that will allow the RFPcommittee a fair opportunity to understand exactly how profiling will work with the vendor will prove worthwhile. Librarians should require the vendor to have a representative come to the library to walk the collection development librarians through the profiling exercise. The librarians might want to consider seriously the way the vendor classifies materials. If it is based on a classification system such as Dewey Decimal or Library of Congress, the librarians might find it easier to indicate what they want included. On the other hand, a vendor-developed system might allow for more specificity and interrelatedness among subjects. Special profiles—perhaps one for novelists or poets or playwrights—might be very appealing to the selector for English and American literature. Having a description of (and perhaps copies of) the profiling tools or documents will be useful in the evaluation process.

The other profiling objective to consider is the use of nonsubject parameters. These parameters are often used to determine whether a book or a form will be sent to the library. A library may want a form on any title costing more than $200, or it may want to exclude completely or receive forms for all reprints of books or anthologies of previously published essays. It may desire books for titles in English but forms for titles in German, French, and Swedish. Some libraries have definite likes and dislikes when it comes to publishers. It may be that the profiling exercise will specify receiving forms from certain publishers because the librarians may want to exclude some publishers entirely.

Some questions in this section should focus on title selection. It is unreasonable to think that a vendor can be 100 percent comprehensive in titles it can and will supply, because too many items are published every year. Some of those items are ones that no library will want. In addition, some publishers, like professional associations or societies, will not deal with a vendor. What the library considers reasonable expectations should be decided, and the RFP requirements and questions should reflect these opinions.

Questions about the sources used for title selection and the degree to which the vendor monitors a publisher's credentials are important. If the vendor limits the tools used for title selection, the library will miss things it wants. On the other hand, having a vendor that will monitor a publisher's credentials can help the library limit mistakes in purchasing titles of poor quality. Many libraries do not want materials unless they are carefully vetted and edited by the publisher's editorial board. The library has responsibilities in this area, too, as it can tell the vendor not to supply materials from a certain publisher. Ultimately, however, the vendor must take responsibility for informing the library of questionable publishing practices. In times of shrinking budgets and high prices, libraries must get the highest quality publications first.

Coverage

Coverage, or the extent to which a vendor will provide a wide array of titles published by a large number of publishers, is important, but the RFP committee should not overemphasize this factor. More important in the long run is the quality of the publishers covered. Often, academic libraries in particular are interested in those materials published by university presses. Having an approval plan with a vendor that can provide all titles both published and distributed by university presses may be very attractive. If so, specific questions about university presses should be included in the RFP.

Materials published by trade publishers are also very important, particularly in the sciences, technology, and engineering. The RFP committee should ask for a list of the trade publishers covered by the vendor. Equally important to many academic, special, and research libraries are the publications of societies, associations, research institutes, and the like. Include pointed questions about these because their publications are often very difficult to acquire through a vendor.

Asking about the kinds of publishers not included can generate very interesting responses. Often, it is societies and professional organizations that will not deal with a vendor of any kind. This question can also provide information about the kinds of formats covered, which is very important in this day of expanding ways of distributing information. Compact disks, laser disks, videotapes, and audiotapes are often important to a library's collection. Asking about Canadian publishers is necessary if the library wants Canadian publications, even if only sporadically.

Information about how the vendor avoids the duplication of U.S., Canadian, and British simultaneous publications is essential. It can be coupled with a question about how the vendor prevents the duplication of titles treated within the approval plan. Unless the vendor can provide specific information about what mechanisms are in place, duplication may be a problem that will drive the acquisitions staff crazy.

Numbered series and sets need to be treated with caution because they can wreak havoc with standing orders if the vendor cannot differentiate between a library's approval profile and its standing orders. "It is incumbent on the approval vendor to identify whether a title is part of a series or a serial, since the decision made may well effect the library's receipt of the book."[16] Finding out about the vendor's standing order and series database is essential. Part of the information needed is whether there are materials the vendor will provide only on standing order. Ask a question about whether or not standing orders come as part of the approval plan or are handled separately.

Bibliographic Data

Most approval plan vendors supply a library with some sort of bibliographic form, whether it be on paper or in an electronic format. Questions about the forms, therefore, will be necessary. As it is very useful to have forms accompany the books, the library may wish to make this a requirement in the RFP. Selectors will often want to take one part of the form for future reference. Until a library is satisfied with an electronic shelf list, the slips could be used as temporary shelf list cards. Forms for materials that will not automatically arrive as books provide librarians with a convenient way to choose what to order. Asking for samples in the RFP is a good idea. If the bibliographic information is available electronically, questions about format, completeness, and the source of such records are in order. Electronic availability also leads to questions about electronic ordering and invoicing.

A different kind of question should be formulated to find out how the information is gathered for the form. Is the vendor using the cataloging in publication information or actually looking at the book? Is the vendor using cataloging information provided by a bibliographic utility? If a utility is providing the information to the vendor, would downloading the record as a kind of outsourcing be considered?

Financial Practice and Overall Cost Considerations

Although the final award of a contract will not rest on the financial practices of the vendor, questions about invoicing and discounts must be asked. Otherwise, the library will find itself at a disadvantage when negotiating discount rates. Although questions on some topics might be a trifle vague, requirements and questions related to financial practices should be as specific as possible so that misunderstandings can be avoided.

Ask for a detailed description of invoicing practices and a sample invoice. Ask for information on the procedures. You need to know whether it is acceptable practice for titles being returned to be lined off the invoice, the total adjusted, and the adjusted total paid. The library should require that the information on an invoice be brief, clear, and easy to read. Be certain that the vendor can provide the purchase order number for each title, if that is how you will be accessing your own order records, or, alternatively, enough of the title to make the item easily identifiable in your records. If exchange rates will come into play on any invoices, ask how the rates are computed and shown.

Request specific details on discount rates. Are all materials discounted at the same rate? Does the rate fluctuate? Negotiating discount rates is not always easy. Success may depend on how large the expenditure with the vendor is anticipated to be. The discount rates may go up as the dollars to be spent go up. Part of the negotiation may be contingent on whether the library wants to place some (usually large) amount on deposit with the vendor. It will also depend largely on the mix of publishers the approval plan will cover and the overall discounts the vendor will receive from them; vendors must receive discounts in order to pass them on to libraries. Ask for details about any exceptions to a given discount rate. The way the discounts are shown on invoices should not be opaque. Some vendors discount each title separately, while others take a lump discount at the end of each invoice.

Ask about charges for items needed on a priority basis. Does the vendor prepay the publisher of an item requiring prepayment, or does the vendor ask the library to pay in advance, which may delay fulfillment? How does the vendor handle items that the publisher says are nonreturnable? What other return policies does the vendor have? Shipping charges can be deceptive; ask for details about them. If the library has specific requirements for a shipper, those should be made known to the vendor in the RFP. Any requirements for a minimum annual expenditure should be explained. Some states will allow libraries to deposit funds with a vendor to take advantage of escalating discounts. Ask about this possibility.

Customer Service

Customer service is important to every library. Librarians need to know that there is always someone at the other end of the telephone or computer to help. Nothing is more frustrating than service representatives who will not return calls, who will not solve problems, or who cannot answer questions. You will have no one to blame except yourself if you do not make your requirements clear and actively solicit information about customer service on the RFP.

One of the most important components of customer service is the fiscal reports the vendor can generate for the library. Ask the vendor to enumerate and describe the fiscal management reports it will provide, and request samples. Ask how often these reports can be supplied. If the library has specific requirements in this area, they should be made known. These kinds of reports are often very useful for supporting requests for additional funds or for supporting the ways in which funds are spent. Some examples of useful reports are those detailing the number of books treated in each subject area during the previous fiscal or calendar year, the average costs of books in various subject areas, and the fulfillment rate and time period required for fulfillment in a specific period.

Very useful for collection development is the vendor's ability to provide lists of books treated in a certain subject area for the last several years. For college and university libraries, these kinds of reports or lists are particularly useful when a new major or program is being considered or when grant proposals are being prepared. If it is important that the reports be provided in an online format, this question should be asked. Some vendors are making their databases available on the World Wide Web, providing one level of access for browsing by collection development staff and a more heavily passworded level of access for use by acquisitions staff when actually ordering materials. Having this access allows library staff to see how individual titles have been treated or to verify dates and prices of publications. Some systems allow library staff to compile lists online and send them to a specified e-mail address. Receiving these reports electronically means that they can be readily passed on to subject bibliographers, faculty, or researchers. Anything that can improve and hasten the communication process is worth asking about.

Another group of important questions should be developed to find out about the contact you will have with the vendor's sales representative and the contact (customer service) person at the home office, who will answer hundreds of questions for the library. These are usually two different people. How contact is made, as well as how often visits or calls are made to the library, must be questioned (or specified) on the RFP.

The RFP committee should develop questions about the claiming of approval items and additional copies. If items can be claimed, it will make the processing of rush orders on approval a viable option. If such items cannot be claimed, the possibility for duplication rises significantly. There are times when items treated by the approval plan will be needed by more than one location in the library. This is particularly true when there are satellite libraries or when the special collections department adds current titles on particular subjects. Detailed explanations of the policies on these two concerns will be valuable.

Other kinds of questions the committee might consider are those dealing with automatic out-of-print searching, publisher's status reports, and the claiming of titles from publishers. Understanding how the library is notified of such activities is important. The time that elapses before each of these activities occurs and their frequency should be determined with specific questions. Also, ask about accessing this sort of information electronically.

Standing Orders

Many libraries place their standing orders with their approval vendors primarily because the opportunities for duplication between something treated for approval and a standing order are significantly decreased. There may be very good vendors, however, who do not supply standing orders, so a forced connection could eliminate these vendors from consideration. The library will have to weigh the options after receiving answers to well-considered questions.

Probably the most significant question is when a library can place a standing order. The library probably hopes that it can do so any time. When and how a standing order could be canceled is perhaps the second most important question to ask. Ask whether a standing order can be canceled at any time of the year and how long it takes the vendor to process the cancellation. Knowing the arrangements for returning volumes received after a cancellation has been completed is essential.

Having access to the vendor's standing order database can be worthwhile, particularly because it can provide information about the status of the series. Can the librarian tell which is the latest volume published, the next expected volume, the price of the latest volume, and similar questions by scanning the database? Because avoiding duplication between standing orders and approval plans is so important, questions specific to this problem must be included in the RFP. Duplications can be as simple as the same title or as complex as duplication between hardcover and paperbound titles. Asking for detailed information about how duplication is avoided is the best way to proceed. If there is no mechanism in place, duplication will be a problem. Also ask if standing order titles can be handled on a rush basis. Ask about the time lag between the publication of a new title in a series and the delivery of the title to the library.

It is necessary to ask if a unit of persons separate from those who service the approval plans would service the standing order customers because if the answer is "yes," duplication again might become a problem. This is also the time to ask if a specific sales or service representative will be assigned to the library to deal with standing orders. Make certain that you can communicate with this representative easily; this person would help with a migration from one vendor to another.

Ask questions about claiming mechanisms for volumes on standing order. Ask what the expected response time to a claim would be and how often the vendor will submit reports on outstanding claims. If electronic access is important to the library, a question about the provision of an online claim service would be pertinent.

Again, questions about invoices can be grouped in a separate section or combined with the questions in the approval section of the RFP if a combined document is sent to publishers. The questions will be much the same. The same holds true for management reports. Finally, ask in detail about discount policies and options.

Outsourcing

Outsourcing is defined by Hirshon and Winters as "the contracting of an outside vendor or agency to perform some aspect of its work (usually non-core mission related function) that the library is unable to or uninterested in providing for itself."[17] "Perhaps many librarians think of outsourcing as mainly relevant for cataloging activities;"[18] but there are many outsourcing opportunities associated with acquiring library materials. In this context, outsourcing is not new,[19] but "just a new name for a familiar process."[20] An approval plan is, actually, an outsourcing activity,[21] because the vendor is providing books (or standing orders) that the library once ordered on its own, title by title, directly from the publisher. When the vendor is asked to provide fiscal reports of all sorts, the library is outsourcing an activity that could be done, albeit with a great deal of time and effort, in the library. A variety of other computer-based services are available through most vendors (see chapter 5, "Library System Interfaces and Electronic Services from Book and Serials Vendors" for information about library systems interfaces and electronic services). Other acquisitions and collection development functions are outsourced, with varying and debatable degrees of success.[22, 23, 24]

Asking questions about the outsourcing of cataloging and other operations in the RFP may be worthwhile for some libraries. Vendors can often provide full MARC cataloging records tailored to a library's needs, as well as shelf-ready books. The records provided can be downloaded into a customer's online catalog, with the library's symbol added to records in OCLC or other bibliographic utilities. Also, table-of-contents notes are often provided by the vendor. However, books that have been fully processed and are marked so that they are shelf-ready are not considered to be part of an approval plan any longer as they cannot be returned.[25]

In addition, questions concerning any kind of activity now handled in the library that the library's administration might want to consider outsourcing in the future, can be asked in the RFP. Together with questions about specific activities, the RFP might include questions about costs and about whether the vendor would consider working with the library to provide locally specific information at some future time. Using the RFP to ask about enhancements the library might want several years in the future is an intelligent way to proceed. Such questions also let vendors know the library's considerations for the future. It is counterproductive to have to change vendors just because the library needs to outsource some kind of work the current vendor cannot supply. However, if the library plans to outsource selected activities immediately, it is more appropriate to write a separate RFP for outsourcing and award a separate contract for it.

Notes

1. Charles R. Wittenberg, "The Approval Plan: An Idea Whose Time Has Gone? And Come Again?" *Library Acquisitions: Practice & Theory* 12, no. 2 (1988): 241.

2. John H. Reidelbach and Gary M. Shirk, "Selecting an Approval Plan Vendor II: Comparative Vendor Data," *Library Acquisitions: Practice & Theory* 8, no. 3 (1984): 164.

3. See Karen A. Schmidt, "Capturing the Mainstream: Publisher-Based and Subject-Based Approval Plans in Academic Libraries," *College and Research Libraries* 47, no. 4 (1986): 365–69, for a reasonable discussion of the relative merits of approval plans based on publisher inclusion or subject specificity.

4. See Beau David Case, "Approval Plan Evaluation Studies: A Selected Annotated Bibliography, 1969-1996," *Against the Grain* 8, no. 4 (1996): 18–21, 24, for valuable information to use when evaluating approval plans. Many of these articles may help the RFP committee formulate interesting questions for the RFP.

5. Dora Biblarz, "Approval Plan," in *Encyclopedia of Library and Information Science*, vol. 56, suppl. 19, ed. Allen Kent (New York: Marcel Dekker, 1995), 21–28. An informative article that discusses the Richard Abel Company, its history, and the evolution of approval plans is Ann L. O'Neill's, "How the Richard Abel Co., Inc. Changed the Way We Work," in *Library Acquisitions: Practice & Theory* 17, no. 1 (1993): 41–46.

6. Biblarz, 21.

7. Biblarz, 24.

8. Biblarz, 22–24. There is interesting information on these pages about various kinds of cooperative buying plans and blanket order plans.

9. Biblarz, 24–26. See these pages for a discussion of the rise and fall of Richard Abel.

10. Gary J. Rossi, "Library Approval Plans: A Selected, Annotated Bibliography," *Library Acquisitions: Practice & Theory* 11, no. 1 (1987): 4.

11. Jennifer Cargill, "A Report on the Fourth International Conference on Approval Plans," *Library Acquisitions: Practice & Theory* 4, no. 2 (1980): 111.

12. Biblarz, 27.

13. See Gloriana St. Clair and Jane Treadwell, "Science and Technology Approval Plans Compared," *Library Resource and Technical Services* 33, no. 4 (1989): 382–92, for an interesting article on approval plans for science and technology subjects.

14. Peggy Chalaron and Anna Perrault, "Approval Plans: The Multi-Vendor Approach," in *Vendors and Library Acquisitions*, ed. Bill Katz (Binghamton, NY: The Haworth Press, 1991), 151.

15. Mary J. Bostic, "Approval Acquisitions and Vendor Relations: An Overview," in *Vendors and Library Acquisitions*, ed. Bill Katz (New York: Haworth Press, 1991), 132.

16. Dana L. Alessi and Kathleen Goforth, "Standing Orders and Approval Plans: Are They Compatible?" *Serials Librarian* 13, no. 2/3 (1987): 26.

17. Arnold Hirshon and Barbara A. Winters, *Outsourcing Library Technical Services: A How-to-Do-It Manual for Librarians* (New York: Neal-Schuman, 1996), 159.

18. See Gary Shirk, "Outsourced Library Technical Services: The Bookseller's Perspective," *Library Acquisitions: Practice & Theory* 18, 4 (1994): 383–95, for a vendor's point of view on successful outsourcing.

19. Jack G. Montgomery, "Outsourced Acquisitions?—Let's Meet the Challenge," *Against the Grain* 7, no. 2 (1995): 66.

20. Sheila S. Intner, "Outsourcing—What Does It Mean for Technical Services?" *Technicalities* 14, no. 3 (1994): 3.

21. Barbara A. Winters, "Catalog Outsourcing at Wright State University: Implications for Acquisitions Managers," *Library Acquisitions: Practice & Theory* 18, no. 4 (1994): 370.

22. The Hawaii State Public Library System and Baker & Taylor reached an agreement in March 1996 whereby Baker & Taylor would "select, acquire, catalog, process and distribute books, videos, music and spoken-word audio materials for Hawaii's 49 branch libraries." Reported in the ACQNET-L@listserv.appstate.edu. This material is archived for only 12 months, but additional information about the agreement is widely available in the literature.

23. "Outsourcing in Hawaii's PLs, Lessons, Unresolved Issues," *Library Hotline* 25, no. 44 (November 4, 1996): 1–2.

24. Conference Call. "The Outsourcing Dilemma: Polar Opposites Bart Kane and Patricia Wallace Debate the Merits of the Hawaii Model," *American Libraries* 28, no. 5 (1997): 54–55.

25. William Miller, "Outsourcing: Academic Libraries Pioneer Contracting out Services," *Library Issues* 16, no. 2 (1995): 3.

Chapter 4

Domestic and Foreign Serials

Frances C. Wilkinson / Connie Capers Thorson

Serials are remarkably like people in that they are born, change names, marry, divorce, have offspring, and finally die. Serials also have been known to come back from the dead and resume living, often in a different format or with a different focus.[1]

—Joseph A. Puccio

A number of factors are important to consider when writing an RFP for serials. These include the types and formats of serials that will be included in the RFP, the consideration to consolidate all serials with one vendor, the cover letter, the library's requirements, and the types of questions to be included in the RFP. This chapter will discuss both domestic and foreign serials. For our purposes, domestic serials primarily include serials from the United States, but could include some serials from Canada as well.

Considering all available options is vital to deciding the optimum course of action for the library, alliance, or consortium RFP committee. Although continuing with the existing division of vendor contracts may be easier, and even tempting, the committee should explore other possibilities to determine whether the previous methods of conducting business are still the best options for the library. Some libraries may consider slanting the RFP to favor a given vendor; however, this practice not only defeats the spirit of the RFP process, it may also unfairly eliminate potential vendors who could provide sound options for the library. This is not to say that a long, positive relationship with a given vendor should not be valued but, rather, that the committee should keep an open mind to other possibilities. This approach facilitates healthy competition, which is the purpose of the competitive procurement process.

A significant portion of the library's materials budget is spent on serials. Most academic and research libraries spend well over half their total materials budgets on serials, with many spending two-thirds to three-fourths or more on serials.[2,3] Serials prices have increased faster than the Consumer Price Index for the last decade and a half, with serials inflation generally topping 9 percent per year.[4] Even the cancellation of some serials, serials expenditures continue to erode materials budgets. Total annual serials expenditures vary with the type and size of the library, but generally range from a few hundred dollars for school and small public libraries to millions of dollars for medium to large academic, research, and public libraries. With such a large amount of the library's budget going toward the acquisition of serials, writing an RFP with maximum benefit to the library in mind is imperative.

Determining What to Include in the Serials RFP

The first step toward writing an RFP for a serials vendor is to determine what types of serials will be included. To accomplish this, the librarian must first determine what is defined as a serial for that particular library. General definitions for serials abound, and a formal definition that fits all libraries is difficult to find. The *Anglo-American Cataloging Rules* (*AACR2* revised) defines a serial as "a publication in any medium issued in successive parts bearing numerical or chronological designations and intended to continue indefinitely. Serials include periodicals, newspapers, annuals (reports, yearbooks, et cetera); the journals, memoirs, proceedings, transactions, et cetera, of societies; and numbered monographic series."[5]

Many libraries divide serials into two major categories, regardless of the format in which they are issued. The first of these is subscriptions (SUBs), which include periodicals, journals, popular magazines, newspapers, abstracts, and indexes that are generally issued daily, weekly, monthly, or quarterly. They are prepaid as they are generally regular serials publications ordered for a calendar year and for which the publisher has established the price in advance. The calendar year order is the most popular for public, academic, and research libraries. Other billing options often used are nine-month subscription terms for school libraries or multiyear terms to provide savings to such organizations as some corporate and special libraries. The second category of serials is standing orders/continuations (STOs), which include series and annuals and, with the exception of annuals, are often not issued on a regular schedule. They are generally paid on a "bill later" basis, meaning they are billed when the price of the item is known or when the item is shipped. Some libraries prefer to prepay for these items even if the price is estimated and, depending on the arrangement that the library has with the vendor, additional charges may be incurred at a later time. Of course, there are exceptions to the publication schedules and billing arrangements for both categories of serials.

The library RFP committee may wish to include both subscriptions and standing orders in the serials RFP. In cases where the library has no approval plan for a particular category, for example, European books, combining its subscriptions and standing orders into one serials RFP is common. In cases where the library has either a comprehensive approval plan or where the approval plan is divided into segments of publishers (e.g., one plan for trade press books and another separate plan for university press books), the library using a combined serials RFP will need to supply each approval plan vendor with a complete and regularly updated list of standing order titles to avoid duplication by its approval plan vendor(s). However, in cases where the library has an approval plan(s), including standing orders in the approval plan RFP, rather than the serials RFP, may be an option to avoid receiving duplicate copies of standing order titles in approval plan shipments.

Although standing orders are combined with approval plans for the purposes of this book, there is no right or wrong way of doing this; rather, the decision regarding which categories of serials to include in the RFP will depend on individual library needs and preferences.

Serials are produced in a number of formats. These include paper, microfilm and microfiche, CD-ROM, and the increasingly popular electronic versions. Although major vendors can handle all formats of serials, "in traditional . . . serials acquisitions rarely have librarians encountered the restrictions on purchase, use, and placement of materials which are now being seen with the newer technologies."[6] To assist librarians with these restrictions, many vendors provide services to handle various concerns regarding electronic format serials such as assistance with site licensing.[7]

Vendor Consolidation Versus Splitting the Contract

To better understand the advantages and disadvantages involved in the decision to consolidate all the library's serials with one vendor or to split the contract between two or more vendors, one should first have a basic understanding of the subscription agency/vendor business: What it is, what it can provide, what costs are involved, and how it operates.

A serials vendor is a commercial agency that processes serials orders for all types of libraries. It provides a variety of services for the librarian, including placing orders with the publisher, processing renewals, consolidating many publisher invoices into one or several vendor-generated invoices, processing claims, and providing a variety of specialized customer and electronic services. Vendors maintain detailed records and management reports for titles that the library has on order with them. Serials vendors are widely used by nearly all but the smallest libraries. Reasons that libraries use the services of vendors rather than going direct to publishers include (1) bibliographic expertise (especially in monitoring changes in ownership and distribution), (2) economy of scale, and (3) value-added services. Vendors handle one-half to two-thirds of annual serials acquisitions in the United States.[8] The remaining number results from publishers who will not accept orders placed with a vendor and librarians who wish to order some titles directly from the publisher to obtain a special discount or package arrangement not available from the vendor.

Unlike book vendors (wholesalers or jobbers) who provide discounts, domestic serials vendors generally levy a percentage service charge based on the type of serials on order for the library. Although some discounts are available from serials vendors for certain materials such as commercial science, technology, and medical publications (commonly known as STM publications), and mass market titles, service charges have been the norm since the 1960s, when most publisher discounts to vendors were greatly reduced or eliminated. This loss of discount applies to academic and research libraries, government libraries, and large public libraries; however, school libraries and small public libraries often still receive discounts because of the types of serials they have on order.

Serials vending is a highly competitive business, and the continued success or failure of a vendor is based on the relatively low percentage profit margin from which vendors derive their livelihoods. Vendors are constantly seeking new ways to attract customers by providing services that will reduce workloads in library technical services operations, thus providing a net savings to the library. This factor is especially important in an environment of shrinking buying power and staffing reductions. In essence, the serials vendor can be viewed as an extension of the library's staff.

The business has witnessed a number of buyouts, mergers, and changes in the recent past, and there is every indication that this trend will continue.[9] These changes have been of no small concern to serials librarians and, in some cases, have altered their thoughts about consolidation versus splitting serials contracts. The RFP committee will want to determine whether it is open to consolidating all domestic serials, or perhaps all domestic and foreign serials, with one company or whether it would consider dividing its serials among multiple vendors. Advantages and disadvantages exist with both options.

Consolidating Orders

Perhaps the greatest advantage to consolidating all the library's serials with one vendor is the reduction in service charge. This reduction can be up to several percentage points, especially if the library is willing to consolidate all its domestic and foreign serials with a given vendor. Although it is never wise to base a library's contract decisions entirely on price considerations, depending on the library's corporate culture or administrative directives, a reduction in service charge will be a greater advantage for some libraries than for others.[10] Serials vendors are quick to add that there are many other advantages, such as having just one customer service representative to provide one-stop (call, e-mail, or fax) communication on all aspects of a library's account from price/availability quotes for titles not in the vendor's database to complex invoicing/credit questions; in addition, with few exceptions, claims can be sent to one location. Another benefit of using a single serials vendor is its ability to produce consolidated management reports, such as an alphabetic list by title for all subscriptions sorted by subject and division, and broken down by country of origin, and lists illustrating historical price changes for all the library's titles.[11]

Using a single vendor for all the library's titles may be a more viable option for some types of libraries than for others:

> Small libraries and special libraries can perhaps work with a single vendor successfully. Their titles are limited either numerically, geographically, or by subject. Academic and research libraries, on the other hand, have more complex serials collections and may have better results employing more than one agent.[12]

Splitting the Orders

Academic and research libraries and large public libraries generally use a number of vendors. Derthick and Moran reported survey results from 74 members of the Association of Research Libraries and found that 99 percent used more than one vendor, with the average number of vendors used by each library being 17.[13]

Why do so many libraries use more than one vendor? What are the disadvantages of using only one vendor? The reasons appear to fall largely into two broad categories: (1) library preference for vendors who specialize—better service for different types of publications, such as type, format, and subject of material as well as geographic location, and (2) on adherence to the policy of not putting all your eggs in one basket—wanting to maintain a healthy competition among the library's vendors as well as concern over a disastrous vendor failure. For contracts in which both domestic and foreign materials are included, many libraries believe that their accounts are better serviced by vendors experienced with certain types of publications, such as country-of-origin (or at least continent-of-origin) vendors. These vendors speak the language, deal in the currency, and know the customs and publication peculiarities of the country, which are often seen as advantages. Vendors may specialize in particular formats, such as microfilm; thus, purchasing those products from a specialty vendor may also be desirable.

Perhaps the most often-cited reason for not putting all the library's serials business with one vendor is concern over deterioration of vendor service to the account, coupled with fear of possible vendor failure. These concerns are not only a reason to consider splitting the contract between domestic and foreign vendors, but also a possible reason to consider splitting the contract among domestic vendors. Although vendors should be considered partners with the library, and it is to their advantage to provide the library with the highest possible service standards, sometimes problems occur. Most are handled quickly and satisfactorily, but horror stories do abound. Services may slip for a variety of reasons, including reorganization of the company; delayed payment of subscriptions by the vendor to the publisher; and the slow processing of claims by the vendor within the often all-too-brief time allowed by the publisher, causing gaps in journal runs. Concern over vendor failures due to bankruptcy is genuine. Splitting the contract reduces the worry and limits the risk that such a failure will result in all the library's subscription payments for a given year being lost with little chance of recovery.

No definitive answers exist when it comes to the decision of whether or not to split the library's serials contract. Rather, the decision will depend on the individual library's needs and desires.

The Cover Letter

A clear, concise cover letter (or "boilerplate") sets the tone for the RFP document. The letter should include introductory remarks and background information about the library and the larger body that it serves or the consortia of which it is a part; this background information should cover both the size and strength of the library collections as well as the state of its library automation. The letter should conclude with a summary of major points.

Standard information to be included consists of the name of the institution sending the RFP; names of the purchasing officer and library contact persons for questions (usually the RFP committee chair and a systems contact), along with street address, e-mail address, and phone and fax numbers; the type of serials that the RFP covers; the approximate annual dollar value of the contract, along with a statement that this is an anticipated amount that is subject to change and shall not be considered a "commitment to purchase" amount; the period of time the contract covers; the date the contract will take effect; the number of copies of the vendor proposal required and whether the same number of exhibits (e.g., catalogs, samples) are required or if one set is sufficient; the format in which the proposal should be submitted; the person to whom the proposal should be sent; and the date and time by which the proposal must be received.

Stipulations for submitting a proposal may include the following: All information must be word processed, typed, or entered in ink; corrections must be initialed by the authorized individual signing the proposal; and a sealed bid sticker must be attached to the sealed proposal envelope.

The library committee should confer with the purchasing officer to determine whether any, some, or all of this information is included in the written instructions from the purchasing department and adapt the RFP committee's cover letter accordingly. In cases where the library is not working with a purchasing department, all of the above information should be included.

Two other important elements to include are (1) a statement indicating if the library reserves the right to use the services of two or more vendors if it deems the vendors' services to be equal and (2) a list of the factors on which vendor replies will be evaluated. Vendors have a right to know whether the library is considering splitting the serials contract. A vendor will take this into consideration when replying to the RFP. For example, different service charge amounts may be offered for the entire contract versus some percentage of the contract.

Types of Serials

The library should state clearly which type of serials the RFP covers. Does it cover only domestic serials? Does it cover both subscriptions and standing orders? Does it cover some or all of the library's foreign serials and, if so, which ones? If the serials RFP is to cover more than one serial type, the cover letter should include an attachment. The attachment should ask the vendor which of the above types of serials it is proposing to provide to the library. Of course, the vendor may well intend to propose a plan for all of them.

Evaluation Factors

The vendor will need to know the list of factors and their weight or point value by which the RFP will be evaluated. Determining which factors will carry the greatest weight is an important exercise for the RFP committee. These weights indicate to the vendor which aspects of the RFP the library considers to be of greatest importance. The library should explicitly state that "the library is not obligated to award the contract based on the lowest cost proposal submitted." Furthermore, it should indicate whether the vendor must give its "best and final offer" regarding pricing in its proposal, or if its pricing is open to further negotiations.

For a serials RFP, the orders, invoices, and claims components, along with the customer service, are the factors requiring the greatest weight, with computer-based services weighing in closely behind. These factors might consume as much as 80 percent of the weight. The overall cost considerations should not account for a large percentage of the weight, unless otherwise mandated by the institution's purchasing department, because vendors must realize that the bottom line is not the service charge but the service factor. Customer service is at the core of the library–vendor relationship. The remaining percentage of the weight should be assigned to the vendor's background, reputation, and financial stability, referred to as "company data." (A sample cover letter appears in appendix B.)

Format of Vendor Reply

The RFP committee should consider the physical format it would like the vendor to use when responding to the library and then clearly state it in the cover letter. A format consistently applied by all responding vendors will simplify the evaluation process. The committee should consider sending the RFP in both paper and computer diskette (ASCII) formats. The vendor can then respond to the library's required elements and insert its replies to the RFP after each question, using as much or as little space as is needed to fully respond. Thus, vendor proposals will be formatted identically to the RFP, and comparing the vendor's responses with the RFP requirements and questions will require much less effort.[14]

Writing the Serials RFP

Once the library has determined the serials types and formats to be included in the RFP, and whether it will consider consolidating all serials with one vendor or splitting the contract, the process of writing the RFP can begin. The first step is to identify clearly what the library's actual requirements are. These are the making or breaking points for an RFP and will be unique to each library. They include such key elements as the vendor's ability to interface with the library's integrated library system. If a vendor cannot meet all of the required elements, it should not respond to the RFP. Any requirement made by the library must be clearly stated and fully defined. If an element is not mandatory, it should not be included in the requirements section. Instead, the library may wish to have a section for desired elements. The questions asked may even reveal some elements or service components that the library desires and could genuinely benefit from that it was not aware of when writing the RFP.

Regardless of how the library wishes to proceed, carefully plan each question to be asked of the vendor based on the library's needs and how the answer will be evaluated later. The evaluation process is lengthy enough without adding extraneous elements. Neither the library nor the vendor is served by asking unnecessary questions. If the library is not clear on how a question fits its needs or how it will be evaluated later, it should not ask the question.

A number of factors are important to consider when writing an RFP for serials. Specifically, orders, cancellations, invoices, claims, title changes, splits, mergers, and cessation questions should be thoroughly covered, either as one or several factors. Ask the vendor to send samples of all document types that would be sent to the library, for example, cost projections, invoices, credits, claim reports, and management reports. The library should, at a minimum, include a sample list of serials titles that will be placed on order with the vendor to whom the contract is awarded. Generally, the sample list should include approximately 10 percent of the library's serials titles, and it should be a representative sample, accurately reflecting the library's mix of titles (e.g., humanities, social sciences, science, engineering, fine arts). Many libraries and vendors advocate sending a list of *all* periodicals to which the library currently subscribes.[15] This eliminates any guesswork on the part of the vendor and may net a lower quote for service charges for the account. (Sample RFP questions for serials appear in appendix B.)

The Specifications

When determining the library's requirements, desires, and vendor questions, remember three key elements: What do we want today? What will we want tomorrow? and What do we want to avoid from yesterday? When determining the questions to ask, based on what the library requires as well as what it desires, consider the criteria that will be used to evaluate the answer. A point system may be useful, with each factor or category having a maximum number of possible points and all factors adding up to some maximum total. Such a system will assist with rank-ordering the evaluations later. While constructing each RFP factor heading, also construct a draft evaluation form with corresponding headings.

Once the RFP is written and sent to those vendors who have indicated an intention to submit proposals for one or more of the RFPs, the committee has time to develop the evaluation criteria form in-depth. The effort that has gone into constructing the RFP will bear fruit during this process because the criteria that formed the basis for the RFP will now be reflected in the evaluation form.

Company Data

Any library considering contracting with a vendor for serials should include questions in the RFP about the company's background and financial stability. Most RFPs begin with a question concerning how many years the company has been in business. This question is meant to document whether the company is new and possibly unproven (although potentially innovative) or is well established and presumably a safer bet for your serials account. The committee is likely to find that almost all companies, through extremely creative and intricate means, can trace their lineage back to Adam and Eve. Therefore, more valuable opening questions might have to do with how many offices the company has and the location of the one that would service the library's account. Another question might deal with the vendor's staff size and the qualifications for the staff that would be working with your account. A legitimate follow-up question might be about the number and size of accounts each service representative handles. Does the service representative have assistants? If so, how are they trained? What type of services are they authorized to provide? The library wants to ensure that the vendor can provide timely service to the library, which is difficult if the vendor is hampered by overworked or underskilled service representatives. A question about what attributes distinguish the vendor from its competitors may also prove enlightening.

The RFP committee should ask a question regarding the approximate number of libraries the vendor serves, broken down by library type. Although most major serials vendors can handle all types of libraries, it is valuable to know that a given vendor has experience providing service to your type of library. A question regarding the types of serials for which the vendor provides coverage can be illuminating, even when the library is not currently interested in all the areas the vendor covers. Coverage may include subscriptions; standing orders/continuations; various formats such as paper, electronic, CD-ROM, and microfilm; and U.S. Government Printing Office materials, as well as serials from the United States and Canada, United Kingdom, Continental Europe, Russia, Latin America, and Asia and the Pacific Rim.

All prospective vendors should be asked to supply a minimum of three references. These should be libraries comparable in type and size to the library writing the RFP. If possible, one of these should be a library that recently transferred its account to the vendor. This will allow the committee to inquire about the vendor's performance during the transfer, what kind of special assistance the vendor provided to the library, and what could have been done better. The library should also request that at least one of the references use the same type of integrated library system as the library. Ideally, the committee can uncover and avoid potential systems pitfalls.

Finally, ask about the vendor's financial fitness in the form of documentation. Specifically, have the vendor provide a recent statement of its financial condition, an auditor's report, and a letter of credit from its bank. Also, ask if the vendor has ever gone through a reorganization, merger, or bankruptcy, and, if so, to describe it in detail.

Core Areas

These sections cover the most detailed aspects of the RFP: Orders and cancellations, invoicing, claims, and title changes. Developing requirements and questions to assess the vendor's capabilities in the above areas is imperative for a successful library–vendor relationship. The task may seem overwhelming at first, but when broken down into parts, it is more manageable. Not all questions suggested in this section will be of interest to all libraries. As technology advances and electronic data interchange (EDI; discussed in chapter 5) becomes more widespread, many questions of current interest will become unnecessary. The specific requirements and questions to be asked will, of course, depend on your library's individual needs. Whatever the questions, an open-ended question asking what other services the vendor provides in that particular area should conclude each section.

Depending on the library's type, size, and specific requirements as well as its desires, some or all of the following questions will be useful. The RFP committee may wish to consult with staff in the acquisitions and serials departments, asking them to draft questions for consideration for inclusion in the RFP. The staff that work in these areas on a daily basis are generally the best equipped to devise questions that reveal the vendor's potential for meeting the library's needs.

Orders and Cancellations

A logical opening question in the ordering section might be within how many days the vendor processes new orders. Follow-up questions might include these: Will the vendor provide confirmation that a new order was received; and how will the library be notified? How many days should the library generally allow before expecting receipt of the first issue of a new order? Within how many days after the vendor's receipt of an order can the library expect an invoice? If the vendor is unable to supply a title, within how many days will the library be notified, and will the reason be included?

Some of the questions in this and subsequent sections will prove unnecessary if the library has a specific requirement in that area. For example, if the library requires that the vendor provide confirmation within 24 hours of receipt of a new order, then the library will obviously not pose this as a question; however, the vendor will respond to its ability to meet that requirement in its proposal to the library.

A series of questions can be asked regarding the way the vendor handles titles that are ordered on a rush basis. Additional questions should be asked regarding the vendor's treatment of memberships, package deals, and titles that "come with" other titles. How the vendor will deal with a pattern of receipt of duplicate issues of a title is another possible question. Whether the vendor handles back issue orders, single-purchase serials, or sample issue requests may be a pertinent question for your library, especially if you are considering purchasing all your serials from one vendor. A group of questions regarding when and how a single serial may be canceled, as well as how the vendor handles the cancellation of all the library's titles in the event of a vendor transfer, is advisable.

Invoicing

Invoices provided by most major serials vendors contain much more information than the amount to be paid. Customization of invoices by the vendor to better reflect the individual library's needs is one of the goals of the invoicing section of the RFP. The library will generally have minimum requirements regarding invoice data elements, some of which may be mandated by its accounting office, especially if it processes payment via an integrated library system. The library may, however, have additional desired elements or be unsure of what other data element options are available. An opening question regarding the vendor's ability to provide the standard types of invoice information is appropriate. For example, can the vendor supply the following types of information on invoices and credits: Library bill-to/ship-to address, title, library-generated purchase order number, ISSN, period/volume covered, library fund designation, service charge or discount, and (for foreign vendors), price in U.S. dollars? Additional information the library may want to consider are codes for frequency of publication, notice of discontinuation or title changes, reports on delayed publications, and designations indicating that the prices invoiced are firm or subject to additional charges later.

The library should require the vendor to supply paper invoices in quantities specified by the library (usually three copies) if appropriate. If the library has an automated fund accounting system, questions dealing with the vendor's capability to provide electronic invoice options (on diskette or via file transfer protocol) will also be appropriate.

Various payment options should be queried. If desired, does the vendor accept credit cards? Does the vendor have a prepayment plan, and if so, how does it work? For example, what is the prepayment credit percentage amount, and is it broken down by date, such as the library receives a prepayment credit of x percent if it pays its annual invoice between July 1 and July 31 and a lower percentage if it pays its annual invoice between August 1 and August 31? Ask the vendor to specify the details of the plan. Another important question is whether there is a penalty imposed for late payment of an invoice, and if so, what the time period and percentage or amount of the penalty are. Conversely, is there a credit given for paying an invoice promptly, such as prior to 30 days, and if so, what is the percentage amount of the credit?

Foreign vendors should be asked how they handle changes in exchange rates between when the invoice is issued and when it is paid. Do both U.S. and foreign currency amounts appear on the invoice? Is there a conversion fee for paying in U.S. dollars?

The committee may wish to inquire about special payment options available for electronic journals and online publications:

> These may include pay per kilobyte; per view; per minute; local site license (straight out purchase); local site license (yearly subscription); remote site license; subscription per enrollee; subscription per corpus; subscription per institution; or pricing proportional to print purchases. Hybrid combinations of any two or more of these may also be inquired about.[16]

Claims

Claims and the method used by the vendor to handle them will determine whether the library has a complete collection of a particular title or gaps in its holdings. Claims must be processed by the vendor within the time allowed by the publisher, or the claim will not be honored. If the vendor does not make good on the claim, the library will either have to purchase the missing issue, paying twice for it, or have a gap in the run. The library also faces the possibility that the title may have gone out of print, making its price much higher if it can be located at all. How claims are processed by the vendor, within how many days, and how the library will be notified of the status of claims are vital issues for the library to consider.

Title Changes

Title changes (single titles that split into two or more parts) and merged titles (two or more titles that merge together to form one title) are of concern to the serials librarian. The library may know what it requires in this area, for example, the library may wish the vendor to give it the choice of whether or not to subscribe to the new title(s), or it may prefer to have a subscription to the new title(s) entered automatically. If it is unsure, knowing what options are available will help librarians make informed decisions regarding what course of action can be taken. Other questions may include these: Will the library be notified of exactly what the last piece of the old title to be received will be (volume and number)? When a titles ceases, what efforts will be made by the vendor to secure a refund for the remaining issues? Will the vendor notify the library of suspended publications, publication delays, and frequency changes, and if so, what mechanism will it use?

Customer Service

The customer service aspect of the vendor's service provides the core of the library–vendor relationship. The level of the library's satisfaction with the vendor often hinges on this most crucial component. This is also frequently the most difficult area to query adequately. Questions about the method the vendor uses to assign customer service representatives to libraries are needed. What kind of training or experience is required of them? What authority does the customer service representative have to resolve disputes or to assist the library with special services? A question regarding what assistance the vendor provides to negotiate site licenses for CD-ROMs, electronic journals, and online services may be appropriate. If the library staff do not find the representative agreeable to work with, can another representative be quickly and easily assigned to the library's account? Similar types of questions should be asked about the sales representative who will be assigned to the account. Few library–vendor situations are worse than those involving an unknowledgeable or unresponsive vendor representative. The library should ask how the representative can be contacted (phone, e-mail, fax, or through some other means) and how quickly the representative will respond to messages from the library.

Another major component of customer service is the vendor's ability to provide management reports for the library detailing various aspects of the titles on order, such as an alphabetical list; a list by ascending or descending price, fund, or country of origin; or an historical price list. The RFP committee will want to ask whether the reports are provided to the library at no additional cost and if there is a limit on the number of different reports that the library can receive. The library should ask the vendor to list all types of reports and combinations of reports that it can provide and to explain what each report contains. Questions should also be asked regarding the vendor's systems capability to allow the library to generate its own reports in-house if it chooses to do so. Another important aspect of vendor service is computerized services (delineated in chapter 5).

Finally, the RFP committee should ask the vendor what services it provides to facilitate the smooth transfer of the library's account to the vendor and, conversely, away from the vendor, based on the library's decision regarding the award of the contract. Will it send a representative to the library to assist with the transfer? Does it offer barcoding services to speed the transfer process? Does it provide for a lower service charge for the first year or some other period of time to help offset the library's changeover costs?

Outsourcing

Outsourcing is the contracting out of certain library functions to a private enterprise. "Few issues in the world of technical services provoke such intense reactions as does the issue of outsourcing, or contracting to a vendor for technical services operations."[17] Many librarians consider outsourcing to be a new concept. Perhaps they may even think of it as mainly relevant to cataloging activities.[18] However, using a serials vendor's services is itself an outsourcing activity. A serials vendor provides outsourcing services to the library by consolidating the library's orders, payments, and claims, and by performing price and availability checking. The vendor can also provide specialized reports that the library could not provide for itself, such as how the library's buying pattern compares with that of its peers.

As vendor and library systems become more powerful, vendors can add to the services they provide to libraries, such as performing serials check-in and ship-labeled, shelf-ready journals and magazines to the library, with holding information added to the check-in record by the vendor. Routing slips can also be provided. A wide variety of other computer-based services are available. Dispatch data (which is an EDI message from the publisher to the vendors) about when an issue was shipped and via what carrier (to prevent premature claims) are available on most vendors' online systems; some library systems can receive these data as well. In addition, some vendor online systems allow libraries to order sample issues, eliminating the need to contact individual publishers. (See chapter 5 for more information on library systems and vendor electronic services.)

Notes

1. Joseph A. Puccio, *Serials Reference Work* (Englewood, CO: Libraries Unlimited, Inc., 1989), 4.

2. This information was derived from the Association of Research Libraries *ARL Statistics*. This publication is available in paper format, and there is a Web site as well; the address is http://www.lib.virginia.edu/socsci/arl/.

3. Clifford A. Lynch, "Serials Management in the Age of Electronic Access," *Serials Review* 17, no. 1 (1991): 8.

4. Kathryn Hammell Carpenter and Adrian W. Alexander, "U.S. Periodical Price Index for 1996," *American Libraries* 27, no. 5 (1996): 99.

5. Michael Gorman and Paul Winkler, eds., *Anglo-American Cataloging Rules, 2nd ed., 1988 revised* (Chicago: American Library Association, 1988), 622.

6. Meta Nissley, "Taking License: Librarians, Publishers, and the New Media," in *Legal and Ethical Issues in Acquisitions*, ed. Katina Strauch and Bruce Strauch (Binghamton, NY: The Haworth Press, 1990), 72.

7. Frances C. Wilkinson, "Electronic Products Access for Libraries: What Some Companies Are Doing to Help with Site Licenses," *Against the Grain* 8, no. 5 (1996): 20–23.

8. N. Bernard Basch and Judy McQueen, *Buying Serials: A How-to-Do-It Manual for Librarians* (New York: Neal-Schuman, 1990), 9.

9. See Frances C. Wilkinson and Barbara C. Dean, "Who's Buying, Who's Selling, and What Does the Future Hold: CEOs Speak Out," *Against the Grain* 7, no. 4 (1995): cover, 18–20, for CEO opinions on these issues.

10. Jan Anderson, "Order Consolidation: One Step in Containing Serials Prices," in *Vendors and Library Acquisitions,* ed. Bill Katz (Binghamton, NY: The Haworth Press, 1991), 99.

11. Twyla Mueller Racz and Trudie A. Root, "Trends Affecting Vendor Selection: One Academic Library's Experience," in *Vendors and Library Acquisitions,* ed. Bill Katz (Binghamton, NY: The Haworth Press, 1991), 59.

12. Marcia Tuttle, "Serials Control, from an Acquisitions Perspective," *Advances in Serials Management* 2 (1988): 71.

13. Jan Derthick and Barbara B. Moran, "Serials Agent Selection in ARL Libraries," *Advances in Serials Management* 1 (1986): 19.

14. Bob Farries, "Developing a Request for Proposal for an Automated Library System," *Colorado Libraries* 19 (Spring 1993): 43.

15. Arnold Hirshon and Barbara A. Winters, *Outsourcing Library Technical Services: A How-to-Do-It Manual for Librarians* (New York: Neal-Schuman, 1996), 94.

16. Michael Jensen (Johns Hopkins University Press), "Money Talks: Issues in Book and Serials Acquisitions Panel Discussion: Payment and Subscription Models for Online Publications," *College of Charleston Conference, Charleston, S.C.* (November 7, 1996): 3:30–5:00 p.m.

17. Ellen Duranceau (with contributions by Karen Wilhoit et al.), "Vendors and Librarians Speak on Outsourcing, Cataloging, and Acquisitions," *Serials Review* 20, no. 3 (1994): 69.

18. See Gary Shirk, "Outsourced Library Technical Services: The Bookseller's Perspective," *Library Acquisitions: Practice & Theory* 18, no. 4 (1994): 383–95, for a vendor's point of view on successful outsourcing.

Chapter 5

Library System Interfaces and Electronic Services from Book and Serials Vendors

Joan C. Griffith
Manager, Electronic Products, Harrassowitz
Booksellers & Subscription Agents, Wiesbaden,
Germany

Automation in the library can take many forms, ranging from simple bookkeeping to full integration of acquisitions, cataloging, serials control, circulation control, and information retrieval. Hardly anybody is in very deep as yet, but some big dreams are being dreamt.[1]

—Daniel Melcher, 1971

We have come a long way since Melcher described library automation in his landmark work on acquisitions. At that time, library and vendor computer systems played only a small role in awarding the RFP. Today, however, considerations for systems interfaces and electronic services may well be the most critical part of the book and serials RFP process and will certainly play an increasing role in the future. As the business of doing business continues to change, both the librarian and the vendor must thoroughly understand their current system capabilities and specifications to communicate effectively about the RFP requirements.[2] One must understand the traditional book and serials business, and in addition, one should acquire an appreciation for the technical sophistication of computing environments. Online system environments can be multifaceted, homegrown online catalogs or integrated library systems (ILS) available from automation vendors; they can range from PC standalone versions to complex mainframe systems. A good source of information on the latest development in this area is the annual April 1 issue of *Library Journal*, which compiles the latest information on integrated system vendors in the library market.

Electronic services from vendors encompass a wider variety of technologies and formats than ever before. Beyond the library in-house computer system, consider how the Internet and the World Wide Web (WWW) will play an increasing role in daily interaction with book and serials vendors. Many ILS vendors already have WWW versions, and many are integrating Z39.50 capabilities, which allow users to search another system without knowing the commands of the other system, into their products to produce the most powerful range of search and retrieval services to date.

Libraries need to assess their technological needs to make the most of their individual system environments. They should analyze in-house workflows to determine if existing workflows should continue, if redesigned workflows will be needed, or if totally new workflows must be implemented. Librarians should seek educational and informational assistance from not only their vendors, but also from their ILS companies, their computing centers, various Web sites, and their colleagues in the field.

Librarians are now buying more than just books and serials. They are buying system interfaces and electronic services from their book and serials vendors. These services may include access to tables of contents, document delivery, news alerting services, hypertext links to publication databases (whether they be full textbooks or electronic journals), and WWW sites.[3] As the purchasing agent for the library, the librarian needs to know how those electronic services might be included in library operations. As library budgets continue to tighten, serious consideration of these options is paramount. Outsourcing, electronic data interchange (EDI), Z39.50, electronic journals and books, MARC records, and the Internet and WWW have all enhanced the vendor's ability to assume more workload responsibilities in the day-to-day library operations.

The Internet, and especially the WWW, have opened up a once-closed in-house computing environment by allowing libraries direct access to vendors' databases and electronic products and services. As interfaces and gateways become more user-friendly, this access will allow libraries to search the vendor database, download the order information into their library system, order electronically, pay electronically, receive bibliographic and authority records via the Net, and even receive fully processed books at their doorsteps.

Working with Book and Serials Vendors

Developing a good working relationship with book and serials vendors is important. The better the vendor knows the library system requirements, the better it will be able to service them. For technology to work, people with expertise need to communicate. These people may include library staff from acquisitions, serials, collection development, access services, and reference who will work with the vendors' systems staff. In the RFP, librarians should be sure the interfaces and programs they requested are reasonable, cost-effective, and beneficial to a larger group. Otherwise, specific proprietary requests may require developmental and ongoing funding.

Whether you are a newly employed or a longtime library employee, the vendor may be able to assist you in learning more about library systems capabilities and features. In some cases, the vendor may know more about specific features of the computer system than library staff, in part because they deal with many library customers who use the same library system but who have used more of that system's capacity. Often the vendor can assist the library in getting greater benefits by using specific features that relate to enhanced book and serials acquisitions within the library system. If the library uses its systems more effectively, both the library and the vendor may realize cost savings.

Library System Interfaces

Vendors offer a wide range of interfaces to libraries, one of which is bibliographic records in machine-readable form, usually MARC. In preparing the RFP, the libraries should specify the type of record the vendor will need to provide. Most U.S. domestic vendors will provide MARC records; a foreign vendor may supply MARC, or national bibliographic records, or even its own standardized processing records. The library must be clear in the RFP as to what type and level of records it wishes to receive from the vendor, whether it requires full MARC, brief bibliographic records, or processing records. Vendor processing records can and do accommodate some libraries' needs for access to potential new materials. Fuller MARC records can be downloaded at a later date from bibliographic utilities, such as OCLC, RLIN, and WLN, or upgraded from the vendor. Bibliographic data or cataloging interfaces may also include pricing or pricing and invoicing data. For an additional charge, some vendors offer authority records. Serials vendors may provide serials holding data, serials check-in, and barcoding interfaces to libraries.

Format Transitions

Since the late 1960s, vendors have provided electronic information to libraries via multiple formats such as computer punch cards, magnetic tapes, microfiche, floppy diskettes, cartridges, and CD-ROMs, to name but a few. Many of these formats are still in use today, and vendors continue to supply customers with these formats. This state of affairs is becoming increasingly costly for vendors to maintain, however. During the first half of the 1990s, access to the Internet has changed communications patterns dramatically by the use of e-mail, Telnet, file transfer protocol (FTP), and WWW. E-mail has, in many cases, replaced the fax, which may have replaced most phone calls and letters. Access to the vendor's host system has allowed libraries to query the vendor's system as well as look at the library's specific records information. The Internet has also made FTP get-and-put commands highly effective for transferring electronic information from vendors to libraries and vice versa. The WWW has brought access to graphically interfaced databases and searchable resources.

Business Standards

Historically, business transactions between libraries and vendors have been, for the most part, paper based: Paper orders, paper claims, paper renewals, paper invoices, and paper management reports are used. Huge masses of paper reports, often in multiple copies, have been shipped back and forth for critical review and processing. Some interim electronic services, such as barcode services for title transfers, check-in projects, or the adding of vendor numbers to library systems records, are in use. Some libraries and vendors, however, are beginning to migrate to fully electronic procedures that will further enhance formerly paper-based activities.[4]

EDI is beginning to play a larger role in the electronic transmission of business-related information, including quotes, orders, claims and claims responses, invoices, and dispatch data for books and serials. Standards such as the American National Standards Institute, Accredited Standards Committee (ANSI ASC) X12 and the United Nations, Electronic Data Interchange for Administration, Commerce, and Transport (UN-EDIFACT) are being incorporated into ILS and homegrown systems computer programs.[5]

The year 1997 was especially important for global EDI standards alignment, as the standards groups in the United States and Europe jointly agreed to move to the United Nations standards transaction sets for both books and serials. Prior to 1997, X12 had been developed in the United States; it relies on the Serials Industry Systems Advisory Committee (SISAC) barcodes and Serials Item Contribution Identifier (SICI). Meanwhile, EDIFACT had been developed in Europe for book transactions. Another U.S. standard, the Book Industry Systems Advisory Committee (BISAC) fixed field format for books, was created in the mid-1980s.

In the RFP, be sure to specify the correct language to be certain that the vendor can comply with whatever standards version the library requires. Two other points to consider when implementing the EDI are these: (1) Determine how the library would like the transactions to be transmitted, via a value-added network (VAN) or over the Internet or WWW, and (2) establish what type of translation software will be used by either the ILS vendor or the library to convert the EDI message into the native programming language of the library system.

For true EDI to occur, the system (ILS or homegrown) must contain transaction sets of the complete business cycle, everything from quotes to dispatch data. For libraries and vendors to gain the greatest potential efficiencies from this technology, systems must be able to send business data electronically as well as receive the response to that inquiry electronically.[6] As EDI capabilities are incorporated into ILS systems, the whole electronic process becomes transparent to the user.

The Internet

The WWW provides access to text files, databases, and the interactive service of vendors, as well as access via the vendor's server to other databases or online resources. Vendors, whether they be book or serials, may play an increasing role in the authentication of user passwords and IDs for this type of interface, thereby consolidating the process into a seamless, one-stop shopping activity on the Net. Other attractive features of Web access include the ability to use news alerting services or push/pull technologies, for which the library selects types of information or services about which it wishes to automatically be notified as new items or products are available, and interactive communications imbedded in the vendors' home page information. The evolution of Web services is still in its infancy.

Z39.50 (search and retrieval) protocol may also play an increasing role for libraries and vendors as demands increase to find whatever information, wherever it might be in hyperspace, for structured databases. Digital library initiatives are beginning to show how diversified the resources are and how complex searching these resources has become.[7] ILS vendors have begun to incorporate Z39.50 and Web browser technologies into their systems, enabling libraries to access more data sources than ever before. Book and serials vendors are studying the efficiencies of these technologies to determine how they might best use them to assist library customers. Software version and release number are also important for Z39.50 and Web browser technologies, so be sure to include the library's specifications in the RFP. If the ILS does not have Web browser capabilities, the library or its parent organization's computing center may provide these services directly.

Who Is Buying What?

Other aspects to consider in preparing the RFP are related to unit delivery mechanisms. Many libraries are no longer buying solely whole books and journals. They are increasingly purchasing parts and pieces of the whole, as well as multimedia components. Supply and demand will undoubtedly play a role in how effective book and serials vendors can market table of contents services, document delivery services, electronic journals and books, sample issues, news manager services, and site licensing agreements. Interactive Internet and WWW ordering via deposit accounts or credit cards also needs to be considered. The library should determine if and how electronic commerce will play a role in the library procurement process. Keep in mind that services purchased by the library may be received at the library or sent directly to the end user. The library must determine if it or the end user will pay for these services. Currently, the role of procuring document delivery or table of contents services may lie outside acquisitions and serials departments, instead resting with the interlibrary loan, reference, or collection development departments. This determination of work responsibility is an area that must be examined in the larger economies of scale within the library RFP to book and serials vendors. Book and serials vendors can and should play an active role in this arena.

Book and serials vendors have always made a valuable contribution to library operations, chiefly through consolidation/coordination and information/education. It will be just as important in the future for these vendors to assist librarians with these information needs and package them accordingly, as the number of potential electronic procurement sources and service types explodes at an ever-increasing rate.

Customized Electronic Services

The library RFP to book and serials vendors should also consider customized versus the standardized system interfaces described in the preceding paragraphs. If the library has greater systems needs than most of the vendor's other customers, it may need to provide some additional type of remuneration. The RFP should evaluate how much time and money the vendor will need to invest to develop the customized product and how much money the library is willing to pay for it. If the library requests a highly customized product from each of its vendors, and none or few of them can provide it, awarding the RFP contract(s) will be more challenging. If, on the other hand, all the vendors can comply with the library RFP customized systems requests, the library need only select the vendor that best fits its other procurement criteria.

Customized Outsourcing Services

Typical customized outsourcing services include barcode interfaces (multipurpose) for check-in, for transferring titles, or for patron checkout. Receipt of sample periodical issues, electronic quotations on a list of titles, consolidation services for books and serials, and dispatch data from publishers also facilitate serials and acquisitions work. Shelf-ready materials are becoming more and more a priority as libraries analyze the internal cost factors of library workflows. Vendor-assisted processing may include spine marking and labeling, patron barcodes, security strips, book jackets, property stamping, and full bibliographic records.[8] Some library RFPs also include binding services as a vendor requirement.

Customized Reports

Customized report generation has been available for some time now from book and serials vendors. For many years, vendors have generated library reports in-house and shipped them to libraries.[9] The newest feature of this service is customized reports generated by the customer at the customer's site via the WWW. The WWW is providing even more in the way of interactive customized applications. The potential exists for libraries to change their approval profiles online, to update fund codes, to review approval information electronically, and to receive electronically profiled information from vendor news alerting systems downloaded directly into the librarian's e-mail account. Standard Generalized Markup Language (SGML) and Hypertext Markup Language (HTML) may replace existing manual or host applications as libraries experience greater flexibility and ease of use with Internet tools. Java scripts may also bring increased interactivity to the workplace, allowing vendor programs to be downloaded temporarily at the library workstation for ease of access.

Security Issues: Interfaces and Electronic Products

As more and more library catalogs become WWW compatible or Z39.50 compliant, computer security issues are of greater concern. One issue that looms on the horizon is how the library and vendor will ensure data integrity and privacy on the Net.

In the RFP process, just as in day-to-day library work, it is increasingly important to have secure computing systems. Finding out what kind of security measures book and serials vendors have installed on their computing systems may also be important, as well as what kind of security measures the ILS vendor has installed on its computing systems.[10] Do these security measures work together, if at all? Most secure systems include multiple firewalls on all sites. Secure systems can be extremely expensive and inconvenient for the vendor or library to implement and operate. If security is a major concern of the library, it must also understand that this security may come at a high price.

The RFP committee has many relevant security questions to ponder and ramifications to consider during the RFP process, including the following:

- Does the vendor require password or user identification numbers to access the library data held on the book or serials vendor's host system?

- Does the vendor offer varying levels of access, for example, separate passwords for searching only as opposed to searching and ordering?

- How well is the library WWW access controlled by Internet Protocol (IP) address(es) (e.g., user@host.domain)?

- How often do the library and vendor update their passwords?

- What other kinds of encryption or validation procedures are in place?

- How will copyright royalties and licensing agreements be handled?

- What considerations must be taken into account with regard to the security environments of the ILS (or homegrown system) and the parent institution's computing center?

RFP Test Transmissions: To Test or Not to Test?

Theoretically, it might be desirable to conduct testing during the RFP process. Realistically, however, it is difficult to accomplish. Vendors do not generally have test environments set up to supply artificial records to libraries for the RFP process, and most libraries do not have staff waiting to process and test artificial records. Also, most ILSs (or homegrown systems) are not designed to create test environments. A better alternative might be to ask the vendor to supply at least one reference in the list of references that uses the same ILS as your library, and contact the reference to determine how well the vendor's interfaces really work. Also, consider contacting your ILS vendor or ILS vendor user's group with vendor interface questions.

Although the RFP should include information about the library's system specifications, testing may be best reserved for the successful vendor(s) once the RFP contracts have been awarded. This will save the library and the vendor unnecessary costs and delays. The contract should be awarded contingent on the library and vendor being able to interface successfully. Before testing begins, provide the vendor with all the specifications for the test.

State in the RFP which system (ILS or homegrown) the library uses and specify the software version number. This may seem obvious, but many RFPs either fail to include basic necessary information or contain incorrect specifications. These errors can cause delays in testing any interface. If someone from the library's systems area is not already a member of the RFP committee, a member of the committee should work with the library or larger institution systems staff on the technical language to be used in the RFP. Be explicit, give all essential details, and include contact names, addresses, phone numbers, and e-mail addresses. Set up mutually agreeable dates for testing. If critical dates or time frames must be met, be sure to provide this information to the vendor.

Once the testing has been completed successfully, sign off on a statement or e-mail message that authorizes production mode to begin for the given interface or electronic service. If testing is not completed successfully, work with the vendor to determine what specifications must be changed. Although it will almost always be possible to arrive at a mutually agreeable accommodation, if it is not possible, the library will have to reconsider the contract award.

Emerging Trends

Although technology is exciting and offers potentially unlimited opportunities to libraries, many unanswered questions remain. In an era of declining budgets and staffing levels, there are simultaneously increasing demands from users for more electronic products, more shelf-ready materials, and more access to the Internet and the WWW. These trends, in turn, mean more or less may be expected altogether from book and serials vendors.[11]

The role of the book and serials vendors may change over time. The potential role of other information providers is also critical to these emerging trends. Information providers include, but are not limited to, publishers, database and indexing services, information brokers, bibliographic utilities, and ILS vendors. It is not clear, however, that book and serials vendors will be the business partners to provide all of the interfaces and electronic services a library needs for the future. Libraries must confront economic issues that go beyond the traditional materials budget for ordering and processing. They must examine which electronic services and products best meet their needs, and purchase them from the most beneficial source.

This chapter concludes with a question: How can librarians evaluate library systems interfaces and electronic services of book and serials vendors in the RFP process? Librarians should keep in mind both current and future needs for these types of services in an electronic environment that is changing and evolving rapidly. Systems and protocols in place today may not be in place a year from now.

What was once a simple decision-making process has become a complex relationship of understanding the library and vendors' systems capabilities and transaction-based analysis. The library should evaluate the RFP response for library system interfaces and electronic services based on actual and perceived needs for the future, which is no small task, given the rate of change and nonstandardization in electronic options available to libraries in today's marketplace.

The smart buyer is an educated buyer. Know the library systems environment, and know the vendors' systems environment—their capabilities and their limitations. Keep open communications channels with book and serials vendors so that the library can benefit from technological advances. Write the RFP to incorporate the library systems interfaces and electronic services requirements in a clear and precise manner. Work with book and serials vendors to create the best possible systems environment for both parties, during the RFP process as well as on a regular business partner basis.

Notes

1. Daniel Melcher (with Margaret Saul), *Melcher on Acquisitions* (Chicago: American Library Association, 1971), 139–40.

2. Frances C. Wilkinson and Connie Capers Thorson, "The RFP Process: Rational, Educational, Necessary or There Ain't No Such Thing as a Free Lunch," *Library Acquisitions: Practice & Theory* 19, no. 2 (1995): 257.

3. AcqWeb, URL: http://www.library.venderbilt.edu/law/acqs/acqs.html. This site has compiled WWW links to various vendors that directly highlight their electronic services and products.

4. Pamela Bluh, "Selected Bibliography on Electronic Data Interchange," URL: http://www-elf.stanford.edu/biblio.html. This site is an extensive EDI bibliography compiled by a librarian.

5. Friedemann Weigel, "EDI in the Library Market: How Close Are We?" *Library Administration & Management* 10, no. 3 (1996): 143.

6. Bruce Compton, "The ILS Vendor and EDI: A Perspective Library," *Library Administration & Management* 10, no. 3 (1996): 165.

7. Clifford A. Lynch, "Interoperability: The Standards Challenge for the 1990s," *Wilson Library Bulletin* 67, no. 7 (1993): 38.

8. Gary M. Shirk, "Contract Acquisitions: Change, Technology, and the New Library/Vendor Partnership," *Library Acquisitions: Practice & Theory* 17, no. 2 (1993): 148.

9. Roger L. Presley, "Firing an Old Friend, Painful Decisions: The Ethics Between Librarians and Vendors," *Library Acquisitions: Practice & Theory* 17, no. 1 (1993): 56.

10. Richard Boss, "Security Concerns Grow," *Library Systems Newsletter* 16, no. 6 (1996): 45.

11. Stanford University Libraries, "Redesign of Technical Services," URL: http://www-sul.stanford.edu/depts/diroff/ts/redesign/redesign.html. This site details the process and conclusions made by the Stanford University Libraries as they explored and redesigned many workflows to take advantage of the electronic capabilities of their vendors.

PART III

Writing the Subject-Specific RFP

Chapter 6

Latin American Approval Plans: A Case Study

Russ Davidson
Curator of Latin American and Iberian Collections
University of New Mexico, Albuquerque, New Mexico, U.S.A.

Strategy drives structure; structure facilitates strategy
—Montague Brown

This chapter will take a case study approach to outline the steps to be followed when developing an RFP for Latin American approval plans. The experience at the University of New Mexico General Library will be outlined to take the reader through all phases of the Latin American RFP process. Although the examples cited pertain to a single world area—Latin America—the points they illustrate will by and large apply to gathering plans affecting all major foreign language and area studies collections.

Pros and Cons of the RFP Process

The technical services literature of librarianship contains a curious anomaly. On the one hand, no subject has been written about more extensively than that of acquisitions and the management of vendor relations.[1] On the other hand, a vital element of that process for many libraries—the development and submission of requests for proposals, or RFPs, in soliciting bids for awarding contracts for book and serials purchases—has been almost entirely ignored. Moreover, the few studies that have been published on this topic have all reached the same negative conclusions. The dim view taken by librarians and others toward the requirement, faced by various publicly funded libraries, to solicit bids on contracts is perhaps best summed up by Heather Miller in her book entitled *Managing Acquisitions and Vendor Relations*. Miller writes, " 'Putting out for bid' is a dreaded phrase among acquisitions librarians. Those who work for agencies where purchase . . . is preceded by a lengthy process of obtaining bids knows [sic] that even for non-library materials it is a flawed system. . . . Examples of the negative effects of bidding for library materials abound."[2] Clearly, such negative examples do abound, as we all know from both formal and informal discussion of the issue and, in some instances, from actual experience. As Miller notes, when all libraries within a particular state or other jurisdiction are forced to operate under a single contract and to buy from the same vendor, and when the major and sometimes sole criterion in determining which vendor is selected is the percentage of discount, the results—especially for academic libraries—are invariably disadvantageous if not disastrous. In addition, other factors are cited as arguments against the solicitation of bids. The process is seen to be time-consuming and energy-depleting, to distort the free play of market forces (thus stifling competition), to disrupt the continuity of acquisitions (leaving gaps in holdings, especially serials), and to require confrontations with bureaucratic-minded purchasing departments whose staff may see little distinction between buying books and paper clips.[3, 4, 5] In short, going out to bid becomes Miller's "dreaded phrase" for acquisitions librarians, leading her (as well as others) to conclude that "no effort is too great in the attempt to obtain exemption for libraries from all contract and bidding requirements."[6]

Yet is this really true? Should such a monolithic pronouncement be accepted without challenge or qualification? Certainly, the bidding process poses difficulties for libraries, and in those instances where they are compelled to be part of a statewide contract or to accept a bid exclusively on the basis of percentage of discount, all of the criticisms cited above would seem to be valid. This, however, represents the extreme and does not appear to be the condition in which most libraries, particularly academic libraries, find themselves. It is essential to recognize that the bidding process per se, contrary to the impression left by this doctrinaire attitude, does not necessarily lead to a negative outcome or put the library in a disadvantageous position. On the contrary, where the library is an active partner in the process and is able to assume some measure of control, the requirement it faces to obtain bids may actually work to its advantage and result in a strengthened collection, improved vendor relations, and superior service to its patrons.

In this environment, the key ingredient for the library is that it obtain multiple bids, for which the most common and effective mechanism is, of course, the RFP. When the library employs this device and (as will be seen below) exercises control over aspects of it, the process of going out to bid and of awarding contracts through a central purchasing department may yield a number of tangible benefits. And although these will undoubtedly vary from library to library, depending on how the RFP is written and what information the responding vendor is required to provide in it, certain benefits should nevertheless be common to all libraries; for example, a greater knowledge on the part of the library of vendors' service policies and pricing structures, a refined understanding by librarians of the range and depth of coverage sought in particular subject areas, and a belief on the part of the library that contracts have been thoroughly vetted (by both parties) and awarded on the basis of free and open competition. The list, of course, is much longer, but the point to be made here is that the time expended by the library in crafting RFPs is hardly wasted.

Approval Plans for Area Studies Collections: Special Considerations

Within academic libraries, certain types of material—foreign language material especially—have historically been exempted from the requirement that they be obtained via the formal competitive procurement process. The prime example would be area studies collections (with the exception of Western European studies), whose materials often circulate outside normal distribution channels, are issued in very small print runs, and are supplied, in many cases, only by specialist dealers without any access to a functioning national bibliographic infrastructure. The thinking is that these materials are best acquired by methods devised by the library alone, building on the cumulative experience of a network of bibliographers and drawing in the contributions of other knowledgeable sources, such as scholars and publishers with significant country and regional expertise. This model, followed almost universally by U.S. academic research libraries since World War II, has generally been successful in creating strong area studies collections. In turn, the core method of acquisition used by many of these libraries to acquire current scholarly imprints has been a blanket order or approval plan contract maintained with specific country vendors. Under the assumption, however, that foreign acquisitions, and especially acquisitions from third-world countries, were subject to a different set of rules, the contracts were never negotiated on the basis of RFPs and the evaluation of corresponding bids.[7] Until recently, this was the model adhered to by the University of New Mexico General Library with respect to the one foreign area (exclusive of certain Western European countries) from which it collected heavily—Latin America. Since the mid-1970s, approval plans have been the bedrock of the acquisition of UNM's current imprints from Latin America. These plans were established and maintained in the traditional manner, that is, through personal contact and communication between the library and specialist dealers located in one country or another. A dealer capable of servicing a particular plan was identified and was furnished with a profile spelling out, by subject, what type of material the library wished to collect, and in what depth. Every year a budget was given, and the books came in. Communication with the dealer was critical and it was maintained in a variety of ways, from written correspondence and face-to-face meetings at conferences to periodic visits by the library's area specialist to countries in the region. In the last few years, these communications were supplemented and, to some extent, supplanted by fax messages and e-mail. Although the arrangements worked out between the General Library and the dealers were governed by written agreements, or "contracts," these were entirely of the library's own making. They were neither scrutinized by anyone other than the library's acquisitions librarian and its Latin American specialist, nor subject to any of the University's rules and regulations on procurement. This system, highly informal and idiosyncratic, had been in place for some 20 years and generally worked well.

In 1993, however, the General Library was informed by the University's Purchasing department that, so far as many of its approval plans were concerned—including several of the Latin American plans— it would need to undergo the RFP process to operate in accordance with state law. New Mexico state law stipulated that any state-funded department, agency, or office was required to solicit bids for services or contracts that exceeded $10,000 per fiscal year. Although the fine print of the law may have permitted certain exceptions or exemptions, these did not extend to the library's contracts with vendors. The "dreaded phrase" had thus been invoked, and the library—initially with great skepticism—set about writing RFPs for a number of its approval plans. Three of these were for Latin American materials.

As noted above, the idea of engaging in this practice ran completely counter to the opinion and experience of area studies librarians. If Latin American bibliographers in North American research libraries had been polled on this question, they would have reacted, it is fair to say, with a mixture of derision and incredulity. Issuing RFPs, in conformity with central Purchasing department requirements, was (and is) simply not part of the landscape of Latin American acquisitions. This fact notwithstanding, it has of necessity become a central component of UNM's purchasing of current Latin American materials. An explanation of how this was accomplished and a description of its effect on areas of the General Library's collections form the basis of this chapter. However, before turning to this analysis, it may be helpful to offer some further details about UNM's Latin American collections and programs.

The Institutional Context

The University of New Mexico library began acquiring Latin Americana, in a concerted way, approximately 50 years ago. The initial emphasis was on monographs, serials, and manuscripts (both original and photostatic) to support UNM's nationally respected programs in Latin American history, anthropology, geography, and Spanish literature and linguistics. As the University's Latin American studies programs grew, so did the collections acquired to support them. By the late 1970s, the collection numbered some 200,000 volumes—a figure that, by 1995, had grown to an estimated 338,000. Yet if the collections grew rapidly, the teaching and research programs that they served grew even more rapidly. Indeed, UNM's Latin American studies curriculum is the largest of its kind in the country, providing 34 specialized degree and dual-degree options in such professional fields as nursing, international management, and community and regional planning in addition to the more established social science, humanities, and fine arts disciplines. In all, Latin American studies and Spanish- and Portuguese-language courses at the University of New Mexico enroll some 11,000 to 12,000 students annually. The library strives to meet the information needs of this large and diverse population by using all means at its disposal. As in other libraries with comparable Latin American or other foreign area holdings, current scholarly imprints are acquired through three principal channels: Title-by title-purchasing, gift and exchange, and approval plans. Each of these is vital to the overall success of the program, but in terms of sheer size, the approval plans consistently add the largest number of volumes to the collection. At present, the UNM General Library maintains a total of 22 Latin American approval plans, covering 21 countries. These plans are handled by 12 different vendors. A single vendor covers five Central American countries, and two vendors are used in Brazil.

The UNM Latin American collection adds, on average, nearly 8,000 monographic volumes per year. Between two-thirds and three-quarters of this total, or 5,000 to 6,000 imprints, are supplied through the approval plans. The budget for these plans is approximately $105,000, out of a total Latin American allocation (from state monies) of some $205,000. The individual country budgets range from a low of $1,000 per fiscal year to a figure of $25,000. Although a considerable disparity may exist between the budgets for, say, Honduras and Mexico, the range of material supplied on all of the plans is fundamentally the same. In addition to books, materials include government reports and publications, atlases, reference works, party political literature and other ephemera, selected serials, and limited numbers of CD-ROMs, posters, videocassettes, and other media.

Planning for the RFP

New Mexico state law, it will be recalled, mandated that the General Library go out for bid for services in excess of $10,000 per fiscal year. For fiscal year 1994–95, three of the UNM General Library's Latin American approval plans fell into this category. These were the plans for Mexico, Argentina, and Brazil, whose budgets (prior to applying any discounts) were $24,000, $25,000, and $25,000 respectively. In broad terms, the process that was used to write, submit, and evaluate the Latin American RFPs, in conjunction with various University Purchasing department procedures, mirrored that followed by the library as a whole.

First, to ensure overall consistency and coherence, a library-wide committee was formed. The RFP committee's members were the heads of the Systems, Serials, Acquisitions, and Collection Development departments, two additional representatives from Serials and Acquisitions, a representative from the Fiscal Services office, and the collection development coordinators for the General Library's Fine Arts, Science and Technology, and Latin American collections. The committee chair (the head of the Serials department) took primary responsibility for coordinating all of the library's attendant activities with the Purchasing department. Because the process entailed a complex series of steps, it was begun in late 1993, well in advance of the beginning of the 1994–95 fiscal year (July 1, 1994), when the new contracts were required to take effect. The committee's first order of business, other than clarifying its work and reviewing a schedule of deadlines, was to assign responsibility for writing the RFPs and for identifying those vendors to whom the Purchasing department should send them. In the case of the subject-based and area studies collections, this responsibility fell, logically, on the above-mentioned coordinators. In the case of format-based collections, such as North American and Canadian serials, or materials of a broad interdisciplinary nature, such as European and British monographs, the responsibility was shared by two or more people. Each of these clusters in turn became a subcommittee which called on the assistance, if needed, of additional staff. The schedule also included, where possible, visits to the library by interested vendors (these preceded the mailing of the RFPs) to enable them to explain firsthand their business practices and the scope of their coverage and services, as well as to provide the committee (and others with an interest in the matter) the opportunity to ask questions of a similar nature. Once the RFPs were written, they were circulated in draft form to the full committee for review and comment. After final revision, they were forwarded, along with lists of prospective bidders, to the Purchasing department, which mailed them out along with instructions for submission and an explanation of University policies governing contracts and procurement. After the deadline had passed for receipt of responses (a four- to six-week period), the Purchasing department sent all of the submitted responses to the library to be evaluated. The review and evaluation were done as quickly as possible, principally by the same individuals who had written the RFPs, with participation invited on the part of other interested library personnel. The latter comprised mainly Acquisitions and Serials department staff as well as those librarians involved in the selection of materials.

Planning the Evaluation Stage

Whereas the RFPs had all varied to some extent in content and terminology, reflecting the inherent differences between forming a collection, for example, of art exhibition catalogs and science and engineering journals, the methodology used for evaluating and ranking the proposals did not. This followed a standardized format and incorporated both quantitative and qualitative data. All of the criteria to be employed in the evaluation of proposals, and the numerical values assigned to them, had been clearly enumerated on the RFP cover letter and sheets. Each person filling out an evaluation sheet scored the proposal(s) against these predetermined values. This ensured that the process of evaluation was fully documented and made as free of bias as possible. Scores were then tallied and a formal recommendation made to the RFP committee chair by the head of each subcommittee as to which vendor ought to be awarded the contract. These recommendations were sent to the Purchasing department for its review and analysis. Vendors who had submitted responses were then officially notified by the Purchasing department of the University's decision. The vendors making successful bids were issued contracts for one year, with the option (to be exercised by mutual consent) of three (subsequently revised to seven) additional one-year renewals. Such, in brief, was the general RFP process followed by the General Library.

Communicating with the Purchasing Department

Before undertaking a specific analysis of the Latin American approval plan RFPs, a few broad points are in order concerning the roles played, respectively, by the General Library and the University's Purchasing department, and the lessons these hold for judging the process described above. Once the library realized that putting out bids through the Purchasing department on its major approval plans was a fait accompli, it wasted little time in bemoaning or protesting the fact. Rather, it turned its energies toward taking charge of the process, to make sure that it controlled critical aspects of it. Above all, this entailed the development of a positive working relationship with the Purchasing department. The lines of communication needed to be kept open at all times, with the General Library asserting itself, albeit subtly, as the lead partner. By adopting this posture, the library was able—to use management parlance—to convert a "threat" into an "opportunity," and to control, consequently, all of the key variables. In the end, it was the General Library that wrote the RFPs and assigned the numerical weights to their various categories (these are discussed more fully below), identified the pool of prospective vendors, carried out the evaluations of the proposals, ranked them, and recommended the vendors of choice. Although the Purchasing department could have theoretically objected to or blocked these choices, in reality there was little or no prospect of this happening. Once the Purchasing department accepted the General Library's position that the acquisition of library materials involved a unique set of problems, to which only librarians knew most of the answers, it had effectively ceded control and agreed to serve an essentially administrative and bookkeeping function. In this fashion, the library's experience was far from what Miller's "dreaded phrase" would imply. The requirement to issue RFPs enabled it to rethink some of its needs and to recustomize its approval plans, including its three largest plans for Latin American materials.

Countries Requiring an RFP

Because, as noted earlier, the literature of area studies librarianship and, in particular, the part of it that applied to Latin America appeared to be devoid of any studies of the use of RFPs in negotiating approval plan contracts, the UNM General Library began this task with a blank slate and developed its own standards and guidelines. The three countries for which RFPs needed to be prepared—Argentina, Brazil, and Mexico—were quite similar in terms of the library's collection development objectives and acquisitions requirements. The aim in each case was (and had been for many years) to develop comprehensive collections, capable of supporting Ph.D.-level research in all of the core social science and humanities disciplines, with the strongest concentrations in history, literature, political science, sociology, and anthropology, accompanied by more selective (but still substantial) coverage in such fields as economics, art history, architecture, communications, religious studies, public administration, and education. To support these and other areas of the curriculum and of faculty and student research, the library needed to collect a wide range of material, including national and state-level census and statistical data, annual government and company reports, conference proceedings, bibliographies and reference works, and publications issued by various noncommercial sources, such as university departments, political and religious groups, NGOs (non-governmental organizations), private- and public-sector research institutes, and literary and historical societies. Expressed quantitatively, the General Library needed to receive between 900 and 1,200 monographs per year from each country to meet these requirements. Because the same acquisitions profile existed, with only minor variations, for all three countries, and because the vendor picture for them was likewise quite similar, the RFP process for the Latin American approval plans turned out to be highly streamlined; to a great extent, it was like filling out a form in triplicate. To describe in detail the library's experience for all three countries would thus be redundant. Instead, the focus will be put on Brazil, the largest and most populous country in Latin America.

Writing the RFP

In keeping with the chronology outlined above, the first task the library faced was to write the RFP. This was done primarily by the Latin American collection development co-ordinator, with assistance from the staff person who supervised the day-to-day work of the library's Latin American approval plan operation.[8] The Brazilian RFP, like the others, required that information be supplied in as much detail as possible and appropriate for six categories, or point factors. These six were (1) Background, Reputation, and Financial Stability (or "Company Data"); (2) Profiling and Title Selection; (3) Coverage; (4) Bibliographic Data; (5) Financial Practice; and (6) Customer Service. Although these factors were uniform to all of the General Library's approval plan RFPs, the point values assigned to them were not. This was a matter for each subcommittee to decide, taking into account the particular dynamics and characteristics of its own area. In the case of Brazil, the greatest weight was given to the point factors of Coverage and Customer Service, and the least to Bibliographic Data. The intent behind the RFP was to gather enough information about each vendor's services and products to permit meaningful comparative evaluation. Consultation of appendix B of this book will provide the reader with a core list of questions pertaining to the Brazilian RFP. Although each question figured in the total count, the most important elements for the library, in the Brazilian RFP, dealt with the range and extent of subject coverage and types of publications provided, the number of other comprehensive approval plans maintained by each vendor with North American research libraries (the latter, it was made clear, would be contacted as references), whether the vendor also offered a separate subscription service for serials, the range of customer services provided (including provision for visits to the United States), and pricing structure and discounts.

The next step, following consideration by the full Committee of the Brazilian RFP, was to give it to the Purchasing department along with a list of those vendors to whom it should be sent. This list contained the names of five companies, three located in Brazil and two in the United States. Because RFPs on approval plan contracts, at least for academic libraries, were unknown to Brazilian vendors and book dealers, the library took the additional step of informing the three Brazilian companies about the impending arrival of the RFPs and of explaining in brief what these entailed. (The same action was taken with respect to the RFPs sent to vendors in Mexico and Argentina.)

Evaluating Vendor Proposals

When the deadline had passed for receipt of proposals, the Purchasing department sent them to the library, and they were evaluated in accordance with the procedures outlined above. All three Brazilian vendors submitted proposals, as well as one of the North American companies. The proposal from the North American company, however, was disqualified, as it referred only to a prospective subscription service on Brazilian serials, whereas the RFP had specified in its requirements that the approval plan would be primarily for current monographic imprints. The evaluation of the three Brazilian proposals was carried out by the same team that had written the RFPs (no other library personnel chose to participate, probably because they felt they lacked the technical knowledge and expertise). After tallying up the scores and reviewing all supporting documentation, the Latin American collection development coordinator recommended a choice of vendors for Brazil to the chair of the committee (the two-vendors plan for Brazil is explained in the concluding section below). This recommendation was shared with the library administration and given to the Purchasing department, which approved it and notified the vendors of the University's decision. The new contracts for Brazilian approval plans went into effect as of July 1, 1994.

Assessment of the RFP Process: What Did the Library Learn?

It remains to analyze more fully the value of this process for the UNM General Library. As might be surmised, the three Brazilian vendors who submitted bids were not unknown to the library. On the contrary, the library had been doing business with them for years. As such, it already knew certain things about the scope and organization of their services. The library had, in fact, used one of the companies as its principal supplier of Brazilian imprints via a blanket order plan over a 10-year span, from the mid-1970s to 1984. It had then employed the services of one of the other companies, on the same basis, between 1987 and 1993. Given this background, what further gain did the library hope to realize from complying with the Purchasing department's requirement?

The benefits to be realized were both tangible and intangible. In the first instance, the RFP was a convenient way in which to elicit current and detailed information from each of the companies concerning the scope and range of their services. For example, with regard to experience, client base, and human and financial resources, each company was asked to supply information concerning the length of time it had been in business and had offered approval plans to academic libraries, the size of its staff and special qualifications of members selecting materials, and the number of approval plans it currently maintains. The UNM General Library, despite its history of buying books from these companies, did not have this type of broad-based information about them. Each company was further asked to supply a list of large research libraries (both new and more established approval plan clients) who could be contacted to supply firsthand information and a recent statement of its financial condition.

Coverage Provided

Under the category of Coverage, questions were posed concerning the companies' abilities to supply, systematically and comprehensively, such non-mainstream material as official documents and government publications, monographs issued by provincial and local-level publishers, and books and pamphlets distributed by political parties and avant-garde presses. Also requested was the exact number of titles that each company had supplied, in fiscal year 1993, to its largest approval plan clients as well as to those of medium size. These are but examples of the questions, reproduced in appendix B, on which the library's evaluation and choice of vendors were ultimately based. In the case of Brazil, it was apparent after analyzing each of the bids that none of the vendors (despite sharply varying capabilities among them) could ensure the depth of coverage sought by the library for all parts of the country. For Brazil, the controlling factor was geography, not type of publication (e.g., trade vs. university press) or format (e.g., serials vs. monographs). The country was simply too far-flung and the distribution system too poorly developed to enable one vendor to operate successfully on a countrywide basis. We thus elected to split Brazil in half and to award two contracts, one to a vendor who would cover the southeast (the area around

Rio de Janeiro and São Paulo, the country's major publishing centers, and cities to the south of them) and the other to a vendor located in the northeastern city of Recife (capital of Brazil's other regional publishing center), who, from this local base, blanketed the rest of the area through regular buying trips.[9]

Advantages to the Library

It is true, as critics of the bid process might assert, that much if not all of the foregoing could have been learned, and could have occurred, without subjecting either party to the time-consuming formalities of the RFP. The process, however, brought other advantages, centering on communication, vendor relations, and the use of good business practice. For example, it ensured that the methods used for both gathering information from vendors and evaluating their proposals would be uniform. Each vendor would be asked the same questions in the same way, with corresponding answers judged according to the same scale. This in turn helps to generate a more businesslike atmosphere and to promote the notion of fair play. The vendors not awarded contracts may be disappointed in the University's decision but still believe (to the extent that human nature will allow) that the system was not rigged against them. Moreover, for the vendor who does win the contract, fulfillment of the RFP has helped both to clarify the library's general expectations and requirements at a very early stage and to establish the framework for successful communication at a later stage. For Latin American collections (as no doubt for other area studies collections), this last point cannot be emphasized too strongly. Where dealer lists substitute for national bibliographies and other standard selection tools are frequently lacking, personal communication with the vendor is absolutely critical in determining the success or failure of an acquisitions program.

The other principal advantage accruing to the library from the RFP is that which is derived from Latin American approval plans in general, namely, "crafting arrangements that take advantage of the presence or absence of vendor competition."[10] A competitive procurement process whose outcome is determined solely by unit cost, or percentage of discount, will, as has been noted earlier, distort the market and thus undermine the broader interests of the library. On the other hand, where the cost of material and the availability of discounts count as only two factors among many, the opposite will be true; they will act as a spur to competition and thus benefit the library. The experience of the UNM General Library with regard to the Brazilian RFP clearly bears this out. The document asked the vendors two questions on this score: First, to enumerate what basic discount they offered; and second, to state whether they provided (or would provide) escalating discounts for monies deposited on account against approval shipments. From the responses received (excluding the North American vendor), it was clear that only one of the Brazilian vendors had any experience servicing deposit accounts. However, the other two indicated that they would be willing to provide a discount (the percentage of which was not specified) in return for receiving prepayment of the year's budget. The two vendors clearly perceived that they would lose some competitive edge unless they were willing to adopt this practice. They were right in thinking so, as the UNM General Library has increasingly been managing its Latin American approval plans as deposit accounts in order to stretch the available dollars as far as possible. That the RFP can be an effective instrument in this process appears to be widely recognized (if not much written about). As Frank Dowd states, speaking of the pressure for accountability arising from ever-tighter budgets, "Purchasing by competitive bid is becoming an issue that more and more acquisitions librarians must deal with. . . . The purpose of developing bid specifications is to get control of the process of the bid and define the product in such a way that competitive purchasing may take place."[11]

To "get control of the process of the bid"—that is the heart of the matter. Where libraries do not face the legal requirement to issue bids through a central Purchasing department, they will understandably opt for simpler, less bureaucratic arrangements. However, where they do, the emphasis—as the experience of the University of New Mexico with its Latin American approval plans shows—should be put less on rearguard actions designed to obtain exemptions from bidding requirements than on proactive actions that enable the library to operate successfully within the RFP environment.

Notes

1. Peggy Johnson and Sheila S. Intner, *Guide to Technical Services Resources* (Chicago: American Library Association, 1994), 29.

2. Heather S. Miller, *Managing Acquisitions and Vendor Relations: A How to Do It Manual* (New York; London: Neal–Schuman, 1992), 62–63.

3. Daniel Melcher (with Margaret Saul) *Melcher on Acquisition* (Chicago: American Library Association, 1971), 46–55.

4. Calvin J. Boyer, "State-Wide Contracts for Library Materials: An Analysis of the Attendant Dysfunctional Consequences," *College and Research Libraries* 35, no. 2 (1974): 86–94.

5. Miller, 61–65.

6. Miller, 67.

7. Two other possibilities may exist; first, that RFPs were used in managing approval plan contracts for materials from third-world areas but were not written about, or, second, that some analyses of their use in area studies acquisitions were published but have escaped my detection. These possibilities notwithstanding, I feel safe in concluding, based on an extensive review of the literature, that the theme has not been addressed so far as Latin American librarianship is concerned. On this point, see in particular the anthology edited by Cecily Johns, *Selection of Library Materials for Area Studies. Part I*, which contains more than a dozen essays covering all of the Caribbean and Latin American nations, none of which makes any mention of the use of RFPs. See also the articles by Hazen, Gibbs, and Gutierrez-Witt, cited in the bibliography at the end of this book.

8. In addition to the coordinator, this operation was overseen by full-time employees (FTEs), who comprised a separate unit of the Gifts/Exchange Team of the Serials department (now the Acquisitions and Serials department).

9. This arrangement, it should be noted, did not translate into an even division of the budget. Rather, the vendor given the Southeast Brazil contract received approximately 90 percent of the allocation, a percentage mirroring the region's preeminence in trade and other publishing.

10. Dan Hazen, "Approval Plans for Latin American Acquisitions: Some Aspects of Theory, Strategy, and Cost," in *SALALM and the Area Studies Community: Papers of the Thirty Seventh Annual Meeting of the Seminar on the Acquisition of Latin American Library Materials,* ed. David Block (Albuquerque, NM: SALALM Secretariat, University of New Mexico, 1994), 170.

11. Frank B. Dowd, "Awarding Acquisitions Contracts by Bid or the Perils and Rewards of Shopping by Mail," *The Acquisitions Librarian* 5 (1991): 63–64.

Chapter 7

Fine Arts Approval Plans

Nancy Pistorius
Associate Director, Fine Arts Library, University of
New Mexico, Albuquerque, New Mexico

Great art is as irrational as great music. It is mad with its own loveliness.

—George Jean Nathan

The fine arts encompass a wide range of materials in both the visual and performing arts. Within this range are select types of materials for which title-by-title acquisition is problematic. In such cases, specialized or customized approval plans facilitate the acquisition of materials. Because of this, approval plans for fine arts subject areas have the potential of covering different types of library materials varying in format, type, and genre. In some cases, RFPs for fine arts materials become essential to reveal plans that may be available and to identify potential vendors that are able and willing to refine or customize approval plans so they meet the needs of a client institution or fulfill institutional or legal requirements concerning funding expenditures with a single vendor.

With specific focus on visual and performing arts materials, this chapter will explore the range of traditional and nontraditional print and nonprint materials available, review the characteristics of various library collections, present considerations for libraries and vendors when customizing the approval plan, and discuss writing the RFP to assist libraries in acquiring these often specialized materials.

Materials for the Visual and Performing Arts

Although most libraries rely on traditional monographs and serials to sustain the core of their collections, academic, research, and some large public libraries require a broader range of materials to meet the needs of their clientele. Many libraries include visual and performing arts materials in their collections, but the strength and numbers of their holdings will differ greatly contingent on the local needs of those using the collections. Institutions serving academic programs or a research-based clientele, for example, will tend to have more extensive collections of these scholarly materials. Collections of this nature tend to include both traditional and nontraditional print and nonprint materials.

Many publications, both print and nonprint, exist beyond the scope of standard identifying sources and are not easily recognized for acquisition purposes. These include art exhibition catalogs, music scores, plays, sound recordings, artists' books, video formats, and other nonprint documentation forms. Many of these materials will eventually appear in RLIN, OCLC, and WorldCat; however, originally identifying them for acquisition purposes often presents difficulties.

The variety of materials in the visual and performing arts can be categorized as follows: (1) easily identifiable monographs and serials, which are accommodated by broad approval plans of academic and trade publications; (2) materials of problematic identification that require item-by-item selection and purchase; and (3) materials of problematic identification that can be accommodated by specialized approval plans.

The materials in the first group include university press monographs and trade publications. These can be identified through traditional sources such as *Books in Print* in its various formats and international equivalents. These materials include art, dance, music, and theater arts histories; biographical publications on artists, musicians, and performers; and critical and theoretical writings on the visual and performing arts. Also now a part of this group are materials on which documentation has been in transition during the past decade. Some formats have moved into mainstream verification sources, while others remain in a limbo or alternative identification status. In addition to trade and university press monographs and serials, plays, play scripts, and copublished art exhibition catalogs have moved into the mainstream. Although many broad, multidisciplinary approval plans intend to supply these materials, some vendors are better at doing this than others. Thus, the possibility exists that various types of mainstream visual and performing arts materials may be inadvertently omitted from acquisition. Such an instance might occur when an institution contracts with a vendor that is more social science and science oriented than humanities and fine arts oriented. In this case, it may be necessary for the institution to locate specialized vendors to supply the materials not provided in the larger multidisciplinary plan. Some specialized publishers, such as publishers of art books, offer approval-type plans for their publications. However, care must be taken to match the publisher's publications with the institution's collection needs.

Once fairly unverifiable and confined to a limited group of publishers, plays and play scripts have made the transition into traditional verification sources, making verification of availability and subsequent acquisition much easier. Many major approval plan vendors are able to include either bibliographic forms or the actual publications in a broad multidisciplinary approval plan profile. This negates the need for a specialized approval plan to cover these materials.

Similarly, art exhibition catalogs and many general topic exhibition catalogs that are copublished by a trade or university press and a museum or gallery have also made the transition into traditional verification sources. Because these represent only a small percentage of the art exhibition catalogs actually available, however, the need for alternative avenues of identification and acquisition remains.

The second group of visual and performing arts materials includes print as well as nonprint material such as videos, slides, facsimile editions, music scores, and artists' books.[1] The broad range of nonprint materials available for the fine arts presents challenges for identification and acquisition. Videocassettes and videodiscs (including laser disks and CD-ROMs) are generally available through local businesses or major video distributors. Although the media distributors have yet to establish approval plans for academic or research institutions, extensive catalogs and brochures serve as reliable sources for identifying and acquiring their materials. In addition, these distributors will often provide discounts to educational institutions.

Although a recognized genre since the mid-1960s, artists' books are still considered a nontraditional print or print and image form. Artists' books are typically located only through contact with specific presses, book arts centers, individual artists, and vendors of this genre. Their acquisition, thus, requires extensive correspondence on the part of the librarian, the selector, or the acquisitions staff.

This brings us to the third group, art exhibition catalogs and music scores, which will be the focus of the remainder of this chapter. The materials in this group are published by a number of publishers who typically concentrate on specific subject areas. In addition, these publications are frequently produced in small print runs. Specialty vendors actively collect and distribute these publications to institutions with identified needs. Given the documentation and identification problems inherent with materials in this group, these vendors greatly facilitate the acquisitions process and ultimately provide the materials to libraries in a timely manner. The following discussion will focus on issues relating to approval plans and RFPs concerning art exhibition catalogs and music scores.

The Acquisition of Art Exhibition Catalogs and Music Scores

Art exhibition catalogs are described as follows: "When objects are displayed for [the] public, a catalog of the exhibition is usually written to inform visitors about the works of art and to produce a permanent record of the event,"[2] exhibition, or collection. Art exhibition catalogs published by academic and trade presses are numerous, but many small museums, art galleries, and art dealers also publish catalogs of their exhibitions and collections, which are equally as significant as those published by trade publishers and university presses. These catalogs are important for their biographical information, exhibition records, and data on specific works of art which might otherwise remain unpublished and unavailable. Catalogs of this nature are especially difficult to locate because they often lack specific identifying elements such as ISBN, ISSN, and Library of Congress Cataloging-in-Publication details. Other important works include international art exhibition catalogs, especially those from Asia, Europe, Japan and other Pacific rim nations, and Latin America. Reviews of exhibitions and available exhibition catalogs from these geographic areas may be announced in various art publications such as *Gazette des Beaux-Arts,* which lists exhibitions; *Art News,* which provides brief reviews of exhibitions; and *Apollo, Art in America, Art Nexus, Arte en Colombia, Artforum, Burlington Magazine,* and *Kunstchronik,* which provide essay-style reviews of exhibitions. Otherwise, exhibition catalogs typically receive little additional documentation that would facilitate their distribution. This significantly complicates their acquisition for visual arts collections.

Music scores are defined as "the written or printed form of a musical work in which the music for the participating voices and/or instruments appears on two or more staves, one above the other."[3] Although music scores are publications of established trade presses, this nontraditional print form rarely appears in established print sources. This factor seriously complicates verifying scores for acquisition purposes. The most recent edition of *Music in Print Master Composer Index* (and its corresponding *Master Title Index*) was published in 1995, with its previous edition appearing in 1988. Just as monographs go out of print, so do scores, making availability and bibliographic information of a timely nature essential. Because they are difficult to identify and locate in the first place, their consistent acquisition becomes especially critical. A reliable means for acquiring this type of material is necessary to maintain and support academic, research, or special collections gathering this type of material; approval plans help accomplish this goal.

Identifying and Meeting Collection Needs

Before contacting approval plan vendors, it is necessary to evaluate the level of coverage and the nature of the materials needed by a fine arts collection and its clientele. To accomplish this, it is important to have assessed the library collections serving academic or research collections or programs through a collection analysis project and to have developed the appropriate collection development policy statements. The former will assist in determining the strengths and weaknesses of a collection, and the latter will aid in identifying the directions a collection needs to take. Even if no collection development policy exists, it is still possible to identify information that will facilitate a plan by which vendors can develop criteria for including materials in an approval plan.

Vendor Interaction

A rewarding aspect of working with fine arts materials and approval plans is working with the vendors themselves. Although there are a limited number of vendors offering approval plans in the fine arts, those with this specialty are typically very reliable and strive to serve their customers in a positive and cooperative manner. Some vendors are small companies that specialize in a single subject area of the fine arts, and others are divisions of larger companies that may offer a variety of approval plans in various subject areas. In either case, the vendor's staff generally includes fine arts subject specialists. These individuals are willing to work with librarians to refine approval plans to meet the needs of the academic programs or research needs of collections within the institution.

Because the volume of materials with which fine arts vendors and the institutions deal is considerably smaller than with large, multidisciplinary approval plans, they have flexibility in developing criteria and requirements for an approval plan to meet local institutional and research objectives. Often fine arts vendors who work with the institution are willing to meet subject and material needs while working within budgetary allocations. Some fine arts vendors offer a variety of established plans from which an institution can choose. Once these are in place, librarians and vendor representatives work to add or eliminate peripheral subjects and materials. Thus, the customizing of the plans begins.

The Cover Letter

Preparing a cover letter to accompany an RFP for visual or performing arts approval plans must include the general information covered in chapter 3. (See sample cover letter in appendix B.) It must also list the specific art or music areas that are included in the RFP. Providing the equivalent Library of Congress or Dewey Decimal classification numbers may assist the vendor(s) in responding to the RFP.

Writing the RFP

Vendors offer a variety of services and materials that may appeal more to one institution than to another. The RFP process is especially useful when seeking vendors who specialize in specific subject areas or in materials that might otherwise be difficult to identify and locate for acquisition. Including subject specialty questions on the RFP will assist librarians and an institution in determining which vendor will best fulfill its needs. Areas to be queried should include company data and financial practice, profiling and coverage, bibliographic data, and customer service.

Company Data and Financial Practice

In addition to the informational equivalents from chapter 3, the RFP committee should ask questions about approval plans that are operating in comparable fine arts libraries. Other questions might include the following:

How many years has the vendor offered music scores or art exhibition catalogs on approval plans?

How many of these plans is the vendor operating at this time?

What are the vendor's staff size, extent of specialized bibliographic knowledge, and scholarly qualifications?

What discounts on materials, if any, are offered?

Profiling and Coverage

Profiling involves negotiated elements between the vendor and the institution. Because the concept of profiling is presented in greater depth in chapter 3, it will not be described in detail here other than to raise issues directly related to fine arts subject materials.

Art Exhibition Catalogs

Art exhibition catalog approval or standing order plans require similar considerations. Criteria for inclusion or exclusion would be medium (e.g., painting, graphic art, sculpture, architecture, decorative arts, photography); time period (e.g., prehistoric, ancient, early Christian and Byzantine, Medieval, Renaissance, Baroque, Modern); specific individuals (e.g., artists, architects, designers); movements (e.g., surrealism, dada, futurism); language of the publication; and continent, country, or region. Whether an institution desires a broad selection of catalogs representing international coverage or a limited selection with a regional focus, it should let vendors know this and state it as a requirement. This information is equally valuable for use during the vendor selection process. For example, exhibition catalogs published in Mexico and Latin America are often privately published, such as by financial institutions, and usually in very limited print runs. These factors complicate learning about, not to mention acquiring, exhibition catalogs from this geographic area. Profiling RFP requirements and questions may need to focus specifically on the geographic area if these materials are important to a library's or institution's collection.

Another factor relates to the language of materials. Care must be exercised when setting language limits on art materials. The subject matter of an exhibition catalog should take precedent over the language of publication, especially if the subject matter is critical to areas of research within an institution or scholarly environment. Many major and minor art exhibition catalogs are published in non-English languages; however, valuable information such as artist, dates, dimensions, and media is still comprehensible to most students and scholars with limited non-English-language knowledge. Also, many non-English-language exhibition catalogs are now accompanied by an English translation or summary.

To prevent overlapping coverage of art exhibition catalogs received through ongoing standing orders with individual museums and publishers or active museum exchange programs, questions in the profile should ask how the vendor handles this type of overlap and whether certain museums or publishers could be excluded from the profile.

Music Scores

Music scores involve similar considerations. These serve a wide range of purposes for the performing arts. Solos, duets, trios, quartets, symphonies, choirs, chorus, and a variety of other score-based activities use musical scores for study, research, and a range of performances such as opera, ballet, dance, and numerous theatrical presentations. An academic program or research collection focusing primarily on classical music would require different scores from those focusing on ancient, modern (such as rock and roll or popular music), or indigenous (such as country and western or folk) music. A library collecting classical music would need to clarify its needs to the vendor. Even within music time periods there may be specific composers whose work will be more greatly emphasized by the program and collection, which would in turn influence other aspects for consideration when customizing a music score approval plan. Information concerning the process for including or excluding various composers must, therefore, be raised in the RFP; for example, inclusion of composers from specific countries (e.g., those from Germany and Austria but not Scandinavia; no Eastern European composers other than the great Russian composers). The RFP must specify the geographic needs to vendors. Countries and/or continents of importance must be identified, such as the United States, Canada, Mexico, Latin America, and England.

Another complication in acquiring music scores is that they appear in both scores and parts. For example, a trio would include a score and three parts or a score and two parts, enabling all performers in a trio to have a part for his or her particular instrument. A library may not want the parts, or it may want scores and parts up to the quartet level. Similarly, if there are limitations on series, performance scores, or varying editions or options for instrumental, vocal, and stage music, these factors must also be stated in the RFP. A library must decide these and other criteria to be included in the RFP and communicated to the vendor.

Another consideration may involve the availability of other music materials that might be available on the approval plan. These include method books, librettos, sound recordings, and other nonscore materials. The RFP must inquire clearly if these materials are available and state if they are desired for inclusion in an institution's approval plan.

Plays and Play Scripts

Because plays and play scripts have been mainstreamed into multidisciplinary approval plans, there is no longer a need to consider them in separate fine arts approval plans. However, when developing an approval plan profile to include plays or play scripts within a larger multidisciplinary approval plan, the focus of the program and the needs of the drama or theater arts areas are primary considerations. If the main interest is in contemporary plays published in English, then two major factors are obvious: Plays of contemporary playwrights are important, and only English-language material should be supplied. If there is further need to refine the criteria to include only U.S. playwrights or British playwrights or U.S. and British playwrights, then this information is necessary as well. If the library also seeks English translations of foreign language play scripts, it must inform the vendor. Finally, it may prove useful to establish some guidelines for the years covered by the term *contemporary*, as it can be interpreted differently.

Bibliographic Data

Although many fine arts vendors do not typically offer bibliographic forms, they regularly distribute lists or catalogs of current music scores and art exhibition catalogs, which provide full bibliographic citations. Many multidisciplinary approval plans, however, do offer bibliographic forms for fine arts materials.

The possibility exists that the library could have multidisciplinary approval plans that might include art exhibition catalogs and music scores. If so, it is vital to set the parameters on the broader plans to eliminate this material or have it represented by bibliographic forms, if for no other reason than to spare the vendor the effort and expense of sending materials that would be returned because of overlaps with existing specialized subject approval plans. Setting such parameters will also help both the library and vendor staff to better refine the broader profiles.

Customer Service

Customer service needs for music scores and art exhibition catalog approval plans are the same as those for the large multidisciplinary approval plans covered in chapter 3. The library needs to consider what level of vendor contact is necessary to meet its individual requirements. How often will a sales representative call on the library? How quickly will customer service representatives respond to inquiries from the library? What types of fiscal and other management reports does the vendor provide? If the library has special nonstandard customer service or sales representative requirements, these should be specified in the RFP.

After the RFP

Careful examination of the institution's goals and the vendor's abilities is essential both in determining the focus of an RFP and in evaluating the vendor RFP responses. Although preparing RFPs is a labor-intensive and time-consuming process, care in their preparation and in the evaluation of vendor replies will ultimately contribute to the development of an approval plan that best addresses the institution's needs. It is beneficial both to the approval plan and the institution to have the librarian who is the art or music subject specialist work most closely, in concert with the acquisitions staff, with the fine arts vendor once a contract is approved. In this way, both the vendor and the librarian will establish personal contacts to facilitate the implementation and the success of visual and performing arts approval plans.

Notes

1. Clive Phillpot, "An ABC of Artists' Books Collections," *Art Documentation* 1, no. 6 (1982): cover.

2. Lois Swan Jones and Sarah Scott Gibson, *Art Libraries and Information Services: Development, Organization, and Management* (New York: Academic Press, 1986), 90.

3. E. T. Bryant, *Music Leadership: A Practical Guide* (London: James Clarke & Company, 1959), 117.

Chapter 8

Science, Technology, and Engineering Approval Plans

Linda K. Lewis
Director, Collection Management Department. University of New Mexico, Albuquerque, New Mexico

Johann van Reenen
Director, Centennial Science and Engineering Library. University of New Mexico, Albuquerque, New Mexico

The science of today is the technology of tomorrow.

—Edward Teller

Although the literature of science, technology, and engineering relies more heavily on serials than on books, it still makes heavy use of them. This chapter will address some of the issues involved in creating and evaluating an RFP for acquisitions in these areas. The science, technology, and engineering disciplines may include a wide range of subjects from the philosophy of science to biomedical engineering. Because each library may include different subjects in its definition of the sciences, the general phrase *science, technology, and engineering* should be understood to encompass the broad range of subjects related to these disciplines.

Advantages and Disadvantages of Science Approval Plans

Several authors have stated that approval plans do not work well for the science, technology, and engineering areas, while others conclude that they are an effective part of a library's overall collection management plan. John Ryland wrote that "sciences should be excluded. The reasons are obvious."[1] Gloriana St. Clair and Jane Treadwell concluded that plans in these areas require careful structuring, monitoring and evaluating, but that there are major difficulties.[2] One of the major drawbacks stated in the literature is that approval plans did not supply materials that the subject specialists expected, and did supply materials not needed. Because science, technology, and engineering materials are generally more expensive than those in other areas, libraries are often highly selective in the purchasing; approval plans may provide more materials than expected. The subject coverage and the ability to provide materials from societies and associations vary widely among vendors.

Given these concerns, why should libraries consider approval plans specifically for the science, technology, and engineering areas? Edwin D. Posey and Hugh Franklin each conclude that plans can indeed work well, rationalizing that the effort required to make these plans function effectively is the same as that needed for approval plans in any subject area.[3, 4] Approval plans are rarely intended as the only method of acquiring materials; they must be supplemented by other materials identified by collection development personnel.[5] When approval plans are designed well, they are a valuable component of a library's collecting program. They can supply most trade and university press materials very shortly after publication, and save time for both acquisitions and collection development personnel by reducing the need to check numerous review sources and place individual orders for the books. This allows the library to concentrate on acquiring specialized materials outside the scope of the approval plan. The success of an approval plan depends on writing a good RFP, selecting the best vendor, creating a working profile, and monitoring and adjusting the plan when necessary.

The Cover Letter

A cover letter for a science, technology, and engineering approval RFP must include the general information covered in chapter 3. (See sample cover letter in appendix B.) The cover letter must also tell the vendor exactly what specific subjects are to be included. For some libraries, *science, technology, and engineering* includes medicine, agriculture, or psychology titles; others will exclude these materials completely from the RFP. It may be useful to list the appropriate Library of Congress or Dewey Decimal classification numbers so that vendors can provide a more informed response.

Writing the RFP

Vendors offer a variety of services and materials to libraries. The RFP process allows the library to put forth specific requirements and ask each prospective vendor subject-specific questions, in this case questions dealing with science, technology, and engineering, to determine which vendor can best meet its needs. The information covered in chapter 3 should serve as the basis for an RFP in the science, technology, and engineering areas. Because of the nature of the subject areas, an RFP aimed at these subjects should address some additional factors in company data; profiling, title selection, and coverage; bibliographic data; electronic services; customer services; and financial practice and overall cost considerations.

Company Data

In addition to addressing the information covered in chapter 3, ask questions specifically targeted to the company's experience in the relevant subject areas. Ask for references from libraries that have separate science, technology, or engineering plans. Also ask for references from libraries that may have more general plans that include science, technology, and engineering as a major portion of their plans. When asking about the qualifications of the people who do the profiling, ask specifically about their relevant subject background.

Profiling, Title Selection, and Coverage

The success or failure of an approval plan depends largely upon the profile; the ability of the vendor to meet the needs of the library is crucial. This is true in all subjects, but the science, technology, and engineering disciplines present some particular concerns that must be addressed.[6]

The library must identify clearly what subject areas it wishes to include. Ask the vendor what methods it uses to assign subject headings, and request copies of the classification documentation. Because interdisciplinary subjects are increasingly important in the science, technology, and engineering areas, ask how the vendor handles these materials. The vendor and the library must agree, for example, on whether or not materials about the economic impact of ecological programs fall under the heading of "science." Other areas that the library and vendor may need to explore are the history of ideas and technology; health promotion, prevention, and management; and memory, cognition, and neuroscience. All these areas, as well as others, may be included in a science, technology, and engineering plan for some libraries. If medicine is to be included, specify whether the profile should include both clinical materials and biomedical research materials.

Many books in science, technology, and engineering are now being published with computer disks or CD-ROMs included, while other monographs are being issued only on disk or CD-ROM. Vendors profile the varying formats of materials through their nonsubject parameters. Ask for the documentation for them; these parameters are as crucial as the subject terms in the success of an approval plan.

Vendors also use nonsubject parameters to describe the academic level of materials. Most vendors have a scale of levels that ranges from "popular" to "research." The library must decide what levels are appropriate for which subjects, considering the needs of their undergraduates for representative core materials as well as the needs of researchers for highly specialized materials. Ask for the definitions of the various levels used by the vendor.

Another nonsubject parameter should relate to series. Because many publishers in the science, technology, and engineering arenas issue monographs in publishers' series, the ability of the vendor to identify these materials and handle them according to the library's needs is crucial. The vendor must be able to distinguish among volumes of a set, volumes of a serial, and monographs in a publisher's series. The definitions of these terms may vary among vendors and libraries. In very general terms, a set is expected to have a specific number of volumes, after which the publication ceases. Serials do not have an expected ending volume; they may include annual reviews of the literature in a subject or the proceedings of an association; for further explanations, please see chapter 4. Publisher's series are created by the publisher to bring together materials related to a topic; the volumes may or may not be numbered, and the series may continue indefinitely. These series are quite common in the sciences and present particular challenges for libraries and vendors.[7] Each vendor should provide lists of the categories it uses; if the documentation is not sufficiently explicit, the library should ask for specific examples. The vendor may offer the option of receiving the first volume of a new series or set as a book so that the library can decide if a standing order is desirable. The vendor should receive the library's list of serials and standing orders to ensure that those titles are not sent on approval; the library should ask how this process will work.

Most approval plan vendors specialize in the major trade and university presses. Ask for lists of the publishers included and excluded by the vendor. Because much of the material in science, technology, and engineering is published by associations, societies, and governmental and nongovernmental organizations, it is vital to ask the vendors which publishers they can—and cannot—supply. Many associations and societies will not deal with approval plan vendors; in such cases, the library must make arrangements directly with the associations. Proceedings are vital in many areas of science, technology, and engineering; vendors vary in their ability to provide these materials. Finally, vendors generally will not supply technical report literature. Libraries must not assume that an approval plan vendor can supply all desired materials. In all likelihood, libraries will have to supplement approval plans by acquiring these materials through other methods.

Bibliographic Data

In presenting selection options to the library, vendors may supply books or bibliographic forms that describe the books, depending on the library's needs. If the library wishes to involve the faculty in selection, it may wish to have titles in some areas sent on bibliographic forms that can be routed to department staff. Because of the high cost of science, technology, and engineering materials, the library may wish to receive bibliographic forms for any items over a certain price. This may allow for more careful review of the titles and a greater degree of selectivity than if books were sent and automatically accepted. Forms will save the expense of returning unwanted books, but they will delay the arrival of the books. If the science, technology, and engineering plan actually becomes a portion of a larger approval plan, ask if the price limits and other nonsubject parameters can be set specifically for these subjects.

Electronic Services

Electronic journals, indexes, and files are developing rapidly. The role of the vendors in supplying these kinds of materials is still highly fluid. Ask what the vendors are doing in these areas. Will they notify the library of materials in electronic formats just as they do for books? Will they provide assistance in arranging site licenses?

With more vendors making their databases available on the World Wide Web, collection development personnel can search these databases from their personal computers to verify how a title is being handled or to create subject bibliographies for retrospective purchasing or for faculty information. Ask if the database is available for collection development searching as well as for acquisitions ordering. If it is, ask if there are separate levels of authorization and passwords for the collection development and acquisitions personnel, as the authorization for ordering must be restricted to the library acquisitions personnel.

Electronic services is a rapidly changing area, and the library must determine which services are its priorities. Libraries must also be careful to distinguish between what the vendors can currently deliver and what they are hoping to develop.

Customer Services

Any approval plan profile will need adjustments as the financial circumstances and priorities of the library shift. Ask how profiles are created and revised. Will representatives visit the library to structure and revise profiles? After changes have been requested, how long does it take to implement them? For a plan to work well, profiles must be regularly monitored and evaluated.

Science, technology, and engineering areas change rapidly; the profile must shift to meet new developments. Ask if new subject terms are added to the vendor's classification plan. If so, how is the library informed of these additions?

As priorities change and new areas of interest develop, the library may need to do retrospective purchasing to supplement its collection. Ask vendors if they can provide specialized bibliographies on request.

Financial Practice and Overall Cost Considerations

If the library is considering creating one approval plan for science, technology, and engineering and another plan for other areas, it needs to consider the discounts carefully. The discount offered for a separate science plan may be higher than that offered for a plan in the social sciences and humanities; a plan encompassing all subject areas might receive yet another discount. The library should consider how much money will be spent in the various areas, the discount offered on those subjects, and the total benefit to the library. It is possible that the overall discount on a plan covering all subject areas might be lower than the discount offered on a science, technology, and engineering plan; however, if the amount of money allocated to the science, technology, and engineering plan is comparatively small, the library might save money by using the more comprehensive plan.

After the RFP

Careful examination of the institution's goals and the vendor's abilities to supply the materials that the library requires is essential when evaluating the vendor RFP responses. Although preparing the RFP is a labor-intensive and time-consuming process, care in its preparation and in the evaluation of vendor replies will ultimately contribute to the development of an approval plan that best addresses the institution's needs. It is beneficial to both the approval plan and the institution to have the librarian who is the science and engineering subject specialist work most closely, in concert with the acquisitions staff, with the vendor once the contract is awarded. In this way, both the vendor and the librarian will establish personal contacts to facilitate the implementation and the success of the approval plan.

Notes

1. John Ryland, "Collection Development and Selection: Who Should Do It?" *Library Acquisitions: Practice & Theory* 6, no. 1 (1982): 17.

2. Gloriana St. Clair and Jane Treadwell, "Science and Technology Approval Plans Compared," *Library Resources and Technical Services* 33, no. 4 (1989): 390–91.

3. Edwin D. Posey, "Approval Plans: A Subject Specialist's View," in *Approval Plans and Academic Libraries; An Interpretive Survey*, ed. Kathleen McCullough et al. (Phoenix, AZ: Oryx Press, 1977), 135–36.

4. Hugh L. Franklin, "Sci/Tech Book Approval Plans Can Be Effective," *Collection Management* 19, no. 1/2 (1994): 114.

5. Barbara Magnuson, "Science and Technology Book Reviews as Supplements to an Approval Program," *Science and Technology Libraries* 8 (Winter 1987/88): 86–88.

6. Stanley P. Hodge and William Hepfer, "Scientific and Technical Materials: A General Overview," in *Selection of Library Materials in the Humanities, Social Sciences, and Sciences*, ed. Patricia A. McClung (Chicago: American Library Association, 1985), 233–34.

7. Nancy J. Putnam, "The Impact of Series Publishing on the Domestic Approval Plan," in *Shaping Library Collections for the 1980s*, ed. Peter Spyers-Duran and Thomas Mann, Jr. (Phoenix, AZ: Oryx Press, 1980), 117.

PART IV

Evaluation, Implementation, and Follow-Up

Chapter 9

Evaluating Vendor Proposals

Frances C. Wilkinson / Connie Capers Thorson

Always do right; this will gratify some people and astonish the rest.

—Mark Twain

Once the deadline for vendors to respond to the RFP has passed and the purchasing officer has released the vendor proposals to the library's RFP committee, the committee's task is to evaluate the proposals and select a vendor(s). The committee must take this process seriously because the library will have to live with its decision for at least a year or two, and usually longer. Although no one in the library, whether involved in the process or not, wants to see more time invested in the RFP process than absolutely necessary, a thorough, fair evaluation is imperative. It is perhaps the most important part of the RFP process; going through months of planning and writing to then perform a substandard evaluation of vendor responses would be absurd!

The implications of change cannot be ignored either. Transferring serial titles, for instance, is a task requiring a great deal of time and effort on the part of many people, and the possibility for error is real. Changing approval vendors will require a commitment by collection development librarians to spend time developing a new profile. Change for the sake of change is not a good idea. A realistic, objective approach to evaluating the proposals will ensure that any changes will benefit the library.

Evaluation Criteria

The evaluation criteria must be based on the RFP itself, and the percentage of value assigned to a given factor must reflect the best wisdom of the RFP committee. The evaluation criteria should have been previously agreed upon and clearly delineated in the RFP cover letter to prospective vendors. Reminding the Purchasing department that the contract award is not being made entirely on the basis of price may be beneficial to the library. It is foolish to "evaluate mainly on the basis of speed, price, and accuracy,"[1] when the whole rationale for preparing an RFP is to base the choice of a vendor on additional, equally significant criteria. For example, the demands that libraries make for increased automation of acquisitions' procedures make the bells and whistles that a vendor can provide of great interest. A library may find itself providing information to users so rapidly that neither it nor the vendor can keep up unless the automated services provided are of a high standard and the vendor has enough personnel to cope with the increased demands.[2] Conversely, the committee should not be swayed by electronic or other features the library really does not need.

The RFP committee must have a clear picture of what its basic requirements are and what extra services would be useful to have, as well as know what may sound good but not be of use to the library. In the interest of fairness and to ensure the integrity of the procurement process, the committee should eliminate any vendor from consideration that does not meet all its required elements. The library must take care when writing the RFP to ensure that all its required elements are reasonable and truly required, not merely desired. In the event that none of the vendors responding can meet a given requirement, however, usually the Purchasing department will allow that requirement to be disregarded.

Evaluation Form

The evaluation form developed should be specific to each RFP, though some factors will be the same for all RFPs. Several schools of thought have emerged regarding vendor evaluation forms. Although some libraries prefer not to use a numerical rating system,[3] and this is perfectly acceptable, a numerical rating system will be used in the examples in this book. Arguments against numerical rating systems are usually based on two elements. Some committees fear inconsistent ratings among the evaluators. However, if a committee member tends to be either a "tough or easy grader," this member generally evaluates this way across-the-board. Because the committee will average all evaluators' scores together to provide a composite total score, this tendency from a single evaluator is unlikely to create a serious problem. The other concern is that some unscrupulous evaluator will rate one vendor artificially high or low to unfairly sway the award. It is highly unlikely, however, that the committee members would condone such unprofessional tactics.

Preparing an evaluation form for each evaluator to use for each vendor response provides the most consistent and least confusing method for the evaluators to follow. The form should state specifically which RFP it is covering and provide spaces for the date, the name of the vendor, and the evaluator's name and department. Every section in an RFP should be a separate factor (e.g., company data, customer service) with a separate weight. That weight, in the form of a percentage assigned to it, should be clearly indicated. (See appendix C for sample evaluation forms.)

Asking evaluators to assign a percentage score and then to justify or explain it will help the evaluators be objective. Defending their judgments will keep them from saying such things as, "We have had pretty good luck with this vendor in the past." The evaluations should be based primarily on the RFP in hand, not past performance, though one cannot ignore it completely.

The percentages awarded to each category on the form will be based on the evaluation criteria specified in the RFP and should be tailored to each library's particular needs. This is especially true for foreign approval plans and standing orders, whether the library chooses to include them in the approval plan or the serials RFP. They are not intended to be prescriptive but merely serve as an example. To simplify the math portion of the RFP process, all categories should total 100% or 100 points or some other easy-to-interpret multiple such as 10 points. The scenario that follows uses 100 points. For example, if three vendors submit a proposal, the library can present vendor scores (which are the mathematical averages of each committee member's score) that the Purchasing department can interpret at a glance, for example, Vendor A at 92 points, Vendor B at 84 points, and Vendor C at 61 points. These scores will, of course, be corroborated by a narrative justification of why each vendor received a given score in each category.

The Evaluation Process

The evaluation process may take place long after the RFP committee developed the factors and weights for evaluation. Thus, before the evaluation begins, the RFP committee should meet to discuss exactly what each person should be looking for, to set ground rules, and to answer any questions or concerns evaluators have. All committee members must have a clear understanding of what the library is looking for in the vendor proposals and how much weight will be assigned to each response. Inevitably, slight variances in opinion will occur and, in fact, can be desirable; one evaluator might miss some point that another finds. Committee members should embark on the evaluation phase with shared goals and understanding for the process to be both equitable and successful.

The evaluation process itself (including verification of vendor references and the library's recommendation to the Purchasing department) should take no more than three weeks. Allowing more time will permit the margin of error to rise because evaluators will become vague about the details of the first vendor proposals they reviewed. In addition, the library administration will be anxious to conclude the lengthy, time-consuming process to make the awards. The Purchasing department will need enough time to prepare the contracts and notify all the vendors that submitted a proposal. Also, if a change in vendors is being made, it is vital that the library allow itself enough time for a well-executed transfer to occur.

Members of the RFP committee should be reminded that vendor responses must be kept confidential until the contract(s) is awarded. Contact with vendors during this phase should be restricted, if not avoided altogether. The RFP committee chair may wish to consult with the library's purchasing officer to discuss any questions the committee members may have in this regard.

As the committee begins to evaluate the proposals, its composition becomes especially important. If personnel from acquisitions, serials, or collection development do not have considerable systems expertise, and there is not already a member of the Systems department on the committee, adding one at this point to assist in the evaluation of computer-based services is highly desirable. If a person knowledgeable about computers has not been on the committee since its inception, this would be a good time to invite a systems librarian to address the group on what they should be especially aware of when reading the proposal and to explain any computer jargon or buzzwords that the vendor may have used. This person may, indeed, be the best one to assess the vendor responses to the questions on computer-based services.

Vendor References

Other important pieces of the evaluation puzzle are the references that the vendors have supplied. The references should be similar in type and size to the library,[4] and at least one of them should have the same Integrated Library System (ILS). Preferably, one of the references has recently (within the last two years) transferred its account to the vendor. The type of references desired should have been stated in the RFP cover letter to the vendor. The RFP committee should contact references as early as possible in the evaluation phase. Obviously, vendors are not going to provide the names of dissatisfied customers, but developing probing questions will nonetheless help to elicit meaningful responses. The committee should prepare a list of questions specific to the library's particular situation. Thought should be given to what is asked, what bearing it has on the evaluation categories, and how it will be assessed. Be sure to ask each reference the same questions to ensure fairness to all vendors. Also, not rushing references into an opinion will allow for more telling responses.

One particularly interesting question can be framed around the worst problem the reference ever had with the vendor in question and how the problem was discovered, communicated, and finally resolved. Another question might delve into how well the vendor responds to requests for fiscal and management reports or for unusual automated services. If the library is interested in working with the vendor on new automation initiatives, ask whether the reference has had occasion to request similar cooperation. Ask these questions even if the reference's library does not have the same automated system as yours. You are trying to find out how well the vendor works with clients, not necessarily how well the vendor works with a specific system. Call at least one reference that does have the same ILS as your library so that you can ask questions about compatibility. Asking questions about customer service concerns, especially those particular to your library's needs or requirements, is obvious, but pinpointing particular issues will help the reference focus answers: Ask about how the vendor responds to concerns or questions about short shipments or duplication on approval plans or claims for missing issues from serials vendors. If the reference has recently (within the last two years) transferred its account to the vendor, ask about transfer assistance programs. A list of potential reference questions can be found in appendix C.

After the RFP committee has called the references, it should meet to share and discuss the information provided. Responses from the references will influence the weights the committee assigns to each evaluation category; these should be discussed in-depth by the committee.

Individual Evaluations

Evaluators will make their recommendations based on the evaluation criteria. They will not only consider the vendor proposals but also all aspects of the library's experience, the vendor's on-site presentations, and the responses from the references in awarding points for each criterion on the evaluation form.

As discussed earlier, any vendor that cannot meet all the library's required elements should be removed from consideration. "Once this subset has been determined, the application of local needs and priorities will facilitate further deselection on price, service, and/or reputation."[5]

Generally, each RFP committee member will perform initial evaluations individually and privately.[6] All vendor proposals should be located in a secure place (to ensure confidentiality) with adequate space available for committee members to comfortably review and evaluate them. A supply of evaluation forms should be readily available. In cases where the committee is evaluating multiple RFPs, it may wish to use a recommendation form in addition to evaluation forms. The one-page recommendation form makes it clear, at a glance to the person who will be tabulating the results, which vendor is being recommended for each RFP type by the evaluator. (See appendix C for a sample recommendation form.) The process is time-consuming and may require evaluators to read through the vendor proposals more than once to compare vendor services fully.

Overall price considerations are often the most straightforward, though generally not the most important, areas to evaluate. The library cannot, however, ignore the discount rates, the service charges, or any prepayment benefits that are delineated in the vendor proposals. After all, these financial considerations will mean that the library can buy more books and serials than their budgets may have initially indicated. Such considerations must be kept in perspective, however, when assessing the best vendor for a particular part of a library's budget. Negotiating the highest discount rates in the world will not be beneficial if the vendor can only supply materials from well-known publishers or consistently short-ships materials to the library (by not having enough stock on hand to supply all librar-ies at one time with an approval book). Prepayment discounts will soon become unimpor-tant if the vendor cannot arrange for periodical issues to be delivered in an uninterrupted, timely fashion. If a standing order vendor cannot offer the variety and number of series the library is interested in buying, then a high discount rate will not be useful. The RFP commit-tee chair should inquire about whether the vendor raises the discount percentage as the amount of money spent rises, if the vendor did not address this in its proposal. This factor alone may be enough to determine whether a library will decide to invest more of its funds with one vendor rather than split the contract between two vendors.

An area that is less straightforward to evaluate than pricing is service. Both customer service and, increasingly, computer-based service are generally of great importance to the library. The areas specific to different types of RFPs, such as approval plans (which in-clude profiling and title selection, coverage, bibliographic data, and financial practice) and serials (which include orders and cancellations, invoicing, claims, and title changes), boil down to vendor service.

The evaluator will have to consider both the experience that the vendor's customer service and sales staff have with accounts like the library's and how easily accessible they are. Also, if the library will be changing vendors, it must consider what kind of support the vendor would provide during the transition. Such areas as the type of accounting informa-tion the vendor will provide on invoices and whether it can be customized for the library, ar-rangements for multiple bill to/ship to addresses, and the vendor's willingness to intercede with difficult publishers on behalf of the library must all be weighed. Profiling and title se-lection techniques and coverage provided must be considered when evaluating approval plan RFPs. Claims procedures, order entry methods, the lag between order entry and its con-firmation, methods of handling rush orders, and accurate and prompt processing of renew-als are areas to be evaluated on serials RFPs.

Automation support has become central to the needs of most libraries. Evaluators must consider what the vendor's database provides in terms of locating price and availability in-formation, publisher restrictions, ordering, claiming, and information regarding the li-brary's account. Is the database easy to use and accurate, with up-to-date pricing data? Can the vendor provide the fiscal and management reports that the library desired, and, if so, how is this done? Can the library access the vendor's online system and run its own reports if it so desires? Information such as the vendor's ability to interface with the library's ILS usually appears in the required section, but some nuances may be open to consideration: Has the interface been tested, and is it being used at other libraries? Will additional software have to be purchased from the ILS vendor or developed in house? Will the vendor custom-ize the way specific data elements can be manipulated for reports?

The evaluator must also consider the less tangible aspects of company data, back-ground, and reputation. Some aspects to be evaluated are fairly straightforward, such as the vendor's financial soundness, its overall reputation, its representative's knowledge, and its level of respect within the library community. Other aspects such as personality[7] or persona[8] of the vendor—the fit between the library and the vendor—are harder to quantify. Evalua-tion of these factors, if considered in the formal process at all, is usually left to evaluator in-tuition and experience, which are also challenging to quantify.

Negotiation Strategies

After the vendor proposals have been received, and while the evaluation process is in full swing, preliminary negotiations may begin. Be aware that there are no magic strategies involved with vendor negotiations. Before the library contacts any of the vendors, the RFP committee chair should meet with the purchasing officer to seek advice about what is and what is not acceptable negotiation strategy in the organization or in the state. The chair of the RFP committee is probably also the best person to call vendors to initiate negotiations. "Negotiation has two objectives: to reach the best possible service and pricing arrangement and to clarify service requirements and commitments."[9] Generally, it is acceptable and desirable to call a vendor to ask questions regarding any answer on the proposal that is unclear. In some cases, a vendor may have misunderstood the question and thus answered it in a way that is of no use to the library.

Depending on what is permissible in your state, and whether or not the RFP required vendors to submit their best-and-final offer with their initial response, the RFP committee chair may be able to question whether the discount (for monographs) or service charge (for serials) is firm and, if not, negotiate a lower one. Possibly the committee chair can persuade the vendor to waive charges for its vendor online system, if it normally assesses a charge. Other concessions that the library believes are necessary to award the contract can be requested. Remember that "the negotiation must focus on approaches with the potential to reduce library costs without reducing essential services, and without putting the agent out of business."[10] Also, hostile negotiations that pit one vendor against another benefit no one in the long run. The goal is to establish a positive working relationship—a partnership—that serves all parties involved. Finally, regardless of how minor or extensive the changes to the original proposal are, the library should always require that the vendor submit an addendum to the proposal in writing.

RFP Committee Consensus

Once all individual RFP committee members have completed their preliminary evaluations of all the vendor proposals, the full committee will meet to discuss areas of concern and to resolve differences of opinion regarding the strengths and weaknesses of a given vendor. Vendor references discussed in a previous meeting may be referred to again for clarification on some point of interest or concern. Any changes or amendments to the initial vendor proposals as a result of negotiations between the library and the vendor should be considered.

The RFP committee must decide whether or not to split the contract(s) among two or more vendors. Two of the best reasons for splitting an award between two vendors are (1) to increase competition and (2) to ensure good service, particularly if the library thinks it is being taken for granted by the incumbent.[11] Being the library that always gets the book last is one way a library can be taken advantage of. Equally annoying is finding the customer representative never available or rarely responsive. Having a serials vendor that cannot and will not take some responsibility for issues claimed but not received (What does the service charge entitle one to expect, after all?) is another example of a reason a library might want to look for something better. Standing order vendors that cannot supply new volumes quickly are of little use, regardless of the discounts they offer. Most publishers of standing order titles do, after all, also offer substantial savings to individual customers.

Inviting a vendor or vendors to return to the library to answer questions in person, especially when the questions are extensive or the decision to award the contract has been narrowed to two vendors, may be helpful. Some believe that "it is usually desirable to schedule vendor presentations with the 'top cut' of respondents and to undergo vendor negotiation sessions with them."[12] The library must weigh the value of another on-site visit against the cost in time to the library and travel expense to the vendor. Still, in some cases a follow-up visit can prove enlightening. If a follow-up visit is not possible, a conference call might be a useful and speedier alternative.

In addition to discussion, someone on the RFP committee will want to tally the vendor scores from each evaluation form to get the average score for each vendor in each category. The scores will usually not come as a surprise to the committee as a whole as it has a common understanding of what the library is looking for in a vendor and has evaluated the vendors accordingly. Especially in cases where multiple contracts are to be awarded, a one-page recommendation form is useful to make clear at a glance to the person doing the tabulations which vendor is being recommended for each RFP type by each evaluator. Once a consensus is reached, the committee is ready to prepare and forward its recommendations to the library director and the purchasing officer.

RFP Committee Recommendations

After completing the evaluation process, accomplishing negotiations, and reaching consensus in selection of a vendor(s), the RFP committee must prepare its recommendations to present initially to the library director or library's management group and, ultimately, to the Purchasing department. The preparation of the recommendation should not be a particularly onerous task if the RFP process has been handled seriously and comprehensively at each step along the way. Open the recommendation document with an enumeration of the vendors submitting proposals and the criteria used for evaluating them. Follow with a clear and positive statement naming the vendor(s) being recommended for the contract(s) and a discussion of the considerations that led the committee members to their recommendations. Indicate clearly the committee's (averaged) evaluation score for each vendor, along with a detailed justification for each score. If the Purchasing department has not already supplied the library with a cost comparison of all vendors submitting proposals, the RFP committee should produce one.

The committee members need to keep in mind that they have knowledge about the vendors that is vastly superior to that of any person or group that will consider the recommendation. Thus, they should keep their document as free of vague assumptions and complicated jargon as possible while striving for a high degree of specificity. They should consider each section of each RFP, providing information not only about why the weight of each is reasonable but also about why the section was included. The evaluation should also point out that the recommendations have the approval of the entire committee.

Emphasize the reasons why discount rates or service charges were not the overriding consideration on which the recommendations were made. A reasonable explanation of the relevance of discount rates or service charges for the whole RFP process will help those reading the document put such issues in perspective. Explain the negotiations that took place with the vendors for discount rates, service charges, and other fiscal matters such as prepayment or deposit account incentives. Anticipating questions that may arise is good strategy and will ultimately save valuable time.

Inevitably, the committee members will compare the vendor proposals. These comparisons must be as objective as possible; the recommendation should not descend to the subjective. Emphasize the responses that most clearly address the major concerns of the committee members. Spend some time explaining both what the successful vendors have indicated they can do now and what they are suggesting they will offer in the future. If the decision to divide a contract is made, explain in detail why splitting the award will benefit the library. Explain briefly how the split will be handled and indicate the proposed timeline for the changes.

The recommendation to the library director or management group should clearly establish the positive aspects the committee members have experienced throughout the initiation and completion of the process. The benefits that have accrued to the various members of the committee could be mentioned briefly. The committee needs to make clear to the director or management group that the process was taken seriously and of value to the participants so that the management group will have no doubts about the merits of such an extensive and time-consuming process. After all, the process will be repeated in a few years!

Awarding the Contract

After the RFP committee has the dean or director's approval of the RFP, the committee chair forwards the recommendation document to the Purchasing department. Once the purchasing officer has read and agreed to the committee's recommendation, the Purchasing department awards the contract(s).

Generally, the RFP specifications, the vendor proposals, and any amendments to the initial vendor responses will form the contract. Some states or institutions, however, require a separate contract document. Preparing this document is usually the Purchasing department's responsibility because of its complex nature.

In cases where the Purchasing department does not routinely notify all vendors of the library's decision, the library should request that the Purchasing department do so, or if permissible, offer to do it instead. Even though a vendor is not selected at the time, it may be solicited and selected in a future RFP cycle. Keeping a positive, cordial relationship with all vendors is beneficial to everyone involved.

Notes

1. Dana Alessi, "Vendor Selection, Vendor Collection, or Vendor Defection," *Journal of Library Administration* 16, no. 3 (1992): 166.

2. In many libraries, both public and technical services are overwhelmed by the impact of expanded automation on user demands. A patron may request priority cataloging for an item not yet available for use but physically in the library, as well as for an item ordered just moments before! At the University of New Mexico, these requests doubled each year over the previous year after the advent of the online public access catalog. As more tables of contents, abstracts, and summaries are added to records, libraries will see the demand rise even more.

3. Arnold Hirshon and Barbara A. Winters, *Outsourcing Library Technical Services: A How-to-Do-It Manual for Librarians* (New York: Neal-Schuman, 1996), 135.

4. Hirshon and Winters, 136.

5. N. Bernard Basch and Judy McQueen, *Buying Serials: A How-to-Do-It Manual for Librarians* (New York: Neal–Schuman, 1990), 116.

6. Hirshon and Winters, 136.

7. See Kathleen Born, "Strategies for Selecting Vendors and Evaluating Their Performance—From the Vendor's Perspective," *Journal of Library Administration* 16, no. 3 (1992): 111–16, for a discussion on vendor personality as well as pricing and service from the vendor perspective.

8. See Karen A. Schmidt, "Choosing a Serials Vendor," *Serials Librarian* 14, no. 3/4 (1988): 11–16, for a discussion on vendor persona as well as pricing and service.

9. Basch and McQueen, 116.

10. N. Bernard Basch and Judy McQueen, "Stretching the Acquisitions Budget by Negotiating Subscription Agency Service Charges," in *Legal and Ethical Issues in Acquisitions*, ed. Katina Strauch and Bruce Strauch (Binghamton, NY: Haworth Press, 1990), 129.

11. Robert F. Nardini, "Approval Plans: Politics and Performance," *College and Research Libraries* 54 (1993): 418–19.

12. Hirshon and Winters, 137.

Chapter 10

The Vendor Transfer Process

Ruth M. Haest

Paying Team Leader, Acquisitions and Serials Department. University of New Mexico, Albuquerque, New Mexico

The difficult things of this world must once have been easy; the great things of this world must once have been small. Set about difficult things while they are still easy; do great things while they are still small.

—Lao Tzu (6th Century B.C.)

Once the RFP committee has carefully evaluated the vendors' proposals and forwarded its recommendation(s) to the Purchasing department, the vendor contract(s) will be awarded. If the contract goes to one or more vendors not currently under contract with the library, the transfer process must be undertaken. The transfer process, also known as the transition process, may involve transferring titles from one or more vendors to one or more vendors and requires careful planning. The sooner planning for the transfer begins, the smoother the process is likely to be. The library must determine the execution of the transfer process, the materials to be transferred, the method by which they will be transferred, and the follow-up.

Whether the library is changing approval plan vendors, serials vendors, or both, it must allocate sufficient staff resources to ensure a successful transition. Changing approval vendors will require a commitment by collection development librarians to develop a new profile. Acquisitions staff will need to ensure that they and the new vendor(s) coordinate the forms and procedures, including timing of invoices, return of rejected approval titles, and development of rejection forms. If the approval vendor is providing electronic access to its database or if it is transmitting records to the library's integrated library system, systems staff may also be involved. Transferring serial titles is also a task requiring much time and effort on the part of acquisitions, serials, and possibly systems staff. In short, changing vendors is not a process to be taken lightly. Vendor-hopping based on whim or even a charismatic sales presentation is never a sound managerial strategy. On the other hand, changing vendors based on well-reasoned purpose can benefit the library.[1] Although few librarians would embrace the thought of a major vendor transfer with glee, careful planning of the transfer process can minimize problems and disruption to library staff.

Planning the Transfer Project

Vendor transfers will usually take more time and effort than expected, and even when everything seems under control, another problem is likely to arise! To minimize the impact of unexpected problems, always plan well in advance. If possible, undertake a series of database cleanup and enhancement projects before the actual transfer process begins. These projects might include updating fund codes and other internal library codes as well as attending to title changes. Having a clean database will save time, which is likely to be at a premium during the transfer project.[2]

Preliminary planning can begin as much as a year before the library decides which vendor(s) will be awarded the contract(s) or the actual transfer occurs. However, as soon as this decision is in place, the transfer process should become a top priority. Planning for the transfer should reflect the requirements and other specifications stated in the RFP and confirmed in the contract signed by both parties. Becoming familiar with the RFP specifications from the successful vendor(s) regarding the services that they will provide to assist with the transition process will help the library make informed decisions regarding the transfer activities that library staff will perform and the activities that the library may be able to assign to the vendor(s).

Involve the library staff that will perform the tasks associated with the transfer project well in advance, soliciting their input throughout the planning process. As the transfer project begins, designate one person to coordinate the entire process; doing so can be very helpful, especially for a large library. Depending on the library's size, this person may enlist a group or at least one other person to work on the project throughout. The leader of this group is then responsible for planning the steps to be taken, meeting with other members of the RFP committee to ensure proper communication and workflow, keeping track of any existing time constraints, and ensuring quality control by monitoring and resolving problems as they arise. Without someone specifically responsible for the success of the transfer project, these issues can easily become problems that will hinder the process.

Planning a vendor transfer presents as many scenarios as there are libraries doing transfers. A library can choose from many options for placing its approval plans, standing orders, and subscriptions. All approval plans could be consolidated with one approval plan vendor, or the approval plan could be divided among two or more vendors who would supply university press titles, trade publications, science and technology titles, fine arts titles, or titles from one or more foreign countries. Bibliographic forms could be supplied by one or more approval plan vendors (either in paper or electronic formats). Standing orders could be supplied by approval plan or serials vendors. All serials titles could be consolidated under one vendor; all foreign and domestic subscription titles could be placed with one or more domestic vendors; all foreign subscription titles could be separated and sent to one or more foreign vendors; or all domestic subscription titles could be sent to one or more domestic vendors. Whatever the scenario, planning the transfer process on the basis of which types of materials are to be transferred to which vendor(s) is crucial.

Planning for Approval Plan Transfers

Once the library knows that the approval plan(s) will shift from one vendor to another, it needs to create a profile with the new vendor. If the contract is being split between two or more approval plan vendors, then, obviously, two or more profiles will have to be created, avoiding overlap between them. The profile(s), created by the library with the aid of the approval vendor(s), establishes specifications and guidelines for the types of books the vendor(s) should send in each shipment. In preparing for the profiling session, librarians must decide on a range of issues affecting the ultimate success of the approval plan, such as publisher scope, subject specifications, duplication control, nonsubject parameters, and budget,[3] as well as paper versus hard copy binding, U.S. imprint versus U.K. or other imprint of the same title, and price parameters.

Assuming that collection development is done by several subject specialists, representatives from all major subject areas should meet with the vendor representative to ensure that interdisciplinary areas are covered appropriately under the new profile. If this is impractical because the group would be too large, selectors could be divided into broad cluster areas such as social sciences, humanities, education, and science. In any case, the profile is crucial; a poor profiling session dooms a plan. Allow at least one day, preferably two, for the entire profiling process to take place, especially if this is a new approach for the library.

If the vendor is transmitting records electronically or providing access to its database via the World Wide Web, the library systems staff and the vendor systems staff need to work together to identify and resolve technical details. Any new electronic program will have some problems; allow enough time to resolve them.

Each vendor has slightly different needs and expectations concerning ways that invoices are processed, books are returned, and communication is established. The library's acquisitions staff and the vendor's customer service representatives should establish the basic practices to ensure a good beginning to the relationship.

Planning for Serials Transfers

Most serials vendors market themselves as partners with the library and as an extension of the library's staff, and are, therefore, usually more than willing to contribute to the transfer process in any number of ways. At a minimum, most domestic vendors, and many foreign ones as well, assign a primary contact person to the library (usually the customer service representative who will handle the library's account) to ease the transition either to or from the company. Virtually every vendor has a toll-free telephone number, fax number, and e-mail address, ensuring access to customer information and assistance. Do not underestimate the importance of maintaining a positive tone with the outgoing, as well as incoming, vendor. Keeping communication on a professional note will make the process go smoother and more pleasantly for all concerned. After all, the library may do business again with this vendor at some future date.

When a library is switching its serials orders from one vendor to another, the new vendor is likely to offer a significant level of clerical and systems support for the changeover. If such assistance is not forthcoming, it should be required as a condition of the new vendor selection,[4] assuming this condition was specified in the contract. The library will want to plan for the amount of library staff time needed during the transfer process while taking into account the types and amount of vendor assistance it wishes to receive.

Types of Vendor Assistance

Vendors will generally offer to help the library with the transfer process in a variety of ways. If the library has a manual system, vendors may offer to provide customized barcode labels to affix to manual records. If the library has an automated system, vendors may offer programming assistance (for a homegrown automated system) or data input assistance (for an integrated library system). Depending on the size and complexity of the account being transferred, the vendor may offer to send a representative to the library for several days to help with the hands-on portion of the transfer for either manual or automated systems. This type of assistance is generally negotiated on a case-by-case basis.

Conversely, if the library prefers, some vendors will authorize library staff access to the vendor's online system to transfer their titles. In such cases, they will give library staff passwords to perform data entry of their titles into the vendor's database. Some libraries prefer their staff to do the data entry themselves to reduce possible vendor error and to ensure that library time frames are met.

Some vendors may offer a one-time transfer assistance allowance or a temporarily reduced service charge to help defray the library's cost to transfer its account. The money saved might be used by the library to hire additional temporary staff, pay overtime for existing staff, or purchase equipment such as scanners for barcoding projects.

The vendor can also make the process easier by creating and sending a program to the library that can scan into the existing system the title or subscription number that identifies each title. Barcodes speed up the manual process of entering ISSNs, fund codes, and unique vendor title numbers. This can save an incredible amount of hands-on staff time. In the future, in an ideal EDI world, libraries will ask the vendor to run an electronic quote containing the unique vendor number, as well as bibliographic information about the title. The library system will then load this information automatically, thus eliminating the need for the barcode process.

The transfer of a subscription from one vendor to another is not an unusual occurrence. Most publishers are fairly adept at recognizing this when one vendor ceases to pay for a given title for a given library and another vendor begins to pay for that title. Also, many vendors and publishers communicate with each other the status of orders transfers, and cancellations for libraries. Renewals appear to flow more smoothly if the new vendor submits them using the form of library name and address used by the previous vendor and annotates the renewal to indicate that it is for an order previously canceled through another vendor.[5]

In some cases, the outgoing vendor may be willing to send letters (using library letterhead, if desired) or in some other way let each publisher for each title know that the library is not canceling the title, just transferring it to another vendor. If the publisher receives such notice, there will be no need for the publisher to contact the outgoing vendor asking why something was not renewed for the client, and the vendor will not have to deal with dozens of messages from individual publishers. Notification may also reduce the incidence of bogus renewal notices being sent directly from the publisher to the library. Notification helps eliminate extra work for the outgoing vendor, the incoming vendor, and the library; most important, it may help prevent future missing issues and duplicates. This procedure is especially useful when dealing with smaller publishers. Larger publishers can be notified electronically by the vendor. This electronic transmission includes the vendor number and the library reference numbers as well as pertinent information about the title. This is the most common way these publishers find out about transfers and cancellations.

The number of titles to be moved will also affect the planning process. The number may be a major or minor issue, depending on the size of the collection and the size of the transfer list. In fact, if every title is being transferred, as opposed to half of the collection or a partial list, the whole process becomes less complicated and certain steps can be eliminated.

Identifying Serials Titles to Be Transferred

After the library decides the number of subscription titles to transfer, it must determine which of the titles (some or all) with the existing vendor will be transferred. This decision can be reached in a variety of ways, depending on the length of the list and the contractual agreement between the library and the vendor. If the library's serials records are automated, run a list from the library's own integrated library system of the eligible titles, based on the guidelines set up in the RFP. For example, if you plan to split all domestic subscription titles between two or more domestic vendors (i.e., away from the existing vendor or leaving some with the existing vendor and placing some with the new vendor), compile a list of every title with the current vendor(s).

When splitting the business equally between two or more vendors, you will want to ensure an equitable mix. The mix is simply the combination of types of serials by subject that reside with each vendor. For example, a factor to consider when dividing the titles to be transferred is that those titles whose publishers provide discounts to vendors (generally publishers in the science, technology, and medical fields) and those titles that carry little or no discount to vendors (typically humanities and social sciences titles) be divided evenly between vendors. Using care in this regard ensures that each vendor receives an equitable share of both discounted and undiscounted titles as well as an equitable share of the total monetary account value. This same procedure would also be followed if all or some of the titles to be transferred to a vendor were previously on order directly from the publisher.

Another helpful tool to use in deciding which titles to transfer is a management report listing from the existing vendor's system of all titles currently ordered through that vendor. This list can be requested in a variety of profiles, such as by country of origin, alphabetically, or by the monetary fund assigned by the library. The guidelines of the RFP will determine what type of list is needed. Libraries that have the capability to receive and use an electronic list should always request one. An electronic list is faster to generate and easier for the library to manipulate or further customize than a paper list. Once these lists (in either electronic or paper format) are developed, the process of picking out titles to be moved can begin, keeping in mind the equality of division. If the decision is to transfer all titles to one vendor, obviously this procedure will be unnecessary.

Executing the Transfer

The exact steps to be taken for executing the library's approval plan versus transferring its serials, as well as managing the details of the transition from the outgoing to the incoming vendor(s), will vary depending on the types of material to be transferred and the library's needs. However, understanding the basic steps that are necessary for each type of transfer is vital to a successful transfer process. These steps follow.

Transferring Approval Plans

The first step in executing an approval plan transfer is to create the profile for which books are to be received on approval by the library and, if appropriate, which titles are to be sent to the library for consideration via bibliographic forms or slips (either in paper or electronic/e-mail formats). Selectors must be involved in the profiling process so that they can comment on exactly what is needed. Those comments can then be translated into the vendor's terms. Typically, after the selectors (or bibliographers) have filled out the profile, the vendor's representative will review the document with the selectors and explain any discrepancies, resolve conflicts, and provide additional information that the selectors may need.

Working with the vendor's representative, selectors must decide what subjects are to be covered. The degree of specificity will vary greatly; one library may wish all materials on literature, including first novels and genre fiction, while another may want only literary criticism and history. The selectors must review the vendor's subject classification lists and identify the desired areas.

The library must also decide which nonsubject parameters are needed. These will determine the formats, academic levels, and publishers from which materials will come. These facts are vital; they must be reviewed carefully with the vendor. An error in this area can result in a library missing items it wants or receiving materials that it neither expected nor desired.

Profiling should be done as a collaborative process with representatives for the appropriate subject areas. This helps ensure that areas are not accidentally omitted and that interdisciplinary areas are covered.

Once a profile is in place, the next step in transferring an approval plan is deciding when business will end with one vendor and begin with the new one. When dealing with books, often the cleanest way is to start and end with the calendar year, using the copyright date in the book. It must be realized, however, that even in the month of March the library may receive an occasional book with a copyright date from the previous year. On the other hand, as early as September of the previous year, the library may receive books with the next year's copyright date in them. Overlaps and duplicates can be expected for a short period, because of the vagaries and delays in book publishing. Selectors may wish to keep a file of titles that they become aware of from other sources so that they can then order them if they do not appear in the early months of the new approval plan.

In certain situations, the library must take steps to prevent duplication as well as to avoid gaps in coverage. If a new approval plan is replacing another one, for example, the departing vendor may handle a given title before the new vendor does, and the library may receive the book from both.[6] The solution is to instruct the incoming vendor to block recent titles that may have been received at the library. The library can supply the new vendor with invoices from the previous vendor or with a list of recent receipts, while coordinating stop and start dates for the two.[7] As with any new plan, there will be a period of adjustment.

According to most vendors, the average return rate is well below 10 percent for established accounts, with a somewhat higher rate during the first year. Of course, this number will vary from customer to customer. During the first six months, the plan should be closely watched and evaluated as to what is received. In this way, the plan can be fine-tuned or changed if it is not meeting the library's needs, and a return rate can be negotiated that is acceptable to everyone. In general, changing the approval plan from one vendor to another should not affect the return rate much, especially if the library has constructed a well-considered profile with the new vendor. If the approval plan is the first a library has ever had, the return rate may be fairly high until the profile can be refined.

Depending on the outcome of the evaluations for the vendor proposals, the contract for the library's standing orders will be placed either with the vendor handling foreign or domestic subscriptions or the approval plan vendor, either foreign or domestic. The standing orders could be used in some combination of the above options; for example, domestic standing orders might be placed with the domestic or approval plan vendor while foreign standing orders could be placed with the foreign subscription vendor.

In previous chapters, standing order serials have generally been discussed with approval plans rather than with subscription-based serials. When transferring standing orders, many of the tenets put forth for subscription-based serials also apply; however, there are notable differences. If the standing orders are placed with the serials vendor, the library may receive duplicate issues covered by both the approval plan vendor and the serials vendor. To avoid this, the library should send a complete list of its standing orders to the approval plan vendor and update it regularly so the approval plan vendor can avoid duplicates. The vendor should also be queried on its handling of overlapping issues and its return policy.

It is sometimes difficult to determine with what volume a standing order should begin. It is important, therefore, to confer with the previous standing order vendor on each title to verify the last volume it will provide. This will help to avoid the problem of receiving duplicate issues after the transfer.

Transferring Serials

After the library has chosen the serials titles to be transferred, it must gather the appropriate identifying information for each title as it is sent to its respective new home. The vendors will need specific facts regarding each title to ensure they are ordering the correct title. Information should include title, publisher, ISSN, start date, and start volume or issue. Ship to/bill to addresses can also be useful, especially when dealing with multiple branches, campuses, or offices. The majority of serials are published in a calendar year cycle; however, many publishers require split-year start-ups. These titles should be clearly noted to avoid future receipt problems. The outgoing vendor should also be queried on overlapping issues and its return policy.

A valuable piece of information that can be of immense help in making sure the new vendor is ordering the appropriate title is a vendor catalog listing the unique title number assigned to each title. If the vendor has such a catalog, this number should be used because it will virtually guarantee that the vendor will order the correct title. The library will want to store other unique numbers in its integrated library system. An example is the vendor's unique subscription number for the individual library, which is the number used by the publisher to answer claims.

As the various lists are readied (either via computer diskettes, printouts, or manually) to be transferred, all memberships and every title included with each membership should be pulled or separated from the main list. When dealing with memberships (i.e., groups of titles published by societies, groups, or organizations billed at one membership price, which is generally lower than the cost of purchasing each title individually), it is helpful to have a special list that includes very specific bibliographic detail. This list will ensure that the vendor orders only the membership while preventing the duplication of payments and receipts that separate orders for the titles that come with the membership would generate. This list will also guarantee that the vendor applies the payment in its system to the membership only and not to one of the titles included. Performing this task carefully will leave little room for confusion on the part of the vendor as to the title needed and will help to eliminate many problems that could occur later. The library may also want to separate titles from the main list that come in packages (two or more titles that are billed at one price) and those that have parts or other titles, such as newsletters, which come with a title (at no additional cost beyond the cost of the main title). Fewer problems will arise later if these are dealt with in the same way as the memberships.

Vendor Records

Staying in close contact with the various vendor representatives, both old and new, regarding the status and schedule of the transfer project is very important. As each step is accomplished, it is helpful to confer with the customer service representative to be aware of any problems at either vendor's end or to learn of areas the vendor can help run more smoothly. This is especially true when the list(s) are ready to be transferred. Many questions will need to be answered by the incoming vendor before this part of the procedure takes place. It is important to know what electronic capabilities the library has and how the vendor prefers transfers to be handled. Assuming that the library has the capability, the following questions are worth asking: Can the vendor accept file transfer protocol (FTP)? Is faxing a preferred option? Can the vendor work with a computer disk? If so, what kind, and is it compatible with the library's automated system? Would the vendor prefer a word-processed list? Is e-mail a possibility? What special problems or criteria do the foreign vendors have? Almost all larger vendors, including many foreign ones, will want to receive these data electronically if the library can supply them in that format. Knowing what method the vendor will be using to input the data is helpful. Negotiate a workable time frame for receipt and input of information.

After these issues are handled and final decisions are made, the actual transfer of the titles finally takes place. Let the vendor know the list is coming and stay in close contact with the customer service representative. As with everything else, paying attention to detail is a key factor in transferring titles. Carelessness in placing new subscription orders will result in missing issues, interrupted service, increased numbers of claims, payment problems, binding problems, and annoyed library users. These problems are costly in terms of staff time and funds.[8]

Internal Library Records

At this stage of the process, attention should turn to internal records. Different integrated library systems do different things when it comes to record structure and options for updating. The exact method that the library will use will depend on its unique situation. Some possibilities follow.

When the library knows which titles will be going to which vendors, it needs to attach appropriate order records to each title reflecting this information. Several routes can be taken to apply the information properly. First, if the library's records are automated, the decision needs to be made as to whether the existing order record will be used with field adjustments and appropriate notes or whether the existing order record will be canceled and a new order record created. If the existing order record is used, certain fields can be globally changed. In a global change, a staff member can change existing data in certain fields on a record virtually with the push of a button. The computer does all the work, saving staff time and avoiding human error. If it is impossible to identify the appropriate titles, or if some other problem prevents a global change, using rapid update might be an option if a system can support it. With rapid update, information can be added quickly to each record, one after the other. A list is made of all titles to be amended, and the needed information is rapidly added to each record on the list by library staff. New order records can be created for each title if so desired; however, this process is very time-consuming and usually costly as well. If new order records are created, the added step of canceling the old order record will also need to be included. If the library uses a manual system, the vendor may be able to produce customized labels to affix to the library's manual files.

Another record type affected by the transfer is the check-in record. Whether the library uses an integrated library system or a manual system, those staff dealing with check-in and claiming will need to know with what volume and year the transfer takes place. They will then be able to adjust the vendor field on the check-in record (or Kardex card) at the appropriate time to claim from the proper source.

Follow-Up After the Transfer

The process of transferring approval plans from one vendor to another is not easy. Being careful and paying attention to detail, however, will mean fewer problems. If the library is discontinuing an approval plan with a vendor, then it must make certain that there are no unanswered questions, claims, shipments in process, or outstanding invoices associated with the library's account. Also, because of uncertainties about the actual publication and copyright dates, there may be overlapping approval plan shipments, for a time, when shifting from one vendor to another. Even in February or March, a library may receive books published in the prior calendar year along with books published in the current year.

Selectors need to be intimately involved with monitoring the approval plans once the transfer has taken place. Selectors will review the approval books regularly and, therefore, have a good idea whether there are problems with publication dates or the like. They will also begin to learn the details of the new profiles so that they can readily assess whether the books received fit the profiles. It is not practical for acquisitions staff to do this kind of monitoring.

Another method to monitor what is being received from the new approval plan vendor is for selectors to check occasionally catalogs from particularly important publishers. If books are being missed, the selectors need to modify the profile for the subject. If the vendor has some kind of online or microform list of what books it treats, the selectors can check it from time to time to determine whether short shipments are becoming a problem. Usually these lists tell when the vendor received and shipped a book. If the library has not yet received its copy, though copies were mailed to some libraries several weeks before, the library is probably experiencing short shipments. Being shorted for a book may not pose a major problem if it happens sporadically, but if it is a frequent occurrence, the library must take action to prevent it from continuing. If the approval plans are split, monitoring will have to take place for both plans.

After the serials transfer process takes place, the library should take several additional steps as a follow-up. First, the library should request from the old vendor a confirming list of serials titles removed from its account, as well as a confirming list of all the new titles added to your account from the new vendors. These lists should be examined, title by title, and compared against the internal lists used during the entire transfer process. This step can point out apparent problems that otherwise might not be noticed for months. Reviewing everything that was just completed and double-checking the work will reveal possible lapses or duplications. This step is time-consuming, but in the long run it will prove to be one of the most useful in preventing future problems and interruptions in service. Another necessary follow-up step is conferring with the person(s) in the library who will be approving the invoices for payment or actually paying the invoices to the new vendor(s). These people will be in a position to notice problems and conflicts on the serials records.

The time-consuming and necessary steps explained in this chapter can ensure that the entire transfer process will proceed smoothly and with as little aggravation as possible. A thorough process will reward the library with fewer errors in the long run that could cost even more time and money than doing the process correctly in the first place would have. Follow-up and evaluation procedures should be ongoing and performed regularly when dealing with approval plan and serials vendors alike.

Notes

1. Sharon C. Bonk, "Towards a Methodology of Evaluating Serials Vendors," *Library Acquisitions: Practice & Theory* 9, no. 1 (1985): 52.

2. Doris E. New, "Serials Agency Conversion in an Academic Library," *Serials Librarian* 2, no. 3 (1978): 282.

3.   Robert F. Nardini, "The Approval Plan Profiling Session," *Library Acquisitions: Practice & Theory* 18, no. 3 (1994): 289.

4.   N. Bernard Basch and Judy McQueen, *Buying Serials: A How-to-Do-It Manual for Librarians* (New York: Neal–Schuman, 1990), 129.

5.   Basch and McQueen, 130.

6.   Gloriana St. Clair and Jane Treadwell, "Science and Technology Approval Plans Compared," *Library Resources & Technical Services* 33 (October 1989): 390.

7.   Nardini, 292.

8.   Margaret McKinley, "Vendor Selection: Strategic Choices," *Serials Review* 16, no. 2 (1990): 50.

Chapter 11

The Vendor Evaluation Process

Frances C. Wilkinson / Connie Capers Thorson

[K]eep it simple and beware of analysis paralysis.[1]

—Anita Crotty

After all the contracts have been awarded and have gone into effect, after the new approval profiles have been created, after all the serials have been transferred, a time arrives when, though vigilance is still required, there is some breathing room. Although it may be tempting to relax completely and trust that everything is working properly, this is the time when the library should be scrutinizing the performances of the vendors.

Why Evaluate Vendor Performance?

The library has a responsibility to itself and to the larger organization to which it reports to spend its money wisely. The purpose of the RFP is to contract the best services for the library at the best overall cost. The RFP process requires much time and effort on everyone's part for proper planning, writing, evaluating, and executing. For a library not to follow through by monitoring contract compliance and evaluating vendor performance would be unfortunate indeed.

The library is the only entity that can truly ensure that it is getting what it bargained for from the vendor. "The library must ensure that the vendor meets all the mandatory conditions of the contract."[2] If the library does not ensure that the vendor meets all the mandatory conditions of the contract from the start, it may risk forfeiting the right to do so later. Some purchasing departments contend that if the library does not enforce the contract over a long period of time, it may be considered to be acting in an "arbitrary and capricious" manner when it eventually does try to enforce it. For the good of all concerned, detecting and resolving problems quickly ensures that the relationship between the library and the vendor will be much more successful. New approval profiles often need adjustment after the library begins to review the shipments. After serials are transferred, they must be monitored to determine that they have started to arrive in the library, that the correct starting issue is received, and that there are no gaps between issues.

Once a contract has been in effect for the period of time predetermined by the library (ranging from a few months to a year, depending on the contract type), an evaluation of the vendors, whether new or not, should take place. The librarians in acquisitions, serials, and collection development can and should determine whether or not vendors are living up to both the detail and spirit of the contract. If subject-specific plans are involved, for example, Latin American or Fine Arts approval plans, the subject specialists must be involved and perhaps responsible for much of the evaluation. It is important that the evaluation process be kept as simple as possible. Because many different people from different areas of the library

99

may participate, an overly complicated process is likely to fail. Regardless of what process is decided on, Crotty counsels that the library avoid "any process that will create a bureaucratic and statistical nightmare."[3] This advice is important. After all, the evaluation process must fit into the daily routines of many different people, and one more project is often difficult to fit into already busy schedules.

Factors to Consider

The library must determine whether it will initially conduct an informal or a formal evaluation. One possibility is to have discussions within each department about the vendor's performance, asking personnel to consider their experiences with the vendor. This subjective method may have merit in the early phase of the contract; however, a formal quantitative evaluation is more likely to be required.

When considering the factors to be evaluated, the library may want to start by asking, " 'What are the library's priorities?' The answer will give you the questions to ask about your suppliers' performance."[4] Of course, the requirements stated and the questions asked in the RFP will also give significant clues about what is most important to the library.

Perhaps the most important question to ask is whether the vendor is providing what is needed (i.e., the materials requested by the library's patrons) in a reasonable amount of time. Librarians sometimes lose sight of the fact that all of the work of buying materials is to provide the informational, research, and leisure materials that the library patrons desire. Are patrons still complaining to the collection development officer that there are no books in their field? Are issues of some important serials published but not yet in the library? Are patrons finding titles they would like to use on order but not yet received? Is the library waiting too long for materials that are on "hot button" issues, and are patrons complaining? All the electronic gadgets available or all the schmoozing in the world by vendor representatives will not make up for slow delivery of needed materials to the patron.

The other issue in any vendor evaluation is whether the librarians are spending the funds for materials in the best way possible—getting the most bang for the buck! Although the discount percentage or the service charge was not the sole reason for choosing the vendor, both merit careful evaluation once the contract is signed. Vendors should be queried if the negotiated discount rate is not being applied to all materials as assumed by the library staff, or if journal issues are being repeatedly claimed but not supplied. The collection development officer and the acquisitions and serials librarians must all be concerned about discounts and service charges.

Very often today's library automation systems make it much simpler to evaluate some specific items—the length of time it takes for books to be supplied on the approval plan or after order on bibliographic forms, the average discount rate, the length of time it takes a new journal title to start arriving, the number of claims of journal issues sent to the vendor—than it was in the past. Thus, do not attempt to measure everything.[5] Trying to look at every possible component available will prove too time-consuming and will distract evaluators from the key issues. A better approach is to pick a few elements and examine them very carefully.

Performing the Vendor Evaluation

Once the library has determined to perform a formal vendor performance evaluation, it must make several key decisions. The first decision is to determine who will perform the evaluation. It may be desirable for members of the original RFP committee to form an ad hoc vendor evaluation committee. Clearly, members of the acquisitions and serials departments will want to be involved. Also, staff from the collection development and systems departments may be appropriate members.

Next, the evaluator or committee must determine when the evaluation will take place and the method of evaluation that will be used. A determination regarding when and how the vendor is to be notified when it is out of compliance with the contract should also be made,[6] if this is not already prescribed in the contract.

Numerous articles and some books have detailed the vendor evaluation process, outlining a number of possible models for libraries to use when evaluating vendors. Some include sample evaluation forms. Among the sources most frequently cited in the literature are *Guide to Performance Evaluation of Library Materials Vendors*; a series of vendor performance and evaluation articles covering nearly every type of vendor evaluation including serials, appearing in *Library Acquisitions: Practice & Theory*, volume 18, number 1 (1994); and an annotated bibliography of vendor evaluation appearing in *Library Acquisitions: Practice & Theory*, volume 12, number 1 (1988). Many other excellent, descriptive materials on this topic appear in the bibliography at the end of this book.

The type and depth of the vendor evaluation will depend on the type of library and its unique requirements as specified in the RFP. "Despite the numerous published accounts of performance studies, there is no perfect tool; there are too many variables."[7] Instead of endorsing a particular model, some common areas for evaluation in most libraries, for both approval plans and serials, are discussed below.

Approval Plans

Several scenarios might dictate the ways in which the library should evaluate vendor performance. Whether the approval plan is chosen as a new venture, is with a new vendor, is with the current vendor, or is an existing approval plan split into two or more plans, the library must monitor it closely. The collection development librarians must establish profiles that reflect the collection needs of the library and then be prepared to monitor what is coming in. It is important that a current vendor chosen for one or more of the new contracts be treated as if a new vendor. That vendor may have always done things well, but common sense says that it should be held up to the same scrutiny as any other vendor.

A new approval profile needs a reasonable amount of time to prove itself. At first, the number of books coming in will probably be small; it takes time for the trickle to become a flood. If a contract is to take effect in January, a vendor may be treating titles published in the last months of the prior year for several weeks. The shipments may not reach the "normal" level until February or March, simply because of the patterns of publication. The vendor's representative should keep the library informed about the shipments and answer questions about the slow growth of the shipments.

It may be advisable to post or make available in the approval display area a copy of the nonsubject parameters that were agreed upon. It takes time to be truly comfortable with all of these parameters, and nothing is more frustrating than having to go somewhere to track down such information. Also consider providing a notebook into which selectors can note their observations about the plan(s). Sometimes selectors have difficulty in remembering what struck them as odd when finally back in the office.

Once approval plan materials begin arriving in expected numbers, the library will want to examine the fulfillment rate. Is the library getting what it wants? Are titles that should be sent to the library, based on its profile, being missed? It should also examine speed of delivery. Is the library getting materials in a timely fashion? How quickly after publication does the vendor treat titles and send them to the library? Does the vendor provide electronic reports on fulfillment time? Return rates must be quantified. Is the return rate high? What are the reasons for so many approval books being rejected by the library? Does the vendor provide electronic diagnosis for approval plan returns on its online system? Approval vendors expect that new profiles will need adjustment to succeed. The evaluation process should enable the library to determine whether there are minor problems that can be readily resolved by adjusting the profile or major problems that must be addressed.

The discount rate and other costs must be monitored. Is the library always getting the contracted discount rate? This is one of the most clear-cut and most frequently monitored factors in the approval plan. Invoices should be spot-checked to ensure that the discount is being applied consistently. Handling and freight charges should also be monitored. Prepayment credits should be reviewed. Does the vendor issue prepayment and refund credits promptly, and are they clear and easy to understand?

The library should evaluate both customer and computer-based services. It may want to consider how promptly customer service representatives respond to questions and problems. Are sales visits regular and informative? Is there follow-up on library concerns? The library will surely wish to evaluate the vendor's ability to interface with the library's Integrated Library System in terms of approval transmissions and invoicing. Also important are the components of the vendor's online system. Is the database easy to navigate? Is it accurate and up-to-date? When problems arise, are the vendor's technical support staff helpful? Are the customized reports that the library requires complete? Do they arrive in a timely fashion? These are just some of the areas that the library can consider when evaluating approval plan vendor performance.

Serials

In previous chapters, standing order serials have generally been discussed with approval plans rather than with subscription-based serials. However, as in the case of transferring standing orders, many of the tenets put forth for subscription-based serials also apply in evaluating standing orders.

One of the most immediately apparent areas for evaluating a new serials vendor is how smoothly or poorly the transfer process progressed. Transferring a library's serials titles, especially a large number of titles, is no small undertaking. Even with the best-planned and best-executed process, the possibility for error is great. The level of assistance the vendor provides during the transition sets the tone for the library–vendor relationship in the future. How easy was it for the library to forward its title list to the new vendor? Were a number of options available for doing this? What steps did the vendor take to ensure uninterrupted issues from the publisher, and were the steps successful? How many titles "slipped through the cracks"? How were memberships and packages handled? Did the library receive any first-year service charge discounts to offset some of the transfer costs in staff time to the library? If the transfer was large, did the vendor offer to send a representative to the library to assist with the process?

After the initial transfer process, evaluations turn to other service factors and pricing considerations. Pricing is perhaps the most easily quantifiable of the two. Libraries should spot-check their invoices, especially the annual renewal invoice, to be sure that they are getting the agreed-upon service charge. If the contract is with a foreign vendor, the handling of exchange rates may be a factor to evaluate. The amount of prepayment credits will often be of interest to the library. In cases where the serials account is large, the amount of the prepayment credit can be substantial. This can provide the library with additional buying power, which, in a time of runaway serials inflation, is important. A difference of just one or two prepayment percentage points can make a big difference in the evaluation. Another area to consider along with the service charge and prepayment credits is the percentage and frequency of added charges. Vendors are encouraging publishers to provide them with firm pricing as early as possible in the fiscal year. Early, accurate pricing not only makes it easier for the collection development librarians to expend their budgets responsibly, it also reduces the number of additional charges to be processed by serials staff. It takes as long to process an additional charge as it does to process the initial charge. Additional charges literally double the workload. Prompt handling of refund credits may also be important to the library.

Service factors are perhaps the most important elements in the evaluation process. Service includes not only direct customer service and computer-based services, but also speed and accuracy of order placement and renewals; processing of cancellations; invoicing practices; fulfillment and claims handling; and attention to title changes, cessations, and delays in publication.

Evaluation of direct customer service might focus on the promptness and courtesy of customer service representatives when responding to the library's questions and problems. Are they willing to, and adept at, interceding with a publisher to resolve a complex problem for the library? Customer service can be measured by the amount of voice, electronic, and paper correspondence required to resolve problems, along with the amount of time required and the final resolution rate. Are sales representatives knowledgeable about new company services and programs? As with approval plans, the library will wish to evaluate the vendor's ability to interface with the library's Integrated Library System for invoicing and credits, and perhaps electronic claims.

Of special importance when evaluating serials vendors are the components of the vendors' online systems. Their database is at the core of their service. The library must determine if the database is user-friendly. Is it easy to learn and navigate? Is it accurate and up-to-date, especially for serials pricing toward the end of the calendar year? When problems arise, are the vendor's technical support staff available and helpful? Are the customized reports that the library requires complete, and do they arrive in a timely fashion without reminders from the library? Does the vendor reliably provide historical price analyses, including the percentage of price increases for several previous years and average prices?

The core factors for serials from the RFP should be scrutinized. The speed and accuracy of order placement and renewal are crucial. Information in serials is more timely than in books, so patrons expect to find paper serials on the shelf and electronic serials on the library's computers rapidly. Fulfillment of orders—the percentage of issues received versus the number of issues published—is a key consideration in the evaluation process. A vendor that cannot supply them is of little use to the library and the patrons it serves. The vendor's speed in processing new serials subscriptions should also be examined. In addition, does the vendor quickly notify the library of receipt and placement of a new order, if the library so desires? Are cancellations handled promptly, or does the library receive unwanted issues? Does the vendor make every effort to obtain a refund for the library when titles are canceled or cease? Are invoices clear and accurate, and do they contain all the data elements that the library requires? How are claims handled? What are the number and types of claims generated? What is the percentage of second and third claims? Who initiated the claims? What is the ultimate fulfillment rate? When the publisher does not honor a claim that was claimed with the vendor within the appropriate time frame, does the vendor supply it at no additional direct cost to the library? How does the publisher handle title changes and delays in publication? Does it notify the library and, if so, by serials bulletins or some other means? At what point does the vendor consider a title ceased and begin a refund request? These are just some of the areas that the library may consider when evaluating serials vendor performance.

Notes

1.   Anita Crotty, "Why Bother with Evaluation?" *Library Acquisitions: Practice & Theory* 18, no. 1 (1994): 54.

2.   Arnold Hirshon and Barbara A. Winters, *Outsourcing Library Technical Services: A How-to-Do-It Manual for Librarians* (New York: Neal–Schuman, 1996), 140.

3.   Crotty, 54.

4.   Crotty, 53.

5.   Hirshon and Winters, 140.

6.   Carol E. Chamberlain, "Evaluating Library Acquisitions Service," in *Encyclopedia of Library and Information Science*, vol. 56, suppl. 19, ed. Allen Kent (New York: Marcel Dekker, 1995), 123.

7.   Hirshon and Winters, 140.

PART V

The Vendor Perspective

Chapter 12

Vendor Interviews

Frances C. Wilkinson / Connie Capers Thorson

An RFP can be the most effective way to set the tone between a library and a vendor.[1]

—Stuart Glogoff

Discussion of the RFP process would not be complete without the vendor perspective. Vendors serve in a partnership with the library to provide library services and materials; they are an extension of the library's staff.

Library–Vendor Relationships: Past and Present

In reviewing the literature, it appears that library–vendor relationships have changed over the last 30 years; however, some similarities endure. The literature in general makes frequent references and analogies to the library–vendor relationship as a marriage. Recent literature refers to it as a partnership, or even a symbiotic relationship,[2,3] with libraries relying on vendors for goods and, increasingly, services, and vendors relying on libraries for their continued existence.

A quick trip back to the late 1950s indicates that libraries were entering the information age with a great outflowing of state and federal funding to encourage education and technological development. Demand increased for materials and new ways to create, reproduce, and disseminate them. The library–vendor relationship centered largely around vendors supplying libraries with print materials in various formats, primarily books and serials. This modus operandi lasted for about 15 years. In the mid-1970s, runaway inflation and eroding buying power, combined with a continued increase in the number of materials being produced and the demand for them, altered significantly the purchasing patterns of libraries. Vendors affected by all the events that influenced the library and the publishing industries were caught in the middle.[4] By the 1980s, two major events occurred to change library–vendor relationships forever: The escalating cost of serials publications and the rapid introduction of automation into all areas of library operations. Not only did libraries begin to expect the vendors to fight for them against price increases, they required that vendors be forerunners in automation.[5]

The 1990s introduced a new consumerism, further altering the library–vendor relationship. Librarians were canceling serials, conducting tougher price negotiations, shifting information access to new formats, and outsourcing (contracting out library functions to private firms).[6] Thus, library–vendor relationships were being buffeted by both economic and technological upheaval. As we move toward the next century, what are the basic characteristics of the ideal library–vendor relationship? Richards posits that they are communication, joint interest, mutual benefit, understanding, and trust, with the factors assuming greater or lesser importance in different types of library–vendor relationships.[7] Bostic states that "a library's relationship to a vendor depends on its own requirements and is partly the library's responsibility" and argues that the vendor "must mediate attempts to standardize the individual practices and demands of thousands of libraries, at the same time allowing as much latitude for individual preferences as possible."[8]

The RFP process, when done well, can provide a firm foundation for the library–vendor relationship. The information outlined in this book thus far has been presented largely from the perspective of the library. An understanding of the vendor's perspective, however, is crucial to "prevent the misunderstandings which arise among us."[9] Therefore, this chapter considers the RFP process from the vendor's point of view.

The Vendors Speak Out

Following are comments from seven book and serials vendors in response to questions posed to them. In addition to their responses are comments the vendors often added on topics that weren't addressed directly. The seven participating vendors are as follows:

N. Bernard "Buzzy" Basch, Chief Executive Officer, Basch Subscriptions, Inc.[10]

Kit Kennedy, Director of Academic Sales, Blackwell's Information Services

David S. Kerin, Vice President and General Manager, EBSCO Information Services

Janice McIntyre, Federal Contracts Manager, The Faxon Co.

Susan B. Hillson, Senior Manager, Market Development, The Faxon Co.

Jane Maddox, Director of Library Services for North America, Harrassowitz Booksellers & Subscription Agents, U.S.

Michael Markwith, Chief Executive Officer, Swets & Zeitlinger, U.S.

Brian Noone, Sales Administrator, Swets & Zeitlinger, U.S.

Mark F. Kendall, Director of North American Sales, Yankee Book Peddler (YBP), Inc.

Lynne Branche Brown, Chief Operations Officer, Yankee Book Peddler (YBP), Inc.

Although the vendors who responded represent a diverse group—domestic and foreign as well as book and serials vendors—noting the similarities in their answers regarding the RFP process is revealing. The vendor responses clearly indicate, as was outlined in the previous chapters, some factors that are of critical importance for inclusion in a successful RFP.

The remainder of this chapter lists the questions and the vendors' responses to them, quoted in their entirety, in a panel interview format. As on a panel, not all vendors responded to all of the questions, and some questions elicited either longer or shorter replies from some vendors than others.

What are the most important areas or questions for librarians to include in approval plan and serials RFPs?

According to Buzzy Basch, "The biggest thing for libraries to do is to define their needs! They should define their needs, requirements, and when they pay their invoices, et cetera."

Jane Maddox agrees and states, "The required specifications for services is the most important section. If the vendors cannot comply with this section, they need not read any further."

Kit Kennedy believes that "The library should be able to answer one three-part critical question before submitting RFPs to vendors: Why is the library entering in the RFP process, what does the library want to gain, and how will the RFP be evaluated?" Furthermore, Kennedy feels that RFPs should contain the following:

- Concise and consolidated instructions (indicating mandatory requirements)
- Library contact person(s)
- Reason for the RFP
- Brief description of the library and institution
- Description of the evaluation process and who the decision makers are
- Time frame in which to respond
- Description of the business (including list of titles on disk) covered by this RFP with an estimated dollar amount of the anticipated expenditure and any plans for major cancellations or redirection of monies to electronic or other format subscriptions, including document delivery
- Length of contract, and expectations of vendors (i.e., presentations: Pre- and post-RFP)

In addition, RFPs should ask vendors to provide the following:

- Company organization and mission
- Financial strength (including supporting documentation, e.g., audited balance sheet or bank letter of credit but not a performance bond as this adds to the cost of doing business for both the library and vendor)
- Detailed information on customer service (benchmarks)
- Detailed information on technical servicing of accounting (e.g., ordering, claiming, cancellations, refunds)
- Strengths in handling particular materials
- Experience in handling electronic subscriptions
- Technical expertise (e.g., access to vendor system; vendor interfacing with ILS systems, especially the library's ILS system)
- Experience with similar business and libraries

- References

- Terms and conditions (e.g., service charge, prepayment plans, transfer assistance, additional charges for value-added services)

Janice McIntyre and Susan Hillson largely agree and add, "Serials RFPs should clearly spell out all work to be performed and terms of the contract so the vendor and client know exactly what to expect." They recommend that the following be included:

- Terms and conditions of the contract

- Length of contract

- Pricing scheme (e.g., vendor price plus a service charge percentage or dollar-per-line-item)

- Detailed technical requirements, including what to expect from a vendor for service

- Level, responsiveness, management tools, et cetera

- A clear description of how offers will be evaluated and the weighing factors and how they will be applied to various sections of the RFP

- The requirement that the vendors quote your list of titles so you can determine which can provide the majority of your subscription needs

- Requirements for services or products you anticipate needing in the future

- Establishment of the service requirements as the primary evaluation criteria, with pricing secondary.

David Kerin states, "The single most important step for any librarian is to decide what is wanted when engaging the services of any vendor, not just a serials vendor. Most of the major serials vendors have valuable services that can save the library staff many hours of work. These services range from 'outsourcing' everything to the point where the serials arrive at the library ready to be placed on the shelf, to, at the other end of the spectrum, simply performing a 'consolidation' function which is limited to a consolidated invoice and little else in the way of service. Rather than list every conceivable question that might possibly be asked which may be important to a librarian, listed below are certain areas or questions which should be addressed in an RFP."

- Does the vendor have a sufficient online database to cover the full scope of journals required by the library?

- Is the vendor's database available for the library's use, is it user-friendly, and what useful information does it contain?

- Does the vendor have a time-proven working relationship with the publishers that is in good standing?

Is the representative who calls on the library knowledgeable of matters that pertain to the vendor's services?

- How do the vendors' services interact with other systems within the library and with publisher policies or practices?

- Will the library's account be handled by a single inside vendor representative?

- What is the experience level of this person, and what communications options are offered for dealing with this person?

- Does the vendor have automated support services?

- Are the vendor's representatives able to offer assistance in the library with such automated services?

- Does the vendor offer useful serials management reports on paper and in electronic formats?

- What claiming options are offered, how are claims communicated to the publisher, and what type of acknowledgment and monitoring system is available?

- Does the vendor handle similar libraries with similar needs, and how can that experience be rated?

According to Michael Markwith and Brian Noone, "The library should ask specific questions about customer service, order and claim processing, management reports, billing/invoicing, and electronic services. We will always include detailed information about the services we provide, but having specific questions helps us to identify the library's needs. This is especially important when technical issues are being discussed: by providing information to us about the library's check-in system and asking specific questions on how we can work with their system, we can reply with detailed information on how we can (or cannot) integrate our services with their existing technology.

"Another important area is the vendor's staff and company organizational philosophy. It is very important for the librarians to know who they will be working with at all levels in the vendor organization. This is primarily important in a service business relationship with customer service personnel and support staff. Specific questions of staff education, training, experience, and expertise should be explored. Also, the vendor should be required to explain the company philosophy (mission statement), provide an organization chart showing management and staff allocation of personnel and resources, and be able to demonstrate complete financial stability."

While the previous answers have primarily addressed serials, Mark Kendall and Lynne Branche Brown share insights regarding the implications of this question for approval plans. They state, "First, it is critical for the vendor to have an understanding of the individual library's expectations in an approval (or continuations) plan. Questions that provide background information about the library, anticipated annual expenditures, title 'mix' and types of materials to be purchased (science/technical, scholarly trade, university press, peripheral press works, et cetera), and what the library values in a vendor are all key areas to help increase the understanding of the library's needs. Questions vendors ask about a library when reviewing an RFP include: Is the library seeking a partnership with a vendor? Are they seeking 'cutting edge' technology? Are they simply seeking the highest discount?

"Libraries also should not hesitate to provide a 'wish list' of services that they would like to see vendors provide as long as it is clearly stated which items are required for the vendor to provide to even warrant consideration by the library, as well as describe which items or services are preferred and/or desired, that is, not mandatory for consideration.

"In an approval RFP, specific questions that libraries could ask to gain a better understanding of the services a vendor could provide would include the number and type of publishers covered, [the] vendor's experience at managing approval plans and experience of staff that would work with the library, how approval plans are established and profiled, and at least three approval plan references from existing approval plan customers as well as two references of 'new' approval plan customers. Additional questions could include how flexible the vendor is in implementing profile changes and what types of management reports are available."

What types of questions/considerations should be included in specialty RFPs (e.g., Latin American, fine arts, or science and technology plans)?

Janice McIntyre suggests that libraries "ask vendors to describe their experience with the appropriate field and ask for references for the same type of materials."

Kit Kennedy recommends that "the RFP should specify the type and estimate of dollar amount of materials covered in this partnership." They both believe the RFP should ask questions relating to the following:

- Vendor experience with specific materials

- Staff experience with appropriate languages

- What partnerships or subcontracts the vendor might enter into to ensure good service (i.e., using other specialized vendors)

- Realistic expectations for fulfillment and claiming

- Vendor claiming policies

- Ability of the vendor to handle rush orders and at what price

- References of libraries who use this vendor for these materials

- Vendor participation in the appropriate international organizations to ensure the vendor's commitment to handling specialized materials

- Vendor policy in recommending when the library orders direct

- Vendor bibliographic expertise with this material

David Kerin comments, "This question applies more to approval plans than serials. However, there are certain questions that one should ask of a serials vendor in order to assess its ability to acquire specialty journals. These questions pertain to the range of publishers with which the serials vendor can demonstrate experience and, in the event of problems, the geographic proximity of the agency to such publishers. For example, if you order a large number of Latin American journals you would want to select a vendor that has experience with such journals and personnel on staff who speak the native language of the publisher. It would also be helpful to have a presence in that part of the world, although not imperative."

Jane Maddox adds, "In areas of specialized approval plan services, the main concern for the library is whether or not the vendor has the specialized expertise/education/training required to provide quality service in this area. Therefore, some 'special' questions about the education or training of the staff involved with the selection of the materials, as well as a request for specific details in regard to any special agents/distributors or acquisition procedures employed by the vendor, would be helpful to have for evaluation. In some cases, the library might want to include a small listing of sample titles they have acquired over the past 12 months, specifically including some of the 'more-difficult-to-obtain materials,' and ask the vendors to quote the date they 'treated' the title on their approval plan and the price and invoicing date to libraries who had an approval plan. Of course, it is definitely helpful to ask for two or three library contacts for you to contact as references."

Mark Kendall and Lynne Branche Brown believe that "questions such as how would the vendor develop a profile for the specific subject area as well as how complex would it be for the vendor to maintain such a profile would be good questions. It would also be useful for the library to obtain the annual number of titles and dollar output by publisher in each specific subject area to determine the vendor's coverage of the subject area, as well as potential cost to maintain an approval plan in the selected area."

What is the single most important element of a good RFP?

Buzzy Basch answered, "A clear definition of the requirements." David Kerin agrees and goes on to add, "The single most important element of a good RFP is to clearly state what you expect from your vendor. By clearly stating your expectations, you position yourself to better evaluate the responses to your RFP and, more importantly, evaluate performance after the selected vendor begins servicing your account."

Michael Markwith and Brian Noone state that "a single most important element is difficult to identify. However, an often overlooked and yet very important element of a good RFP is clear instructions for the formal response: Clearly listing the deadline for the RFP reply, including the name and phone number of a contact that can respond to questions about the RFP, and providing the address the reply should be sent to (if necessary, specifying different addresses for mailed responses and those sent via courier, such as Federal Express) and a contact name and phone number of the individual who should receive the reply."

Jane Maddox believes that RFPs should include information that applies to the situation at hand. She states, "I have trouble coming up with a single element. If it must be singular, then I would have to say that the most important element is the omission of extraneous or unnecessary data elements. To turn it around the other way, it cannot be reduced to a singular item, as I would have to say the most important elements of a good RFP are brevity and clarity. The area where this is usually the biggest problem is within the 'Boilerplate' section, especially where government RFPs are concerned. It is daunting enough to receive a bundle of 250 pages, but when you must read through very carefully and identify that two-thirds of the sections end with a statement indicating that this only applies to RFPs exceeding the value of the RFP in question, then you have wasted so much time and effort trying to understand the section or even reading it in the first place. This also makes it easier to overlook items that are part of what you should read and be in compliance. In this age of word processing, there is no excuse for sending out 'Boilerplate' information that is generic and requires editing by each vendor who processes the document. Any editing that is required should be accomplished by those who know best exactly what applies to the purchasing requirements. The vendors should receive only what is applicable to the specific RFP."

Mark Kendall and Lynne Branche Brown state, "That the RFP being written to allow an even, open 'playing field' among vendors competing for a library's business is, in our opinion, the most important element of a good RFP. Some RFPs are clearly, yet subtly, written to favor one vendor over another. If a vendor invests time and effort in responding to each of a library's RFP questions in-depth, a vendor hopes to be at least equally considered and evaluated among the other vendors that are bidding."

Kit Kennedy agrees and sums up the single most important element: "Spirit. The library's willingness to enter into the RFP process with a well-crafted document and evaluate fairly, based on vendor's response to the RFP, presentations, references, and the library's experience and instinct." She adds that "this is an excellent question and also a perplexing one since it is very difficult to reduce an RFP to its single most important element."

Janice McIntyre and Susan Hillson take a slightly different tact, stating that "without a doubt, detailed technical requirements are the most important element of a good RFP. Technical requirements clearly state what services you expect from the vendor and give the vendor the opportunity to describe exactly how it can fulfill your requirements."

What areas/questions would vendors like to see added more often to RFPs?

Jane Maddox states, "I cannot honestly say that there is anything I would like to see added more often to RFPs, since I do not believe that the RFP is the most effective way to establish a good working relationship between a library and vendor. While some librarians and vendors have utilized the RFP process to clearly communicate the specifications/requirements and terms/conditions of the business relationship, it is the organized communication and commitment that are the important elements, not the RFP. For many institutions, less formal but clearly organized and legally binding communication has been equally as effective and much less costly for establishing mutually beneficial business relationships. In situations where there is a mandate for contracts from the authorities in state governments, the state listing of 'approved' vendors is a cost-effective method for imposing state legal requirements and yet retaining the individual library option for selecting the vendor best qualified to serve its particular requirements."

Mark Kendall and Lynne Branche Brown would like to see several things added more often to RFPs. "Questions that we would like to see added to RFPs would be questions designed to solicit from the vendor an understanding of what type of company the library would be dealing with. Libraries should be encouraged to request a vendor's mission and vision statement. Questions that invite a vendor/library partnership where each party works to forge a 'win-win' relationship for all parties are welcomed. More emphasis on the value-added services a vendor can provide a library would also be ideal, along with an idea of how the proposal will be evaluated (or scored). Will discount drive the decision making? Or will vendor experience combined with other factors such as discount, customer service, et cetera, all be equally considered?"

Kit Kennedy suggests including the following:

- A concise description of what the library is really wishing to gain from this RFP as well as the library's collection development policies, i.e., consolidate business vs. multiple vendors, undecided or under re-evaluation

- A description of the evaluation process—if the library is assigning values to each section, please inform the vendor

- Offer the vendor the opportunity to add comments or describe additional services available

David Kerin also believes that the evaluation criteria need to be included. "It is very helpful to a vendor to understand how his response is to be evaluated. As stated above, if you clearly state your expectations you should be able to identify the value you place on the vendor's ability to comply with your needs. A well-prepared RFP not only states desired services from the vendor, but goes on to indicate a point value associated with the vendor's ability to supply or perform the desired service. Too often an elaborate RFP is prepared by the library listing an extensive array of things that are important for the vendor to supply, only to have the evaluators cast everything aside in favor of the best price. If price is the most important factor to the library, indicate that fact by assigning a high point value to it. At a minimum, your responding vendors will know the value of price or any other factor before responding."

Michael Markwith and Brian Noone state, "From a purely administrative perspective, the most important things are the inclusion of a cover page clearly listing the most important elements plus a summary of the RFP including a description of the titles to be quoted on (domestic, foreign, scientific, medical, engineering, general, et cetera), an estimate of the number of titles involved, and their approximate worth. When a title list is included, ISSN numbers should be provided, and diskette (or FTP) versions of the list in ASCII format are greatly appreciated. It would also be extremely helpful if titles to be sent to individuals (i.e., desk copies) are included in a separate list from the main library's list.

"As far as content is concerned, more detail and background should be provided when asking questions about electronic services. If a library wants to know what services a vendor can provide, it is extremely helpful to know what library systems, local network requirements (hardware, PCs, et cetera) are used so a vendor can explain in detail what options are available."

Janice McIntyre and Susan Hillson suggest, "Due to the changing nature of serials and the information market, it is important that a vendor have sufficient automation to provide you with timely and accurate service." They recommend inquiring into the following areas:

- Vendor knowledge of, and experience in, the information industry

- Vendor references

- Technological achievements and systems capabilities

- The ability of the vendor's system to handle the millennium change

- Future directions and plans

What special instructions should always be included in an RFP?

Mark Kendall and Lynne Branche Brown recommend that "items such as number of copies of the RFP responses to be mailed, contact name(s) at the library, and deadline dates for responses all should be included in the instructions."

Jane Maddox adds, "It is not always clear to whom the completed RFP should be addressed. If there are specific ID elements that should be included on the outside of the envelope, this needs to be emphasized. Also, there should be a specific contact point/person for any questions."

Michael Markwith and Brian Noone suggest, "Any format specifications (page numbering, double-spacing, including a special RFP code on each page, et cetera) should be included, as well as specifying the number of copies of the reply needed."

Janice McIntyre and Susan Hillson also consider format to be an important element. "An RFP should clearly instruct the bidder on the format desired for response. It is also helpful if the requirements are listed in a logical order. For example, list requirements for standard subscription services as separate items, but in logical order; list all automated services as separate items, but in logical order. Basically, it is easier for a vendor to respond and easier for you to evaluate responses if the requirements are broken down into sections such as basic service requirements, reports, automation, specialized requirements, optional requirements."

Kit Kennedy recommends that RFPs should always include the following:

- Contact person

- Scope of the RFP

- Deadlines and a timeline of the process (e.g., Will presentations be required? When will the RFP be awarded?)

- Mandatory requirements

- A limit to the number of special submission requirements (e.g., requiring many copies of the RFP, special bidding instructions)

Finally, Kennedy suggests that prior to mailing the RFP, the library might contact the vendors for intended interest and contact name and address at the vendor site.

David Kerin provides a number of special instructions that should be included. They include:

- Date and time by which the vendor's response must be returned

- Mailing address to which the response must be sent (or fax number, if fax responses are permitted)

- Name of individual (and phone number) to contact with questions related to the RFP

- Number of copies required of the vendor's reply document and whether the copy count includes an equal number of exhibits (e.g., catalogs, booklets) if the vendor's reply contains exhibits

- Date by which the vendor can expect to receive a reply

- Whether the vendor's reply document is considered confidential or public domain

- Whether the library intends to divide its business among more than one vendor and, if so, whether each vendor would be obligated to adhere to the same terms and conditions quoted for all business outlined in the RFP

- Any special vendor disqualification criteria (e.g., the vendor is unable to perform any of the required or desired services specified in the RFP)

- Policy on price, if unit pricing is requested, regarding what is expected to satisfy this requirement so that all vendors are responding in the same manner (for example, are all respondents using institutional rates from the publishers, do they include the publisher's shipping and handling fees, do they include the applicable taxes, et cetera)

- Whether the respondents are required to handle all the journal needs of the library or if they can be selective

- Term for which the library intends to award its business

- Statement that all responses are 'best and final' if the RFP is to be the vendor's one and only submission

> # What areas/questions should NOT be included in an RFP that often are included? What are the most common mistakes that librarians make when compiling an RFP?

Buzzy Basch plainly states that "the most common mistake is not being specific as to the library's requirements." Of course, there is a difference between citing what the library truly requires and rigging the award so that only one vendor can be selected.

Jane Maddox states that libraries should "make sure that what is included in the required section truly are absolute requirements. Otherwise, you may be inadvertently excluding the possibility of some qualified and good agents from consideration. Some libraries include in the required section a very specific description of a report, invoice, or other service, which is so totally vendor-specific that it is obvious that the RFP has been written so that only one vendor could possibly comply with the requirements. This eliminates the possibility of furthering the library awareness of different approaches to the same service. Whereas if this is in the 'desired,' but not 'required' section, it is possible to review samples from various vendors, and if the 'vendor-specific' approach is really the best, it will be obvious from this review and so stated in the evaluation. In this case, the library will still end up with the vendor that is best for them, but they will not have eliminated the possibility of the review of other vendors who could not have possibly complied with such a vendor-specific required specification."

David Kerin also believes that "the most common mistake made in the RFP process is to go through the exercise with the preconceived notion that a given vendor is going to win the award. In such cases, the evaluation committee may even fail to adequately evaluate each vendor's response. This is obviously a disservice to all parties concerned. As for the document itself, the RFP should be clear with instructions to the vendor and should allow for the vendor to elaborate in the more technical areas. Journal pricing is also an area that requires careful structure to ensure a level playing field. For example, if you ask your vendor to supply detailed pricing any time during the period June through December, you may get some prices that are for the current year and some for the upcoming subscription year. Comparing one set of vendor prices to another can be misleading without knowing the details behind the numbers. If journal prices are requested, ask the vendor to state whether the prices are for the current year or for the upcoming year. If they are a mixture of both, many vendors can earmark the newer rates."

Mark Kendall and Lynne Branche Brown assert, "Any question is fair game, and we cannot think of any specific areas or questions that would be considered inappropriate. Again, as long as all vendors are being equally considered in the bid process, any question is fair. Perhaps the most common mistakes that we have seen in RFPs are (1) asking the same question more than once in the RFP, (2) submitting an RFP that is not specifically tailored to the product or service that is being put out to bid. For example, some libraries may use 'boilerplate' RFPs that are virtually identical for the commodity being bid on whether it be photocopiers or library books. For the library to best understand a vendor's capabilities and proficiency in providing the specific service it is seeking, an RFP which asks specific questions unique to the commodity being bid upon is important, (3) disorganized RFPs which create redundancy, and (4) a general lack of focus, that is, the library asks the vendor virtually every question it can imagine while not indicating what areas it is most interested in."

Michael Markwith and Brian Noone indicate that "the most common mistake we have found is repetitive questions. It appears that attempts to be completely thorough can result in the same question posed two or three times. And the vendor cannot reply once but must repeat the answer, which makes for an awkward response."

Janice McIntyre and Susan Hillson suggest that "questions regarding staff salaries or age should not be included in an RFP. It most cases, it is against company policy to divulge such information. However, information that has been published in an annual report of a public company can be requested. Requests for services that are not a general part of a company's business should not be included (i.e., serials RFPs should be for serials services only; book RFPs should be for books only). Common mistakes include the following: pricing requirements are unclear (i.e., current pricing or firm-fixed); a complete or at least a representative title listing is not included for the vendor to quote, which assists in determining service charge; and the type of Integrated Library System or system planned for purchase is not listed, yet if Electronic Data Interchange (EDI) is required, vendors need to know the name of the system to discuss appropriate EDI capabilities."

Kit Kennedy considers the most common mistakes libraries make when compiling the RFP to be:

- Unclear directions on what the RFP is covering and how the vendor responses will be evaluated

- Too short a time frame to respond

- Too short a time frame to arrange presentations and at an inconvenient time of year (peak renewal time or end of the year)

- Too little feedback on the decision

- Document written specifically for a particular vendor

- Request for vendor proprietary information, including a list of all customers

- Boilerplated RFPs; all RFPs should include special areas and questions of importance to that library

How could librarians better negotiate contracts with vendors?

Kit Kennedy suggests a number of areas libraries might consider, including "indicating on the RFP that the service charge provided will be the vendor's best offer and/or indicating that the library wishes to further negotiate terms with the top selected vendor (don't play one vendor against another), multiyear contracts, and contracts for consolidated business—do not siphon off the more profit-generating subscriptions." Buzzy Basch replied they might "be more knowledgeable."

David Kerin asserts that "if 'negotiate' means 'how can librarians get the best price,' then I would have to say they do pretty well already. Vendors know that they must be competitive to even be considered when responding to an RFP. So, negotiating becomes a matter of price, service capability, and service delivery. Just because a vendor 'can provide' service, it does not necessarily mean they 'will deliver' service. When negotiating, look beyond price to see what the vendor can do in a timely way to offset workload in the library."

Mark Kendall and Lynne Branche Brown state, "A vendor can better negotiate with a library if the vendor has a clear understanding of the needs of the library. For example, for a library negotiating a higher monographic book discount, it is imperative that the vendor have an understanding of what the estimated annual book expenditures will be and the 'mix' of titles to be ordered. It is also important for the vendor to communicate to the library and the library to take into consideration what value-added services the vendor can offer the library, including customized services like electronic ordering capabilities, shelf-ready book processing, et cetera. As always, if both parties can work toward a 'win-win' scenario rather than entering into a one-sided agreement (which is almost always disastrous in the long term), the better for all."

Janice McIntyre and Susan Hillson caution, "Be precise when listing services required. By asking just for services needed and no more, you may be able to negotiate the contract based on minimal services and get a better price. Be realistic when listing service requirements and vendor response time. Librarians need to realize that vendors often have certain processes and procedures to follow and that we must often wait for publishers to respond to us before we can resolve an issue. Keep in mind that requirements that cause the vendor to use manual processes rather than allowing automated systems to generate certain types of correspondence with publishers and librarians will be more costly to the vendor and ultimately more costly to the librarian."

Michael Markwith and Brian Noone believe that "if there is any positive benefit to the overall RFP process, it is in this very simple core question. The RFP process in and of itself, when done properly and diligently by both library and vendor, creates a finished document that presents clear library needs specific to the requesting library matched to specific vendor services to meet those needs. Identifying, realizing, and codifying these needs and services then permit both parties to negotiate from a positive position. And the result is better contracts for both the library and the vendor."

Jane Maddox provides a different perspective. She comments, "The best contract negotiation processes I have experienced are situations where there are state contracts, with a list of 'approved vendors.' The vendors' terms and conditions for 'doing business' are on file with the state and available to all libraries affiliated with the state purchasing office or the state agency handling the contract. The idea is that the libraries can only order from vendors included on the state contract, unless there is special justification. No library will be provided less service or less discount, et cetera, than the terms that the vendor included in the state contract. However, the libraries are free to choose from the range of vendors on the listing of 'approved vendors.' The state contract RFP is similar to the individual library RFPs in establishing whether the vendor can provide required products or services, but it differs from the RFP in that it gives the library the flexibility to negotiate for any additional special services or enhancements during the course of the contract, or indeed, even the possibility of switching to another agent on the approved list of vendors, without further contract negotiations."

> # Do you encourage in-person presentations by vendors at library sites as part of the RFP process? Why? Why not? What are the benefits? What are the disadvantages?

Although most vendors approached the questions up to this point from somewhat different points of view, their answers were in basic agreement. This set of questions, however, split the panel; some are for, while others are not in favor of in-person, on-site presentations.

David Kerin states, "If the RFP is to be judged on price alone, then no in-person presentation is necessary. However, if service is an important part of what is required, then an in-person presentation is essential. If possible, the presentation should include the representative who will come into the library to offer assistance on matters that require vendor interface. In-person presentations offer the opportunity to discuss in depth the areas of most concern to the librarian. If for no other reason, an in-person presentation offers the opportunity to get to know the people with whom you may find yourself working over the next several years. About the only disadvantage to an in-person presentation is the risk of being sold on 'form' over 'substance.' In my experience, this is not likely to happen in an academic environment."

Buzzy Basch adds, "If a library does a good job of clearly defining its requirements, a site visit is not necessary."

Janice McIntyre and Susan Hillson also believe that they "would have to discourage in-person presentation because it is time-consuming and it is better for all parties involved to have all information in writing—this leaves little room for misunderstandings and misrepresentations. An in-person presentation included as part of the RFP has some benefits because it allows the library staff to ask questions and gain a complete understanding of vendor services, but this really should be done before the RFP process. The RFP process must also include written technical requirements that vendors must respond to. The written requirements and the vendor's written responses will become part of the contract.

"On the downside, in-person presentations are often hard to coordinate. Vendors should be afforded sufficient time to put together a customized presentation and to rehearse. Presentation guidelines, allotted time for presentation, and presentation topics need to be clearly articulated in writing from the library prior to the start of the process. Also keep in mind that vendors incur significant expense (travel, lodging, et cetera), by participating in presentations.

"Another approach to combining presentations with the RFP process is to first evaluate written responses to the RFP, then to coordinate a conference call with the vendor to discuss certain points for which you may have questions or may want additional information."

Jane Maddox asserts that "in-person presentations are certainly helpful, especially when there are complicated details of services which need to be discussed before an RFP can be written. But whether this should require a special on-site library visit really should be weighed against several factors: (1) What is the value of the proposed contract in relation to the cost for the vendor to make the on-site visit? (2) Are there other possibilities for in-person presentations which would not involve the expense of a special on-site presentation, such as key RFP evaluators who are attending a conference having a special presentation from the vendor representative at the conference, or having the presentations over several weeks, which might allow for the vendor to include the on-site presentation in a regularly scheduled visit to the library? and (3) Are there particularly complicated specifications which need to be discussed before the RFP can be written, or are there only a few questions which could easily be communicated with vendors via e-mail or telephone discussions? (Conference calls or video conferences are possibilities.)

"The disadvantages to the library and vendor are that these on-site visits take a great deal of time and energy and are thus very costly. Given the current-day technology of the WWW and e-mail, et cetera, on-site visits seem to be an outdated method for collecting information on services one might want to consider including in an RFP. If there are other considerations, then the on-site visits may be necessary. At least one library with which we have worked has post-RFP on-site visits, instead of pre-RFP visits. This has been the most effective process that I have seen, in that the review of the bids allows the library to narrow the field to two or three agents, and it is those agents who then are called in for personal discussions. This may be the most cost-effective process for all concerned."

Kit Kennedy believes that a "pre-RFP in-person vendor presentation can assist both the library and vendor in understanding what the library wishes and needs and what the vendor can offer. The vendor often comes away with a clearer way to respond to the RFP, and as a result, the document is more valuable to the library. The library can craft a more useful RFP for its own needs.

"An in-person vendor presentation after the RFP has been submitted is an effective way for the library to ask any questions or probe for additional information. The vendor has a target audience and should welcome the invitation."

Mark Kendall and Lynne Branche Brown state, "We strongly encourage on-site library presentations as part of the RFP process. This process, normally conducted after the RFP responses have been submitted to the library, allows the vendor to present their services and enter into a dialogue with the library staff to clarify questions answered in the RFP. The presentation is an opportunity for the vendor to ask the library for clarification about its needs and the library to further explore written responses it received from the vendor. It also allows the library staff to meet some of the key individuals from the company that they decide to work with. An RFP alone can be somewhat 'arm's length' in terms of evaluating a vendor. The presentation better allows the library and the vendor to get to know each other so that the library can make a more informed decision about which vendor they feel they could best work with.

"One of the limitations of in-person presentations is the danger that nonobjective evaluation criteria may be brought into the decision-making process (such as the degree of 'finesse' the vendor is able to project during the presentation).

"Used as one component of a balanced evaluation process for identifying which vendor is most able to meet the library's needs, the in-person presentation affords the library and the vendors opportunities for dialogue which are not possible through the RFP process."

Michael Markwith and Brian Noone "always prefer on-site library presentations. A formal presentation by the vendor helps clarify any questions and allows both parties to see how and if they can work together. This is especially helpful if the library is not completely familiar with the vendor's services, staff, and organizational philosophy. Recently, libraries have begun to ask for presentations prior to releasing the actual RFP. This has been most beneficial in helping the library staff focus on their needs with a better market understanding of what vendor services are available. I think this is a positive trend, but still does not replace the option of having the vendor return to clarify any unresolved questions by the library staff."

What are the principle benefits to the library and vendor of librarians doing RFPs? What are the disadvantages to both?

Jane Maddox comments, "Some immediate positives that come to mind when I think of what I have seen happen in the industry during the past few years, as we have been experiencing a tremendous growth in the use of the RFP process, are as follows:

- Libraries have more clearly established service requirements and documented this information in a formalized way.

- Booksellers and subscription agents have had to provide organized documentation as well as make financial disclosures.

- Libraries have become much more aware of different booksellers and agents and their respective strengths and weaknesses.

- Booksellers and subscription agents have had to become more involved in professional organizations to stay on top of current developments.

- Both libraries and vendors have had to give more thought to implementation of standards.

"But I have to ask whether these positives are really a part of the RFP process or just a more professional way of doing business. Has this growth in professionalism developed because of the RFP process, or has it simply been natural professional growth and maturation?

"I think the answer is yes and no. For some institutions, the RFP process has been directly related to positive enhancements within the organization and documentation of their procedures and vendor service requirements. However, those same positive enhancements have also developed in some institutions which have not been involved in the RFP process at all."

David Kerin offers, "The RFP gives the librarian a chance to clearly state what is important to the library. This is of value to the library and the vendor. Through this process, both parties can focus in on what is important. An RFP can also set the stage for the working relationship between the two parties since formal contracts with specific performance criteria are uncommon in this business. The only disadvantages of an RFP are related to the investment of time required of both vendor and library to do it correctly."

Michael Markwith and Brian Noone suggest that "the principle benefit for vendors is that they can receive information in an RFP that is essential in deciding whether or not to pursue a library's business, and also to identify what the library's needs are if they do decide to reply to the RFP. The library benefits by receiving precise information on what each vendor can and cannot provide in terms of services and pricing available. The only disadvantage for libraries is the amount of time it takes to prepare the RFP. This is especially relevant for libraries who need to prepare title lists manually."

Janice McIntyre and Susan Hillson state, "The principle benefits to the library of doing RFPs are that they are able to quantify the analysis of each vendor service and can select the vendor that best meets their needs. The benefits to the vendor are that the RFP provides performance guidelines and a clear statement of the work to be performed. A disadvantage in doing an RFP is the fact that most vendors provide the same services and the library may not be able to clearly determine which vendor will provide the services that best meet their needs. Another disadvantage is that the library may be forced to switch vendors on a regular basis each time an RFP is done if technical requirements are not concise or if the RFP is not properly evaluated. The RFP process is time-consuming and, ultimately, costly for the library. A major disadvantage for the vendor is that current business may be lost if the library does not write tight and concise technical requirements. Another disadvantage to a vendor is that responding to an RFP is time-consuming and sufficient time to respond is often not allowed."

Buzzy Basch comments that the advantages of the RFP are "better service, a chance to clarify quality of service, and to gain knowledge."

Mark Kendall and Lynne Branche Brown believe that "perhaps the principle benefit to the library is that it is ensured of receiving, in most cases, a written description of the vendor's abilities to meet the specific needs of the library. By issuing an identical RFP to other vendors for the same commodity, the library can compare responses and evaluate how each vendor might best address the library's needs. The benefit to the vendor is that the vendor can develop a clearer understanding of the library's needs and the key criteria for making the vendor selection. Whether the vendor selection will be made on price (discount), customer service, or technology is often borne out to the vendor in the types of questions asked in the RFP.

"There is a substantial time investment for both the library in preparing the RFP and the vendor in providing a detailed response to it. There are potential disadvantages when the RFP alone is used to make a vendor selection. As stated above, we strongly believe that it is equally critical for the library staff to meet the vendor(s) staffs who, based on the RFP responses, best embody the goals and services outlined in the RFP. This can be done in a presentation format or through individual meetings with library staff."

Kit Kennedy responds that the benefits to the library are "evaluation of service, improved and expanded range of vendor services, improved communication and partnerships with vendors, and improved management of serials. Disadvantages to the library include a drain on resources (a good RFP is hard and time-consuming in addition to the work as usual) if the decision is a foregone conclusion or the committee's recommendation is vetoed by an associate university librarian (AUL) or director, if the purchasing department makes the decision based solely on price, and if the contract is for only one year.

"Benefits to the vendor are new or expanded business, marking intelligence—how a vendor compares to competition, partnership (e.g., electronic services), and vendors enjoy selling and the RFP process and presentation is at the heart of sales (good work is fun). Disadvantages to the vendor include potential loss of existing business and drain and expense of completing RFPs and making in-person presentations."

What makes your company respond to an RFP? What makes your company not respond?

Kit Kennedy answers, "Why do vendors respond to RFPs? Maintaining and/or gaining new business given a sufficient time frame to respond." Why vendors do not respond to RFPs include:

- Evaluation that the RFP is written for a specific vendor
- Sufficient lack of time to meet deadlines or timing of the RFP
- RFPs received too late in the year (for the following renewal year)
- Mix of materials or expenditure covered by RFP

- Past experiences with the library

- Understanding that decision will be based solely on price

- Contracts awarded for one year only

- Technical requirements (e.g., interfacing with local system)

- Mandatory requirements or expectations of service that a vendor might consider unrealistic

- Specialty RFPs outside the expertise of the vendor

Buzzy Basch sums up the reasons as "timing of request, dollar volume, potential, publisher discounts, customer versus prospect, what the library is currently paying in fees, and library reputation."

Mark Kendall and Lynne Branche Brown reveal that "we tend to respond to RFPs that are oriented toward our core competencies and that invite the desire to form a close working relationship, or partnership between the library and vendor. We tend to shy away from RFPs that are based on services that are in areas we do not have expertise in. We also are reluctant to respond to RFPs where the selected vendor will be chosen based on highest discount only. These types of RFPs typically place a lower value on the 'partnership component' described earlier as well as customer service and other value-added benefits."

David Kerin states, "My company responds to every RFP that is judged to be within the scope of our ability to serve the library well. This means we can handle the titles, bring value to the library, be permitted to recover our costs, and earn a reasonable profit. Financial health to a vendor is essential to one's ability to remain in the business. What causes my company not to respond is the belief that the RFP is merely an exercise and the library is using the process to justify a decision that may have been made prior to issuing the RFP. Another reason not to respond is the belief that price will be the only consideration for award, but the service demands by the library may be extensive. In these situations, a vendor may end up serving a library at a loss when all things are considered."

Jane Maddox answered this question along similar lines of reasoning. "We respond to any RFP where it is clear that we would be very qualified to provide the services specified as being required or desired. However, we have limited staff available to work on the RFPs, so it is possible that even though we would like to respond, there may simply not be enough time or staff or both to facilitate the response. Also, when there are very clear preferences for a specific vendor included in the specifications, we may elect to forego the expense of processing the RFP."

Janice McIntyre and Susan Hillson indicate that "several factors assist us in determining whether or not to respond to an RFP. We will respond if there is [a] significant amount of business at stake, the technical requirements and RFP instructions are clear, and there is a fair amount of time in which to respond to the RFP. We will not respond if we have had a bad experience with the client in the past (e.g., payment problems or unrealistic client expectations), technical requirements and RFP instructions are unrealistic or composed in such a way that it is extremely difficult to respond either to the requirements or the format, and if there is not sufficient time to respond to the RFP.

On the average, how much time should be given the vendor to complete an RFP? How much time does it generally take a vendor to complete an RFP?

David Kerin believes that "the length of time necessary to complete an RFP varies based upon the complexity of the RFP and whether a complete list of priced titles must accompany the response. On average, the typical academic RFP should provide a month for the vendor to respond. It could be done in less time, but the library should allow for scheduling conflicts that the vendors may experience."

Kit Kennedy asserts, "The question hinges on three factors: the time of year, the complexity of the RFP, and the market condition (is it a year in which many institutions are submitting RFPs). Generally, outside of peak renewal periods, conference season, and very late in the year, a library should give a vendor a minimum of one month. While it won't take a vendor a solid 30 days to complete, the vendor has to fit this RFP onto its bid-response calendar. Most in-depth RFPs are reviewed and signed off by several personnel within the company. Often, input is needed from several staff within the company.

"It is important to give a vendor sufficient time and, whenever possible, options to schedule in-person presentations. Because of the increasing complexity of in-person presentations, vendors need to coordinate the schedules of both inside staff and field sales representations."

Mark Kendall and Lynne Branche Brown recommend, "preferably, six weeks lead time to prepare an RFP is sufficient. There is no general amount of time required to complete an RFP. Each RFP is unique, and the amount of time required to complete an RFP response usually varies depending upon the complexity and length of the proposal. Some can be completed in as few as two days; others may require input from several key individuals within the company who have proficiency in delivering specific services outlined in the RFP, such as cataloging, physical processing, et cetera, and, therefore, we should like at least four weeks to respond to an RFP—more if it is particularly long and detailed."

Buzzy Basch believes that "the time given the vendor should reflect the library's needs and the amount of time it can afford. Frequently, RFPs are received by the vendor late in the fall. The increased number of RFPs at this time increases the amount of time needed for completion and return. A library might be best served to consider sending its RFP in the spring when there are fewer requests, resulting in RFPs being completed in less time."

Jane Maddox states, "The amount of time needed to complete a response to an RFP can vary greatly, depending on how long or brief the RFP is and whether there are extraneous materials that we have to sort through or edit out. It also depends on whether it is a formal RFP or an informal RFP. For serials RFPs, if the listing of titles is provided electronically, with ISSNs included, this can also cut down on the time needed for processing an RFP response. Also, depending upon whether the vendor already provides all the mandatory requirements or whether they are presently developing or need to modify or enhance a service in order to comply with these requirements, extra time may be required before submitting the response to the RFP. Another factor can be whether the vendor has many other RFPs to be processed at the same time. I would say that the minimum time that should be allowed for response is four weeks, and ideally the RFP should allow eight weeks for a response."

Michael Markwith and Brian Noone say, "We recommend that libraries should give at least one month to complete the RFP. It can take up to two and a half weeks to complete a serials RFP if there are titles to research and quote. Having one month allows vendors to respond to more than one RFP at the same time (which is the rule rather than the exception)."

Janice McIntyre and Susan Hillson agree, stating that "a vendor should be allowed three to four complete weeks to respond to an RFP. The vendor usually has several RFPs to work on at a time. Depending on the complexity of technical requirements and RFP instructions, the vendor will prefer the maximum amount of time so they can submit a good proposal. Generally, it takes a good two weeks to write a good response to an RFP, quote a title list if necessary, and mail the response. A library also needs to factor in at least a week for the RFP to reach the vendor and time for the vendor response to reach the library."

Are automated services underemphasized or overemphasized in RFPs?

Mark Kendall and Lynne Branche Brown say, "We do not believe that automated services are underemphasized by any means in most RFPs. The rapidly changing technological environment that both libraries and vendors exist in today necessitates an understanding on the library's part of what types of services the vendor can offer them. The challenge to the library in writing an RFP that may be designed to establish a contract extending for several years, as well as the vendor in responding, lies in determining what types of questions can be asked of the vendor regarding automation that will still be applicable one, two, and three years into the future. As though trying to anticipate the future of automation through a crystal ball, libraries will occasionally fall into the trap of attempting to look too far out on the horizon and state requirements in the RFP to the vendor regarding automated services that either are developmental in nature or simply not yet planned. For a library to understand a vendor's current and planned automation capabilities, we recommend adding questions to the RFP regarding what developmental projects are currently under way or planned in the next year or two regarding automation, technical services, et cetera."

According to Kit Kennedy, "The library should have a working knowledge of what reports it actually needs at present to manage its operations and should consider what it might need in the future. Vendor reports that satisfy both those conditions are valuable. Increasingly, library systems are providing a richer array of reports, and libraries are no longer as dependent as they were five years ago on vendor reports. Reports for collection development are still an integral part of a vendor's portfolio.

"The RFP should distinguish between a vendor's current interface capabilities with specific ILS systems and a vendor's future plans of interfacing with systems. RFPs should distinguish from what is possible today and what is technically probable in the future. Asking for a vendor's commitment to interface with a specific ILS system (when the ILS system is capable) is a part of a well-crafted RFP."

David Kerin believes that "automated services have a value equal to what the library wishes to place on them. These services are designed to reduce the amount of time spent by library staff on manual activities related to serials management. In my judgment, any service offered by a vendor which enables the library to save time should be emphasized."

Jane Maddox states, "I do not think this judgment could be passed on automated services, or any other for that matter. What does need to be considered very carefully by the author of the RFP is exactly what services are important (mandatory) and which are only desirable. If there are services (either automated or otherwise) which really do not make any difference to the library, then they should be excluded."

Michael Markwith and Brain Noone "think automated services are given the appropriate emphasis in RFPs. However, it is important to differentiate between what is and what will or might be for both the library and vendor. Questions about specific needs with existing systems are relevant. Requests for vendor philosophy on future development are relevant. What is most important is to distinguish between the two. RFPs should not encourage marketing hype unless this is the library's true intention."

Janice McIntyre and Susan Hillson depart from other vendor responses, asserting that "automated services are underemphasized in RFPs. Often, the library is not clear as to what sort of automated services they require. We often see major misunderstandings of Electronic Data Interchange versus proprietary system interfaces versus the format and media (e.g., data in ASCII format versus File Transfer Protocol). If a library is not clear on the type of automation they desire, they should hold a discussion with vendors before the RFP process so they can gain a clear understanding of the various services available and then be able to clearly state their requirements.

"Libraries also need to clearly state which Integrated Library System, including version, they have so the vendor can respond to their needs appropriately. Libraries need to consider the specific serials management software used by the vendor and word their requirements accordingly."

Are customer services and reports underemphasized or overemphasized?

Kit Kennedy states, "I do not think it is possible to overemphasize good customer service. I am keenly interested in how libraries 'interview' the vendor's references and how those responses are interpreted, evaluated.

"I see great value in reports which are really useful to a library. More and more, libraries need reports (information) from vendors on price predictions and budgeting estimates for other-than-paper formats."

Mark Kendall and Lynne Branche Brown also maintain that "both customer service and reports cannot possibly be overemphasized. However, in the last year or two, there has seemed to be less of an RFP emphasis in this area in favor of a greater emphasis on automation. This is perhaps understandable in light of the tremendous pace of automation changes, but ultimately, one of the best measures of a book vendor is the ability to provide accurate book delivery and reports, timely and quality customer service and delivery of the right book, the first time, at a fair price. As stated earlier, it is also critical that the library have an understanding of the staff and the experience of the vendor's staff that will be servicing the library's account."

Buzzy Basch emphatically states that service is "underemphasized—few libraries specify their service requirements!"

Janice McIntyre and Susan Hillson take the middle ground: "Customer services seem to be fairly represented in the RFPs we have seen. On the other hand, reports tend to be overemphasized. Libraries tend to list every possible report and sort option they desire and list report elements, whether or not those options are possible from the vendors. Report requirements should be realistic—required elements that you need and that you know vendors can provide."

David Kerin states, "I would respond to this question in the same manner as indicated for automated services. They have value only if the library makes use of the available services. I would add, however, that many services are activities that are required to maintain one's collection and if not provided by the vendor would fall upon the library to perform."

Jane Maddox agrees and adds, "Again, it would be the libraries who could better answer this question. If libraries are including items which are not relevant to the services they truly require, then there is too much emphasis. If, however, they are leaving out elements which are, in fact, crucial to their operation, then they are underemphasized."

What is the best strategy to use to get the lowest service charges and the highest discounts?

Kit Kennedy explains, "The mix of titles, the estimated expenditure, whether the business is new or retained, whether and when the library can prepay, the length of the contract, whether the library is centralized or decentralized, the complexity of the account, the stability of the list, and any special requirements influence the service charge. The mix of titles and the profitability of the list is a key factor in determining service charge. It is very useful to have the titles under consideration submitted in a disk (including ISSN, title, and, if known, price). In lieu of a reduced service charge, often a library can negotiate for no-charge or reduced charge on a vendor's value-added services (access to vendor system, document delivery, access to electronic journals, et cetera). In addition, on a substantial transfer, the library can negotiate for transfer assistance from the vendor.

"The RFP process is one of partnership. With an understanding of the economics of doing business (how a vendor makes its profit), the library can negotiate realistically with a vendor. Pitting one vendor against another or [using] threats are not useful strategies. After a library has negotiated, it does no harm to ask the vendor, 'What else do you think you can do for us?' "

Michael Markwith and Brian Noone suggest that "the best strategy is to weigh price in terms of the total service provided and not simply on the discount or service charge offered. For example, a high discount or low service charge on prices that have been adjusted upwards to reflect a fair vendor price costs the library more than a lower discount or higher service charge on the true publisher list price. It is true that the mix is a crucial factor in the vendor pricing decision. It is one of many important factors for both the library and the vendor to consider. And when considering the entire service offering and costs involved, it is also very important to remember that the lowest price is not necessarily the least expensive choice."

Janice McIntyre and Susan Hillson state, "Vendors still base service charges on the mix of titles and on the discount we get from publishers. By including the higher discount scientific, technical, and medical titles in your list, those titles will help you to get a lower service charge. Keep in mind that the more labor-intensive technical requirements you list, the higher your service charge may be. Require that the vendor give you the lowest rate for which your institution type qualifies (e.g., academic rates for a university, government rates for federal governments libraries)."

Mark Kendall and Lynne Branche Brown caution that "there is really no one 'strategy' to obtaining the lowest service charges and highest discount. For a vendor to quote their 'best' discount, it is critical in an RFP for the library to provide information on the anticipated dollar amount expenditures. It is preferable that this be done by category, for example, X dollars for approval plan, X dollars for firm orders, X dollars for continuations, et cetera. Next, the 'mix' of the types of materials being ordered must be stated. Ultimately, the highest discounts will be offered to those institutions that select a vendor as the sole vendor. This reflects a commitment on the part of the library to form a deep, working partnership with the vendor, and a higher discount is one way that the vendor reciprocates this commitment."

Jane Maddox states, "I do not think it should be the goal of an RFP to get the lowest service charges or the highest discounts. I have read recommendations that the librarians have to 'talk tough' to their agents to 'demand' the best price, et cetera. But my personal experience has been that the best negotiations are those where there is an informed buyer and informed seller involved, with the goal of providing the best quality service for the best possible price. This price may not be the lowest possible price or the best possible discounts. Both parties should be interested in what is best for both the buyer and the seller, and both should be able to justify their actions within the framework of a long-term plan. Extremely low bids may appear to be attractive in the short term but usually leave the library with not quite the quality of service it expected and the vendor with little or no profit with which to continue as a viable entity in the industry."

David Kerin recommends that the library "simply give service charges and/or discounts a higher point value in your RFP. If this is the most important element of your needs, state it in your RFP."

Does it really come down to "mix" and, for serials, should a representative sample of serials titles to be transferred be included?

Buzzy Basch responds with a clear, simple "yes." Mark Kendall and Lynne Branche Brown go on to add, "As stated above, 'mix' is very important. Yes, a representative sample of serials titles should be included with the RFP to ensure that, if selected, the vendor can actually handle those specific titles. By reviewing the list, this also helps the vendor in quoting their best discount for the serials. It is also worth asking a vendor in an RFP how it would assist the library in the transfer of continuations from its present vendor to the new one."

David Kerin agrees. "Yes, mix is important because the commission, or discount, given by publishers varies by publication. A representative sample is not of value unless it represents the average margin the vendor is to receive from the entire list of titles. By determining what can be expected from the publishers in the form of commissions, a vendor can then accurately calculate the necessary service charge."

Janice McIntyre and Susan Hillson also concur. "Yes, it really does come down to 'mix' to ensure the best possible service charge offered. Either a complete list or a representative sample of serials titles should be included in the RFP to assist the vendor in determining a service charge. Also, keep in mind that the larger the title list, the more time it will take the vendor to quote."

Jane Maddox believes that "library materials contracts are very indefinite entities, because of the nature of the products we are talking about. Anything you can do to narrow the field being considered, such as providing a list of titles currently purchased (electronic file if at all possible), should help to make the contract negotiations on more definite grounds."

What areas of the vendor RFP reply are the most often negotiated, and what are the best strategies to use?

According to Michael Markwith and Brian Noone, "This answer is dependent on accepting the answer offered on the previous question. Service charge and/or discount is usually the most negotiated item in our experience, but the best strategy to use remains the consideration of the entire service and pricing package offered by the vendor. Perhaps a service offered is not needed by the library and the vendor can lower the price by excluding the service. It's not just the discount or service charge. There is an old and wise maxim for libraries (as in real life): You get what you pay for!"

Mark Kendall and Lynne Branche Brown indicate that "discounts, service fees, shipping and handling, and return terms are probably the most commonly negotiated areas. There is no specific strategy to use for negotiating these areas except to say, as stated above, that selecting the vendor as a 'sole vendor' provides the library with the greatest leverage in negotiating terms. Beyond this, the level of expenditures committed to the vendor combined with the 'mix' of titles ordered will also impact each area."

According to David Kerin, "The only aspects of an RFP routinely subject to negotiation are the financial elements. The best strategy to deal with the financial elements of the RFP is to indicate your requirements and the priority of your requirements in the RFP."

Janice McIntyre and Susan Hillson assert that "price and specific technical requirements that the vendor cannot provide exactly as required are most often negotiated. Strategically, the library should be honest and realistic in its approach. To get the best price, do not ask for more services than you realistically need, and do not ask for items that will cause the vendor to manually produce the desired output."

Buzzy Basch believes that "the whole process is a negotiation—make it win-win for the vendor and the library. The best strategy overall is to be knowledgeable. Remember that the lowest cost doesn't ensure the best price. There can be instances where the higher cost and services can be the best price. Special consideration should be given to the price on a per item basis. It is not always the bottom line that is the best indicator."

What other areas of the RFP should be covered?

Mark Kendall and Lynne Branche Brown indicate that "as was alluded to in the question regarding automation, libraries should not hesitate to ask via the RFP what the vendor is considering or planning in the way of development for the future. This would include specialized services that are planned or under consideration, possible areas of expansion, and the vendor's vision for growth. It is important for the library to know that its vendor has a strategic plan for the years ahead and is not a 'here today, gone tomorrow' entity.

We see the RFP process as an opportunity for the library to elicit information from vendors which describes how the unique capabilities of the vendor will meet the needs of the library. An RFP which clearly describes what the library needs, which items are most important to that particular institution, and what criteria will be used in selecting a vendor allows the vendor a better understanding of how well suited its services are to that institution—and thus to respond appropriately."

Buzzy Basch suggests asking these questions: "How are fees assessed? Are there additional fees beyond standard service charges for titles where there is no publisher discount, for Superintendent of Documents materials, et cetera?"

Kit Kennedy says, "Another useful tool that a library can use to evaluate its serials is to issue an RFI (Request for Information). Most of the same topics included in an RFP should appear in an RFI. However, a library can, in a cover letter, state that it is evaluating its vendoring decisions, the reason why it is doing this, and the time frame; ask vendors to submit information about their company; and specify a contact person. Libraries who award business based on an RFI might request the vendor to submit a 'Letter of Agreement' between the library and vendor. A letter of agreement sets forth the terms and conditions, length of anticipated business, benchmarks for customer service, and any special requirements agreed to by library and vendor."

Jane Maddox comments on an area that she would like to see covered. "Standard commercial RFPs involve services or products from either the producers or distributors of these services/products. To use the same vehicle for obtaining services and products from booksellers and subscription agents is a little like the proverbial mixing of apples with oranges. Consider the following comparison of what is involved with the standard commercial producer/distributor (not to be confused with publishing distributors) responding to an RFP for products and/or services as opposed to the bookdealer/subscription agent responding to an RFP: Standard commercial producer/distributor RFPs usually specify a specific volume of specific products required for each year of the proposed contract. Producers have contracts with suppliers of the raw materials, and distributors have contracts for specific gross margin percentages from producers, so they are in a position to calculate their costs for obtaining the products required by the RFP. The costs for the services involved with delivery of the product can more definitely be calculated as the producers are in control of the production line, or the distributor has product availability from more than one producer and can juggle orders to obtain materials where they are available and/or at the best terms.

"Booksellers and subscription agents do not even know what is going to be published in the first year of an RFP, much less year two or three and beyond. And of what is published, there is no way of knowing which titles the library will purchase, cancel, et cetera. The agent/bookseller certainly [has] no contracts with the publishers, who can change the amount of discount granted to the agent from one day to the next, and/or from title to title. The cost involved with getting the materials requested by the RFP is more difficult for the bookseller/subscription agent, as there is no way to gauge how long orders must be kept open, as they cannot simply switch the order to a different publisher when a title ordered is not immediately available for some reason.

"For these reasons, and others stated previously, I think it would be a giant step forward if more states could implement the state contract approach. Also, work done on the national level to coordinate a standard library contract format would help to streamline the contract for services process. By this, I mean simply a format for the various elements so that the libraries and vendors can consistently quickly identify the various sections of the RFP and know to always find certain data elements in specific sections, instead of having to search through all pages just to find the essential information."

Janice McIntyre and Susan Hillson conclude by considering the importance of the evaluation process. "An evaluation team, consisting of several library staff and contract office staff, needs to be assembled. Each member of the team needs to be objective in their evaluation and the evaluation criteria needs to be clearly spelled out and understood by all. Elaborate rating schemes do not benefit anyone and can cause the evaluation process to drag on."

Notes

1. Stuart Glogoff, "Reflections on Dealing with Vendors," *American Libraries* 25, no. 4 (1994): 313.

2. Glogoff, 315.

3. Gary M. Shirk, "The Wondrous Web: Reflections on Library Acquisitions and Vendor Relationships," in *Vendors and Library Acquisitions*, ed. Bill Katz (Binghamton, NY: Haworth Press, 1991), 2–3.

4. See William Fisher, "A Brief History of Library–Vendor Relations Since 1950," *Library Acquisitions: Practice & Theory* 17, no. 1 (1993): 61–69, for an historical overview of library–vendor relationships.

5. Roger L. Presley, "Firing an Old Friend, Painful Decisions: The Ethics Between Librarians and Vendors," *Library Acquisitions: Practice & Theory* 17, no. 1 (1993): 55–56.

6. Gary M. Shirk, "Contract Acquisitions: Change, Technology, and the New Library/Vendor Partnership," *Library Acquisitions: Practice & Theory* 17, no. 2 (1993): 145.

7. Daniel T. Richards, "The Library/Dealer Relationship: Reflections on the Ideal," *Journal of Library Administration* 16, no. 3 (1992): 46.

8. Mary J. Bostic, "Approval Acquisitions and Vendor Relations: An Overview," *Acquisitions Librarian* 5, no. 3 (1991): 136.

9. James R. Coffey, "Contracts and Ethics in Library Acquisitions: The Expressed and Implied," in *Legal and Ethical Issues in Acquisitions,* ed. Katina Strauch and Bruce Strauch (Binghamton, NY: Haworth Press, 1990), 103.

10. N. Bernard "Buzzy" Basch discusses many of the issues raised in the questions to vendors throughout this chapter in his workshop entitled "Negotiating Services and Fees with Subscription Agencies: A Seminar Presented by Basch Associates" and in the book *Buying Serials: A How-to-Do-It Manual for Librarians*, coauthored with Judy McQueen.

Appendix A

Sample Timeline for the RFP Process

This appendix contains a sample timeline covering the various stages of the RFP process. It is presented in July 1–June 30 fiscal year format. It can easily be tailored to fit a different fiscal year (e.g., October 1–September 30), a calendar year (January 1–December 31), a school year (e.g., September 1–May 31), or some other time period. (See chapter 2 for more details.)

October 1
Appoint RFP committee; elect chair

October 5
Meet with purchasing officer

October 10–November 15
Select vendors and arrange site visits

November 16–January 15
Write RFP draft

January 16
Make RFP draft available for review and comment by other library employees (if appropriate)

February 1
Send RFP to Purchasing department for review

February 15
Purchasing department reviews RFP, makes any needed changes, and mails it to all appropriate vendors

Vendors will have 30 to 45 days (depending on mail delivery time) to respond to the RFP

April 1
Purchasing department receives all proposals and forwards them to library for review and selection

April 2–April 15
RFP committee evaluates vendor proposals and calls vendor references

April 16–20

RFP committee reviews and tabulates evaluation forms, discusses reference calls, and selects a vendor(s)

April 21

RFP committee forwards recommendations to Purchasing department

May 1

Purchasing department notifies all vendors

July 1

New vendor contract(s) begins

Appendix B

Sample RFP Materials

The appendix contains (1) a sample cover letter, (2) sample vendor proposal cover sheet, and (3) sample RFP questions. The sample RFP questions are subdivided by RFP type (e.g., questions suitable for all types of RFPs; domestic approval plans; specialty approval plans, including Latin American, fine arts, science, technology, and engineering; standing orders; and serials).

The presentation of the cover letter is generic and should be tailored by the library to fit its unique needs. Sections should be altered, added, or deleted, depending on the library's requirements.

When writing an RFP, the library should first clearly state its requirements in the RFP and then select vendor questions from the samples, altering, adding, or deleting questions to fit its particular needs. The sample questions also serve as a useful tool for the RFP committee to assist it in solidifying its actual requirements as well as what it desires from a vendor. The more general questions may also be useful to libraries writing a Request for Information. (See chapters 3–8 for more details for both the cover letter and the RFP questions.) In addition to the questions presented here, see chapter 12 for the vendor perspective, which contains additional potential questions to include in the RFP.

Fig. A1. Sample Cover Letter.

-----

library letterhead

TO: Vendor Name
FROM: Library Name
SUBJECT: Request for Proposal to Supply [specify material type]
DATE:
INTRODUCTION AND SUMMARY OF MAJOR POINTS

This Request for Proposal (RFP) is to supply [type of material; for example, domestic approval plans, specialty approval plans (state type), standing orders, domestic serials, foreign serials (state type)] for the [library name]. Please indicate which plan(s) you are proposing on the attached "Vendor Proposal Cover Sheet." If your organization chooses to submit a proposal, please note that it must be received by the [university/parent organization] Purchasing Department (address below) no later than [time] on [date]. The format of the response should be [physical format], and [number] copies of the response should be provided [the library should indicate whether the same number of exhibits (e.g., catalogs, samples) should be provided or if one copy of each of these is sufficient].

The [library name] requires three client references (contact and institution name, address, phone number, and e-mail address) similar to itself in type and size; preferably, one of these should have transferred its business to the vendor within the last two years. [If the library has an online system, request that at least one reference be from a library that uses the same system.]

This service will take effect on [date], the beginning of the new fiscal year [or calendar year]. This contract will be valid for [time period] with the option of [number] additional [time period] renewals. Such extensions, if granted, will be by mutual consent of both parties and will be based on the criteria set forth in this proposal and contingent on the availability of funding. The [library name] anticipates spending approximately [dollars] annually on [type of material]. These amounts should not be considered as commitment to purchase but are, rather, intended to provide the vendor with an estimated contract value. The [library name] reserves the right to increase or decrease the amounts as actual needs determine.

All vendor proposals will be jointly evaluated by the [university/parent organization] Purchasing Department and by appropriate [library name] personnel as soon as possible after [closing date]. On the basis of the information received, the vendor(s) that represents the best overall value to the [library name] will be selected. The [library name] reserves the right to use the services of two or more vendors for a single material type if it deems the vendors' services to be of equal overall value. The vendor should submit its best-and-final pricing offer in its proposal and indicate if there are separate offers for all versus part of the library's account [if this does not apply to your library, omit this sentence]. The [library name] is not obligated to award the contract(s) based on the lowest cost proposal submitted. It is the sole responsibility of the vendor to inquire about any sections of the RFP process that are unclear.

BACKGROUND INFORMATION

The [library name] [describe parent organization (and consortium), clientele, programs, size and strength of collections, operating budget, staff size, and other appropriate information pertaining to the library]. The [library name] is a member of the [association, if appropriate], uses [bibliographic utility], and has [integrated library system, in-house system, or no automated system].

EVALUATION FACTORS

The weighted point factors to be used to determine the appropriate vendor will include, but not be limited to, the following: [which are designed to serve as samples only; they are not intended to be prescriptive in any way—weights and factors will vary for each library]

Approval Plan [sample]		**Serials [sample]**	
Weights	Factors	Weights	Factors
10%	Company Data	10%	Company Data
20%	Profiling and Title Selection	10%	Orders and Cancellations
10%	Coverage Provided	15%	Invoicing
5%	Bibliographic Data Provided	20%	Claims and Titles Changes
10%	Financial Practice	20%	Customer Service
20%	Customer Service	15%	Computer-Based Services
15%	Computer-Based Services	10%	Overall Cost Considerations
10%	Overall Cost Considerations		

Please do not minimize the importance of an adequate response to each of the above.

CONTACT NAMES
    Send proposals to Name of Purchasing Officer
    Institution
    Address (including city, state, and zip code)
    Phone Number
    Fax Number
    E-mail Address

If you have any questions regarding this proposal, please contact one of the following:

General Information:
    Name (usually RFP committee chair)
    Address
    Phone Number
    Fax Number
    E-mail Address

Systems Information:
    Name
    Address
    Phone Number
    Fax Number
    E-mail Address

Fig. A2. Sample Vendor Proposal Cover Sheet.

Vendor Name:
Contact Person:
Address:
Phone Number: Fax Number: E-mail:

The above named vendor is submitting this proposal to the [library name] for materials for the areas indicated below (please check all that apply):

Domestic Approval Plan(s)
    Entire Approval Plan:
    Trade Plan:
    University Press Plan:
    Science, Technology, and Engineering Plan:
    Art Exhibition Catalogs Approval Plan:
    Music Scores Approval Plan:
    Approval Plan for Mexico:
    Approval Plan for Brazil:

Standing Orders:
Domestic Serials:
European Serials:
United Kingdom Serials:
South American Serials:
Asian Serials:
African Serials:

Vendor proposals must be received by the [university/parent organization] Purchasing Department by [time and date]. The vendor understands that if it does not submit a proposal by this date the [library name] will conclude that it does not intend to submit a response to this RFP. Not submitting a proposal will not affect the vendor's right to submit a proposal for a future RFP from [library name].

Fig. A3. Sample RFP Questions.

Please note that some of the following RFP questions overlap or are similar to questions in other sections. Also, some questions fit into more than one section. The questions should be tailored to the library's actual situation and requirements; not all questions apply to all libraries' needs. In addition, the library should ask each vendor for samples of all forms, invoices, credit memos, claims reports, and fiscal and management reports that the vendor would supply to the library, based on the library's requirements, should the vendor be awarded the contract. Care should be taken not to make requirements for services (electronic or other) in the RFP that the library does not intend to use. This will simplify the process for the vendor and the library, especially at evaluation time. Finally, the library should be sure to understand the questions it asks, the answers it expects to receive from the vendors, and how it will evaluate these answers.

Questions Suitable for All Types of RFPs

The following are suitable as general questions pertaining to company data, customer service, computer-based services, and overall cost considerations for approval plans, standing orders, and serials.

Questions Suitable for Company Data

- How many years has the vendor been in business?

- How long has the vendor offered [specify: approval plans, standing orders, or serials] to libraries?

- How many offices does the vendor have, where are they located, and which office would handle the library's account?

- What is the vendor's total staff size? Specify where they are located.

- Specify the general qualifications and training of the staff who would be working with this library's account, for example, individuals who select, buy, and profile titles for the approval plans, as well as individuals who handle standing orders and serials services.

- What is the approximate number of libraries the vendor serves in each category: academic and research (specify number that are ARL), public, special/corporate, government, school, and other types of libraries?

- What types of approval plans does the vendor offer (general or specialized), and how many of each are in operation at this time? Specify what percentage are for academic and research, public, special/corporate, government, school, and other types of libraries.

- What serials formats does the vendor handle other than traditional paper journals (e.g., CD-ROMs, microfilm, newspapers, electronic journals)?

- Can the vendor accommodate multiple ship-to/bill-to addresses for the library?

- Include a copy of the vendor's mission statement and vision statement.

- Include a statement regarding the financial condition of the vendor. This statement could be a financial investment prospectus, a statement of financial solvency from the vendor's major lender, or an internal auditor's report. A letter of credit from a financial institution would also be relevant.

- Supply a minimum of three references. These should be libraries comparable in size and type to our library. If possible, one of these should be a library that recently (within the last two years) transferred its account to the vendor. Also, at least one of these libraries should use the same online system as our library [specify the type of online system it uses]. Supply names, addresses, phone numbers, and e-mail addresses of individuals to be contacted in these libraries.

- What distinguishes the vendor from other vendors of its kind?

- Are there other aspects of company data the vendor would like to comment on that have not been thoroughly covered in this section?

Questions Suitable for Customer Service

- Approximately how many accounts does each customer service representative handle? Does this individual have assistants? What are they authorized to handle?

- How quickly will the customer service representative typically respond to a question or problem from the library?

- What form(s) of communication does the vendor provide to the library (e.g., a toll-free phone number, a fax number, an e-mail address, communication via the vendor's online system)?

- Will a sales representative be assigned to work with the library? If yes, where will this individual be located, and how often will the library be called on to discuss new programs, procedures, services, and problems?

- Will the vendor provide fiscal and management reports to the library at no additional cost? Is there a limit on the number of different reports or the number of times the library can receive a single report annually at no cost? List all reports and combinations of reports the vendor can provide, briefly explaining what each contains or covers. Provide samples. List any other reports for which there is a charge and state the amount of the charge.

- In the event that the library transferred its account to the vendor, what services would be provided to facilitate the smooth transfer of the account (e.g., customer service, on-site visits, technical/systems support)? Be specific and detailed.

- In the event that the library transferred its account away from the vendor, how would the vendor handle the cancellation of all titles for the library? Be specific and detailed.

- In the event that the library transferred its account to the vendor, what procedures does the vendor have for notifying publishers of the change of vendors?

- In the event that the library transferred its account away from the vendor, what procedures does the vendor have for notifying publishers of the change of vendors?

- Are there other aspects of customer service the vendor would like to comment on that have not been thoroughly covered in this section?

Questions Suitable for Computer-Based Services

- Does the vendor currently work with other library customers that use [specify the system, software version/release number the library uses]? How many other libraries?

- Does the vendor have e-mail access for systems contacts to library accounts? If yes, provide contact names, addresses, and e-mail addresses.

- Can the vendor coordinate a test-records environment once the RFP contract has been awarded?

- Can the vendor accommodate the library's testing and implementation schedule [specify the library's schedule]?

- Can the vendor assign a specific person for project management and testing of new interfaces or programs?

- What kind of Internet connection does the vendor have? Which Internet provider does it use?

- Does the vendor give libraries online access to its host system? If yes, for which applications, and how is access established?

- Is the vendor's host system view only, or can the library update and change its own records? If yes, what kinds of records and what kinds of updates are possible? Are there varying levels of access and passwords (e.g., for acquisitions staff ordering vs. collection development staff viewing)?

- Does the vendor have a WWW site? What is the URL?

- What does WWW access for libraries include from the vendor (e.g., databases, text files, and other access)?

- Is the vendor using WWW news services applications?

- Are the vendor's online system, databases, and WWW sites Z39.50 compliant? [Ask this only if the library's computing systems are Z39.50 compliant or will be shortly.]

- Does the vendor offer electronic tables of contents, document delivery, WWW news services, and databases? If yes, specify.

- Does the vendor currently support EDI? If yes, what standards, which versions, which transaction sets (via the Internet, or VAN, or structured proprietary formats)?

- What kinds of electronic outsourcing does the vendor do?

- Does the vendor handle e-journals and e-books? If yes, how are these accessed?

- Does the vendor send electronic cataloging records? If yes, what type and level [the library should add what kind of records are acceptable (e.g., MARC, brief bibliographic records, process records)]?

- If the vendor supplies brief or processing records, can the vendor, over time, supply upgraded or enhanced bibliographic records to the library?

- Does the vendor provide authority records? If yes, what types (e.g., subject, names, and series)?

- Does the vendor supply serials holdings records? If so, what format?

- What structure file formats does the vendor supply (e.g., FTP, tapes, or other formats)? [The library should state what it requires.]

- Does the vendor have barcode services? If yes, what types of interfaces?

- Does the vendor use SISAC barcode and SICI?

- Does the vendor handle e-site license agreements for library customers? For consortia?

- Does the vendor use deposit accounts or credit cards for WWW orders or other services?

- Can the vendor deliver e-products to various sites (e.g., the library, end users [patrons])?

- Does the vendor have partnerships with information providers to make e-products available?

- Does the vendor provide electronic access to sample serials issues or sample text files?

- Does the vendor process quotation lists electronically?

- Does the vendor process publisher dispatch data electronically? If yes, with which publishers?

- If the vendor does book or serial technical processing, what electronic services does this include?

- Does the vendor make self-generation of management reports possible via the Internet or WWW?

- Does the vendor allow downloading or access of records or files using SGML, HTML, or Java scripts?

- Describe the system security measures in place on the vendor's systems.

- Does the vendor provide any archival access to publications?

- How does the vendor handle copyright regarding the electronic access environment?

- Does the vendor charge any fees for any e-products or services? If yes, what fees for what services?

- Describe the vendor's interest in "partnering" with the library on future computer or systems innovations.

- Does the library need to supply additional information regarding any systems questions to the vendor?

- Are there other aspects of computer-based services the vendor would like to comment on that have not been thoroughly covered in this section?

Questions Suitable for Overall Cost Considerations

- What discounts are offered for approval plans, bibliographic forms, firm orders, standing orders, and select serials? Enumerate and describe in detail. [The library should indicate if it expects this and other pricing to be the vendor's best and final offer.]

- What would the vendor's flat service charge be for the library's serials account? [To assist the vendor in determining this, the library should state the approximate dollar value of its account in the cover letter and provide either a sample or a full list of titles.]

- What other service charge options does the vendor have besides a flat service charge for the library's serials account? Specify and give examples of how each service charge option would work.

- Are there any other special or blanket fees charged by the vendor for serials either on a per title basis or overall?

- Does the vendor ever add service charges to approval plan or standing order invoices? If yes, please explain.

- Enumerate and describe in detail the costs associated with any value-added services the vendor offers to approval plan customers (e.g., for cataloging, shelf-ready materials, authority control, the binding of soft-cover books).

- Can the vendor provide sample issues of periodicals at the library's request? If yes, is there a fee for this service? Specify.

- Enumerate and explain the charges and fees assessed for any and all computerized services for books and serials, including access to the vendor's online system; electronic or downloadable invoicing; fiscal and management reports; downloading of full MARC records, partial MARC records, table of contents information, dust jacket information; and check-in, holdings, and routing slips for periodicals at the vendor's site, mailed shelf-ready to the library. [The library should only include the services that it is interested in receiving from the vendor.]

- Enumerate and describe postal charges that the vendor passes on to the library.

- Is there a special handling charge for RUSH materials (e.g., approval plan titles, standing orders, serials)?

- How does the vendor handle changes in exchange rates? Be specific.

- In the case of a non-U.S. vendor, is there a conversion fee for paying in U.S. dollars?

- What are the vendor's prepayment discount options for serials? Explain in detail.

- Does the vendor provide escalating discounts for monies deposited on account against approval or standing order shipments?

- Does the vendor require minimum annual expenditures? If yes, enumerate and explain.

- Are there other aspects of overall cost considerations the vendor would like to comment on that have not been thoroughly covered in this section?

Questions Suitable for Approval Plan and Standing Order RFPs

The following questions pertain to general approval plans and include questions on profiling and title selection, coverage, bibliographic data, and financial practice.

Questions Suitable for Profiling and Title Selection

- What is the basis for subject classification for profiling approval plans?

- Can specific publishers be limited by subject or nonsubject treatments via the vendor's profiling method for approval plans? If yes, how?

- How closely does the vendor monitor publisher credentials?

- What are the vendor's sources for title selection for approval plans?

- If approval plan title selection is done solely by hand, is any prepublication notice sent out?

- How are coded approval plan titles matched to a library's profile?

- What sources are used for coding approval plan titles by subject? At what point are titles coded?

- Describe the vendor's primary approval plan profiling tools or documents.

- What techniques are used to monitor the approval plan profile?

- When approval plan profile changes are needed, how are the changes accomplished and how long does it take for shipments to reflect the adjustments in the profile?

- How are new subject terms added to the vendor's subject classification plan? How are libraries notified of the changes?

- If the library provides its standing order list to the vendor, can the vendor prevent the duplication of these items in the approval plan?

- Can the vendor provide special profiles (e.g., literary authors, literary genres, publishers)?

- How does the vendor handle the simultaneous publication of cloth and paperback editions of books treated on the approval plan? On standing order?

- What provisions does the vendor have to supply titles distributed by a publisher?

- Can specific imprints of one publisher be excluded from the approval plan?

- How are titles that are needed on a RUSH basis handled within the approval plan? For standing orders?

- How does the vendor avoid short shipments of new approval titles?

- How does the vendor determine how many copies of a treated book to purchase for its approval customers?

- What is the length of time from receipt of the book by the vendor until it is sent to the library for approval plans? For standing orders?

- What return rate is acceptable for approval plans? Is there a maximum acceptable percentage for new plans? For established plans? If yes, please specify.

- What is the maximum allowable turnaround time for items being returned?

- Are there other aspects of profiling and title selection the vendor would like to comment on that have not been thoroughly covered in this section?

Questions Suitable for Coverage Provided

- Does the vendor provide materials distributed by university presses?

- Does the vendor provide the publications of all university presses, including Oxford and Cambridge?

- Does the vendor treat the publications of all major trade publishers?

- How many trade publishers does the vendor treat?

- Does the vendor provide the publications of the following: Societies, associations, university research institutes/centers/departments, small presses, corporate bodies, personal authors?

- What type(s) of publishers does the vendor exclude?

- Does the vendor supply all formats (e.g., compact disks, videos)?

- Does the vendor supply both United States and Canadian publications?

- Does the vendor supply books in all languages if published in the United States or Canada? If no, please explain.

- How does the vendor avoid duplication of United States, Canadian, and United Kingdom simultaneous publications? How does it prevent the duplication of titles treated within the approval plan?

- How many titles did the vendor treat for approval plans (books and bibliographic forms) in [previous year]?

- How does the vendor treat numbered series or other series? How does it treat sets? Does it provide access to its standing order and series database(s)?

- Are there materials that the vendor will provide only on standing order?

- Does the vendor treat books that are nonreturnable?

- Do standing orders come as part of the approval plan, or would they be handled separately? Please consider ordering, delivery, and invoicing in the response. For example, when can the library place orders for and cancel standing orders, and will invoices for standing orders generally be included with volumes as shipped?

- Does the vendor treat reprints?

- Does the vendor have the capability to provide backruns of title lists for specific subject areas? If yes, what retrospective period is available?

- Does the vendor accept claims on approval items? For standing orders? Does it claim titles from publishers? What is the time frame for claims?

- How does the vendor treat orders for additional copies? Can they be treated as part of the approval plan? If yes, explain.

- Does the vendor provide automatic out-of-print search and notify services when books treated on approval are no longer available? How is this done?

- How does the vendor notify the library of publisher's status reports? Does it provide a readily understandable list of code definitions? With what frequency is this done? Can the publisher's status reports be transmitted to the library electronically?

- Describe the value-added services that the vendor can supply to approval customers. These might include cataloging, shelf-ready materials, authority control, and the binding of softcover books. Please be specific about relevant value-added services that might be outsourced to the vendor.

- Is the vendor willing to work with the library to provide locally specific information in the future? For example, would the vendor consider supplying cataloging that uses local call-number peculiarities?

- Are there other aspects of the coverage provided the vendor would like to comment on that have not been thoroughly covered in this section?

Questions Suitable for Bibliographic Data

- Does the vendor provide bibliographic forms (also referred to as bibliographic slips) at no additional charge for approval books and approval forms?

- Are the bibliographic forms provided multi-part forms?

- Does the bibliographic form follow MARC format?

- Send sample bibliographic forms, explaining the data elements if they are not readily understandable.

- How are bibliographic forms prepared? Book-in-hand? CIP? Other?

- What is the maximum turnaround time the vendor requires for filling 90 percent of bibliographic form selection orders?

- How long does a title remain in the vendor's database?

- Can books ordered on bibliographic forms be returned? If yes, describe the vendor's return policy.

- What is the time lag between date of publication and the library's receipt of a bibliographic form selection notification?

- Are there other aspects of bibliographic data the vendor would like to comment on that have not been thoroughly covered in this section?

Questions Suitable for Financial Practice

- Describe the vendor's invoicing practices in detail and send a sample invoice. Also, cover any online, tape-based, or disk-based invoicing procedures or capabilities that the vendor uses.

- Describe the vendor's practices for credits in detail and send a sample credit. Also, cover any online, tape-based, or disk-based procedures or capabilities for credits that the vendor uses.

- How are discounts shown on invoices?

- For returns, can titles to be returned be lined off an invoice, the total adjusted, and the adjusted total paid? Or does the vendor use some other procedure? If yes, specify.

- Describe the vendor's return policy?

- Which delivery services does the vendor use (e.g., U.S. mail, UPS, Federal Express)?

- Can the vendor provide expenditure estimates, based on the profiles, each year?

- Are there other aspects of financial practice the vendor would like to comment on that have not been thoroughly covered in this section?

Questions Suitable for Specialized Approval Plan RFPs

The following questions pertain to specialized approval plans, including Latin American (Brazil will be used as the Latin American country for the sample questions), fine arts, and science, technology, and engineering. They include questions on company data, profiling and title selection, coverage, bibliographic data, financial practice, customer service, computer-based services, and overall cost considerations as they pertain to a specialized plan. General questions on company data, customer service, computer-based services, and overall cost considerations can be found in the earlier section on "Questions Suitable for All Types of RFPs." General questions on profiling and title selection, coverage, bibliographic data, and financial practice can be found in the earlier section on "Questions Suitable for Approval Plan and Standing Order RFPs."

Questions Suitable for Latin American Approval Plan RFPs

(Brazil is used as the country example)

- Describe how the Brazilian approval plan would be developed.

- What are the vendor's sources for title selection of Brazilian materials?

- Is the vendor able to provide comprehensive coverage of new monographic imprints issued by all major Brazilian publishers?

- Is the vendor able to provide comprehensive coverage of new Brazilian monographic imprints issued by specialist dealers and publishers, such as small presses, historical and literary societies, public and private research institutes and foundations, and university departments and faculties?

- Is the vendor able to provide materials published on a regional or provincial level?

- Does the vendor supply Brazilian government publications and official documents, including censuses, annual reports of ministries and other large government bodies, national statistical data, and statistical yearbooks, as part of its approval plan service? Describe any specific limitations the vendor faces in providing material of this general nature.

- Will the vendor include regularly published periodicals, revistas, serials, and books in series, as specified by the library, in the approval plan service?

- Does the vendor also provide a separate service, if requested, for serials subscriptions and standing orders?

- Will the vendor obtain and supply, based on specific instructions from the library and to the extent possible, political pamphlets, party literature, and *hojas sueltas* under the approval plan?

- How frequently does the vendor ship Brazilian material?

- Does (or would) the vendor compile and distribute regularly to the library a list of new Brazilian titles, giving full bibliographic information and clearly indicating which have been selected for shipment? If yes, provide a sample copy and specify any fees involved with this service.

- What types of delivery service does the vendor use for Brazilian materials?

- If the vendor is not based in the United States, does it have a U.S.-based representative, and does it provide for any personal contact with its library customers? If yes, how frequently?

- Does the vendor have the capability to provide lists of Brazilian titles from previous years that are still in stock for specific subject areas? If yes, what retrospective period is available?

- Does the vendor stock or search for older and out-of-print Brazilian materials, and does it accept want lists?

Questions Suitable for Art Exhibition Catalogs and Music Score Approval Plan RFPs

- How long has the vendor offered [specify: art exhibition catalogs or music scores] through approval plans, and how many plans with [type of library] are currently operating?

- What is the range of geographic coverage of the [specify: art exhibition catalogs or music scores] included in the vendors approval plan?

- What is the specialized bibliographic knowledge and scholarly qualifications of staff selecting [specify: art exhibition catalogs or music scores]?

- What are the return options available through the vendor?

- What publishers are represented in the art book approval plan? Describe the process for excluding or including publishers.

- Are nonbook formats (e.g., CD-ROMs, videocassette, slides) included in the art book approval plan? If so, describe the formats available and how they are identified for inclusion in the plan.

- What museums, galleries, and dealers are represented in the art exhibition catalog approval plan?

- Describe the exclusion or inclusion options available concerning catalogs of museums, galleries, or publishers. Also address exclusion options when standing order or museum exchange programs are already functioning at the library.

- Describe the coverage that the vendor will provide for [specify: newly published art exhibition catalogs or music scores] in the United States. What coverage is available for Canada, Mexico, and Latin America?

- How are simultaneous art exhibition catalogs, including cloth and paperback editions and translations, handled?

- Identify the time lag between date of publication and final delivery of art books and art exhibition catalogs?

- Is a list available of composers covered by the vendor's music scores approval plan? If yes, provide the list to the library.

- Describe how composers are identified for inclusion in the vendor's music scores approval plan.

- How does the vendor differentiate between classical and contemporary composers for the music scores approval plan?

- Will the vendor provide the music score alone without the parts, scores and parts, or scores and parts up to an agreed upon level, such as quartets?

- How does the vendor handle series, performance scores, and varying editions, and what options are available for instrumental, vocal, and stage music in the plan?

- Are other types of music scores available, such as country and western, blues, rock and roll, and folk music? If yes, describe the extent of coverage.

- Describe the exclusion or inclusion options available concerning nonmusic score-specific materials such as method books, librettos, and sound recordings.

Questions Suitable for Science, Technology, and Engineering Approval Plan RFPs

- What are the science, technology, or engineering backgrounds of the people doing the profiling for the vendor?

- How does the vendor assign subject headings to science, technology, and engineering books? Provide a copy of the classification documentation used by the vendor.

- Provide a copy of the documentation for the vendor's nonsubject parameters that covers such factors as format, publication history, or price for science, technology, and engineering books.

- What assistance does the vendor provide in creating the initial science, technology, and engineering profile? If revisions are necessary, how quickly will they take effect?

- Does the vendor provide bibliographic forms as well as books for its science, technology, and engineering plans?

- Can the vendor provide specialized science, technology, and engineering subject bibliographies?

Questions Suitable for Serials RFPs

The following are questions on orders and cancellations, invoicing, claims, and title changes as they pertain to serials. General questions on company data, customer service, computer-based services, and overall cost considerations can be found in the earlier section on "Questions Suitable for All Types of RFPs."

Orders and Cancellations

- Within how many days does the vendor process new serials orders?

- Will the vendor provide confirmation that a new serials order has been placed? How will the library be notified (e.g., mail, phone, fax, e-mail)? Within how many days?

- How many days should the library generally allow before expecting receipt of the first issue of a new order?

- Within how many days after the vendor's receipt of a serials order should the library expect an invoice?

- If the vendor is unable to supply a title, within how many days will the library be notified? Will the reason be included?

- Will the vendor accept RUSH orders for serials? How does the vendor define "RUSH"?

- Will the vendor supply information about "comes with" titles and memberships, and will the vendor notify the library of options to buy titles in combination, when available?

- Will the vendor seek a common start date for all periodical titles (e.g., January) and a common expiration date (e.g., December)?

- Is the vendor willing to accept orders for back issues of periodicals for past years, for any previous year, for single-purchase issues, and other?

- When can a single serials title be canceled? Are there restrictions? If so, specify.

- In the event of a cancellation, will the vendor notify the library of exactly what the last piece to be received will be (e.g., volume, number, year, month)?

- Are there other aspects of orders and cancellations the vendor would like to comment on that have not been thoroughly covered in this section?

Invoicing

- What information will the vendor supply on serials invoices and credits? Describe the options in detail.

- How are service charges shown on serials invoices?

- In the case of a non-U.S. vendor, do both U.S. and foreign currency amounts appear on serials invoices and credits?

- Can the vendor provide serials invoices in multiple paper copies?

- Will supplementary serials invoices state the reason for additional charges?

- Is there a discount for expedited payment of a serials invoice (e.g., paid within 30 days)? If yes, indicate the time period and amount of the discount.

- Is a penalty imposed for late payment of a serials invoice? If yes, indicate the time period and amount of the penalty.

- Are there other aspects of invoicing the vendor would like to comment on that have not been thoroughly covered in this section?

Claims

- How are claims for serials processed by the vendor?

- Within how many days of receipt are serials claims processed, and what is the average turn-around time for processing claims?

- Are serials claims ever held and batched by the vendor?

- How is the library notified as to the status of its claims? Within how many days will the library be notified of the status of outstanding claims?

- Describe the vendor's serials claims reports. Provide a sample.

- Does the vendor provide the library with any type of statistics on its serials claims?

- For serials claims submitted to the vendor within the time period designated by the publisher, will the vendor agree to supply the missing issue(s) at no additional cost to the library, even if the publisher does not honor the claim?

- How will the vendor deal with a pattern of receipt of duplicate serials issues?

- Are there other aspects of claims the vendor would like to comment on that have not been thoroughly covered in this section?

Title Changes

- In the event of a title change, cessation, split, or merger, will the vendor notify the library of exactly what the last piece to be received will be (e.g., volume, number, year, month)?

- When a title changes, will the library be given a choice of not subscribing to the new title, or will the vendor automatically enter a subscription to the new title for the library?

- When a title ceases, what efforts will the vendor make to secure a refund for the library?

- Will the vendor notify the library of suspended publications? If yes, at what point is the serial considered "dead" and procedures for a refund initiated?

- Are there other aspects of title changes, cessations, splits, or mergers the vendor would like to comment on that have not been thoroughly covered in this section?

Appendix C

Sample Evaluation Materials

This appendix contains (1) sample questions to ask the references, given by and for each vendor during the vendor evaluation phase of the RFP process, (2) sample vendor evaluation forms for approval plans and serials, and (3) a sample vendor recommendation form for libraries that are undergoing more than one type of RFP.

The sample questions to be asked of each reference for each vendor are generic in nature, somewhat overlapping, and should be tailored (by altering, adding, or deleting them) to fit each library's particular needs. They are grouped into the following broad sections: Library background, customer service, computer-based service, and vendor strengths and weaknesses.

Included are two sample vendor evaluation forms: One suitable for approval plans and one suitable for serials. The categories and percentages awarded to each category will be based on the evaluation criteria specified in the RFP and should be tailored to each library's particular needs. This is especially true for foreign approval plans and standing orders, whether the library chooses to include them in the approval plan or the serials RFP. They are not intended to be prescriptive but merely serve as an example. To simplify the math portion of the RFP process, it is desirable for all categories to add up to a maximum of 100% or 100 points or some other easy-to-interpret multiple such as 10 points (100 points are used in the sample form).

The sample vendor recommendation form is used primarily when the library is using RFPs for more than one type of material (e.g., a domestic approval plan and serials subscriptions, or either of the above with one or more specialty approval plans, or two or more specialty plans). This type of form will simplify the process for the library and the Purchasing department because, although each evaluator will still complete a separate evaluation form for each vendor and for each type of RFP, a recommendation will be clearly made as to which vendor the evaluator believes should be awarded the contract for each type of RFP. The award will obviously go to the vendor that receives the highest point total for a given material type (e.g., for the domestic approval plan, Vendor X with 92 points should be awarded the contract; for domestic serials subscriptions, Vendor Y with 89 points should be awarded the contract). Chapter 9 contains additional information on evaluating vendor proposals.

151

Fig. A4. Evaluating Vendor Proposals: Sample Questions for References.

Library Background

- What kind(s) of approval, subscription, or standing order plans does your library have with the vendor?

- How long have these plans been in place?

- Has your library ever split a contract for approval, subscription, or standing order plans?

- How did you arrive at this decision?

- Has time shown that it was the right decision? Why? Why not?

- Does your library have an automated system? If so, is it an in-house system or a commercial Integrated Library System (ILS)? If it is an ILS, what type?

Customer Service

- How does this vendor respond to questions of immediate importance such as those about short shipments, duplication of materials or claims of missing periodical issues? For example, is the response (and follow-up, if needed) prompt, knowledgeable, courteous, and is the problem quickly resolved?

- Is customer service as good and as reliable as the vendor would have us believe? Explain.

- Does a sales or other type of representative visit your library regularly to share new developments, answer questions, and resolve problems? Is this individual effective? Is follow-up provided when needed?

- Is your library satisfied with the vendor? For example, the experience of library staff that have direct, regular contact with the vendor and the experience librarians have may be quite different. If your library has experienced this discrepancy in service, would you discuss your experiences?

- Have you experienced significant delays in the receipt of approval plan titles, in the fulfillment of book orders, or in the delivery of periodical issues or standing orders? For example, in what period of time are orders generally filled? Have monographic orders remained unfilled after 8, 12, or more weeks? Have periodicals not received been reported unclaimable, even if your library claimed them with the vendor within the time period specified by the publisher? Have these problems been resolved to your satisfaction?

- [For libraries that have recently transferred to the vendor] Did the vendor provide your library with satisfactory transfer assistance? For example, if you transferred your approval plan, how was the vendor's profiling assistance service to your library? If you transferred your serials, describe the vendor's transfer assistance program for your library. How much assistance did it provide? Was it useful? Describe in detail.

Computer-Based Service

- How does the vendor respond to requests for fiscal and management reports? For example, will this approval vendor supply lists of books treated on approval for a given period in a given subject? Will this serials vendor supply lists of periodicals sorted by publishers or library fund or some other method that is needed? Are they received in a timely fashion? Can the library create its own reports using the vendor's online system? If so, does this work well?

- Is the vendor's online system of value to your library and easy to use? Is it easy to access?

- Have you worked with this vendor on any special projects, especially in the area of increasing or improving electronic services? Please explain and describe any special problems or benefits that you have experienced.

- Can the vendor really provide all the computer-based services it says it can provide? [Give specific examples to the reference, such as interfacing with the library's system for tape or electronic invoices for books and serials; approval plan transmissions; full MARC records; fully cataloged and bound books.]

Vendor Strengths and Weaknesses

- What has been the most significant, distressing problem your library has had with this vendor? How was the problem discovered, handled, and finally resolved?

- What does this vendor do best?

- If you had it to do over again, would you select this vendor? Why? Why not?

Fig. A5. Vendor Proposal Evaluation Form: Approval Plans.

Name of vendor being evaluated:
Evaluator's name and department:
Date:

FACTOR: Company Data (10%)

Percentage Score (0-10%): _____

Why did you assign this percentage score? Other comments:

_____

FACTOR: Profiling and Title Selection (20%)

Percentage Score (0-20%): _____

Why did you assign this percentage score? Other comments:

_____

FACTOR: Coverage Provided (10%)

Percentage Score (0-10%): _____

Why did you assign this percentage score? Other comments:

_____

FACTOR: Bibliographic Data Provided (5%)

Percentage Score (0-5%): _____

Why did you assign this percentage score? Other comments:

_____

FACTOR: Financial Practice (10%)

Percentage Score (0-10%): _____

Why did you assign this percentage score? Other comments:

_____

FACTOR: Customer Service (20%)

Percentage Score (0-20%): _____

Why did you assign this percentage score? Other comments:

_____

FACTOR: Computer-Based Services (15%)

Percentage Score (0-15%): _____

Why did you assign this percentage score? Other comments:

_____

FACTOR: Overall Cost Considerations (10%)

Percentage Score (0-10%): _____

Why did you assign this percentage score? Other comments:

_____

Total Percentage Score for this Vendor _____

Fig. A6. Vendor Proposal Evaluation Form: Serials.

Name of vendor being evaluated:
Evaluator's name and department:
Date:

FACTOR: Company Data (10%)

Percentage Score (0-10%): _____

Why did you assign this percentage score? Other comments:

_____

FACTOR: Orders and Cancellations (10%)

Percentage Score (0-10%): _____

Why did you assign this percentage score? Other comments:

_____

FACTOR: Invoicing (15%)

Percentage Score (0-15%): _____

Why did you assign this percentage score? Other comments:

_____

FACTOR: Claims and Title Changes (20%)

Percentage Score (0-20%): _____

Why did you assign this percentage score? Other comments:

_____

FACTOR: Customer Service (20%)

Percentage Score (0-20%): _____

Why did you assign this percentage score? Other comments:

_____

FACTOR: Computer-Based Services (15%)

Percentage Score (0-15%): _____

Why did you assign this percentage score? Other comments:

_____

FACTOR: Overall Cost Considerations (10%)

Percentage Score (0-10%): _____

Why did you assign this percentage score? Other comments:

_____

Total Percentage Score for this vendor: _____

Fig. A.7. Vendor Recommendation Form.

Evaluator's name and department:
Date:

   I recommend the following vendor(s) be awarded the contract for the following plans. Please specify vendor name in the space provided.

Domestic Approval Plan(s)
       Entire Approval Plan:
       Trade Plan:
       University Press Plan:
       Science, Technology, and Engineering Plan:
       Art Exhibition Catalogs Approval Plan:
       Music Scores Approval Plan:
       Approval Plan for Mexico:
       Approval Plan for Brazil:

Standing Orders:
Domestic Serials:
European Serials:
United Kingdom Serials:
South American Serials:
Asian Serials:
African Serials:

   On the back of this form please specify why you would award the contract to the vendor you specified for each category. Use additional sheets if necessary.

THANK YOU FOR YOUR PARTICIPATION

Glossary

Please note: All glossary entries contain original definitions except where otherwise noted using brief citations; the full citations appear in the bibliography of this book. Definitions are not all-inclusive. Rather, terms and phrases are defined in the context of how they relate to or are used as part of the RFP process.

ACQNET The Acquisitions Librarians Electronic Network. Started in December 1990, it is a managed/edited listserv providing a medium for acquisitions librarians and others interested in acquisitions work to exchange information and ideas, and to find solutions to common problems. (Definition taken from ACQNET's online welcome message: acqnet-l@listserv.appstate.edu).

Administrative services Offices, often found in large libraries, that handle both accounting and personnel. Members of these operations have knowledge of institutional regulations and policies regarding accounts payable. They can contribute much to the RFP initiative.

Agent A person or company retained by many book and serial publishers to represent their business interests to libraries and other clients.

Alliances Groups of libraries or other entities that work together for a common goal or interest. Such groups can often negotiate contracts for their members for various library services at greatly reduced prices. Also known as *consortia*.

Annual value of the award The dollar amount the library projects that it will spend annually with the vendor for books or serials. This is an important part of the cover letter that will help the vendor provide an informed response to the RFP.

ANSI ASC X12 An acronym for American National Standards Institute, Accredited Standards Committee. The ASC develops standards in telecommunications and international trade. X12, the subcommittee of the ASC, is charged with developing electronic data interchange (EDI) standards. This standard structure for electronic communication specifies a hierarchical structure of transaction sets. Each transaction set is a different kind of document (e.g., purchase orders). The X12 standard is being incorporated into integrated library systems and homegrown systems computer programs.

Approval plan Approval plans provide books matched to a preapproved profile of subjects desired by the library or institution. Librarians and other personnel physically review copies of the books and make their selections. Books not selected are returned to the vendor. Libraries receive shipments of approval books at predetermined intervals, generally weekly. Many approval plans also provide selection forms for other books the librarians may want to consider for purchase. The forms for titles chosen are returned to the vendor for fulfillment.

157

ARL   *See* Association of Research Libraries.

Art exhibition catalogs   Highly specialized publications that are published in conjunction with an exhibition at a gallery or museum. They provide a record of the exhibit and often contain commentary, photographs of works in the exhibit, biographical information about the artist(s), a brief bibliography, and a catalog of the artist's(s') other work and exhibits.

ASCII   American Standard Code for Information Interchange. This text file comes from the ASCII code, which is a specification that defines how various characters are represented as computer data.

Association of Research Libraries (ARL)   ARL is an organization consisting of more than 100 of the largest research and academic libraries in the United States and Canada. It operates as a forum for the exchange of ideas and action, as well as providing information via its statistics and measurement program.

Authentication   A security technique in which computer systems authenticate the identity of the user so that unauthorized personnel cannot perform functions such as order materials or add unwanted material to a library database. Password/user ID or IP number/address access is commonly used on the World Wide Web as well.

Authority records   Records in a bibliographic database that verify the accuracy of a personal or corporate name, the uniform title of a work, subject headings, and other important cataloging information. These records ensure that an author's name, for example, is always listed the same way in the card or online catalog.

Automated fund accounting   An automated system that uses an order record to track fund accounting, which allows the library's system to make an intelligible record of the funds spent or to be spent for any item. The aggregate of this information is the fund accounting record. Many integrated library systems offer elaborate fund accounting subsystems in addition to the online catalog or inventory subsystems. The entire fund accounting process is greatly enhanced by automation.

Average return rate   The average number of titles returned to a vendor under an approval plan. The average rate of return for an established plan is well below 10 percent. The rate may be somewhat higher for a new plan until the profile is adjusted to the wants and needs of the library.

Award of the contract letter   A letter sent to the successful vendor(s), usually by the institution's Purchasing department, at the conclusion of the RFP process.

Back issue orders   Orders for any issue of a periodical other than the current issue. If the back issue order is for material more than six months old, the publisher will often require payment for the issue. Older issues of periodicals are often difficult to obtain. Some dealers specialize in supplying back issues to libraries.

Barcode   A machine-readable code that appears as a pattern of vertical lines or stripes printed on a book or serial to identify it. It is used in libraries to check in or transfer titles, add vendor numbers to order records, or facilitate patron checkout.

Bibliographic data   The information found in the cataloging record for a book, serial, or other piece of library material that pertains to the publication of the piece. Such data provide the basis for the card or online catalog record.

Bibliographic form   A form available from most approval vendors containing bibliographic and other data for books not intended to be supplied automatically as part of the plan's profile. These data can be supplied on printed paper or in an electronic format.

Bibliographic records in machine-readable form   Machine-readable records of bibliographic information. For U.S. libraries, these are usually called MARC records.

Bibliographic utilities   Entities such as OCLC, RLIN, and WLN that are the major providers of bibliographic and cataloging records to libraries for their online public access catalogs.

Bill-to/ship-to address   The library address that the vendor uses to send its invoices (bill-to) or its books or serials (ship-to). The addresses for each can be the same or different.

BISAC   *Book Industry Systems Advisory Committee*. Its membership consists of publishers and others in the book industry. BISAC was responsible for creating the BISAC fixed field for book electronic ordering and, more recently, has worked with the Serials Industry Systems Advisory Committee (SISAC) to develop X12 joint book and serial purchase orders.

Bit stream   A series of bits. *Bit* is an abbreviation for *binary digit*. In computer science terms, a bit is an element that can contain either one of two values, *0* or *1*.

Blanket order plans   A vendor plan that does not provide for the return of unwanted titles by the library. The library must keep every title selected for and sent to it. Blanket order plans are designed to encompass numerous broad subject or geographical areas.

Boilerplate   *See* Cover letter.

Book Industry Systems Advisory Committee   *See* BISAC.

Bookseller   A person or company that sells books. Booksellers are known by various names, including *jobber*, *vendor*, and *agent*. The bookseller has a long and distinguished history; booksellers range in size from the corner bookstore to a large corporation with offices around the world.

Cataloging-in-Publication Information   *See* CIP.

Cataloging records   The permanent record for any publication, regardless of format. It includes information about the author(s), the title, the publisher, the physical description, the edition, the subjects addressed in the publication, and any other facts perceived as important for a specific item.

CD-ROM   *Compact disk—read only memory*. One CD-ROM can hold the equivalent of 700 floppy disks.

Cessation   The demise of a publication. When a periodical is no longer published, it has ceased. A vendor of periodical materials should notify its customers when titles have ceased publication so that the library may adjust its records accordingly.

CIP   *Cataloging-in-Publication* information. Publishers provide specified information to the Library of Congress when supplying the details required for the registration of copyright. This information is used by the Library of Congress to develop a preliminary cataloging record for the title (regardless of format), which is returned to the publisher. This information gives the vendor, library, or reader information about the probable cataloging and classification information for the title and is usually the first cataloging record provided to and by a bibliographic utility. It is often printed on the verso of the title page of a book.

Claim   A report generated by the library and sent to the vendor when an item ordered is not received by the library. Some integrated library systems provide claims after a specified time has passed. How the claims are processed by the vendor, within how many days, and how the library will be notified of the status of claims are vital areas for the library to consider when choosing a vendor.

Claim reports   Documentation relating to claims. There are two kinds: Reports supplied by the integrated library system (recording the claims generated) and reports by the vendor (responding to specific claims).

Classification systems   Systems such as the Dewey Decimal system or the Library of Congress system that streamlined the arrangement of library materials. An item's classification is normally within a subject area denoted by a regularized combination of Roman letters and Arabic numerals. These classifications provide what are commonly known as call numbers. Such numbers are also used to provide information about the location of the material within the library.

Codes   The mechanism in integrated library systems that accommodates bibliographic, order, check-in, and item records functions. Although this information is generally masked in the public record, it is available to library staff who use the coded information in a variety of ways. For example, there can be codes for frequency of publication, for vendors, for languages of publication, for title changes, for funds, for locations, for reports on delayed publications, or for whether or not the prices invoiced are firm or subject to additional charges later. Codes are often the mechanism provided by the system to generate management reports.

Collection development officer   A librarian who directs the efforts of a group of colleagues in managing and building the many diverse collections for the library. Most often found in large research, academic, and public libraries.

Collection development policy statement   A policy statement describing the collecting philosophy of the library and defining the relative importance of specific subjects. The statement may include information on the existing level of the collection for a subject as well as plans for future changes. The level is defined by the depth and strength of the collection; for example, a research-level collection would support doctoral and advanced independent research in a given subject.

Comes-with titles   Titles that come at no additional charge as a result of purchasing other titles. For example, some publishers, particularly societies and associations, will supply a newsletter or other publication with a subscription to a journal.

Company data   Information related to the history of a company, the locations of its offices, the number of libraries similar to the library that the vendor seeks to serve, what distinguishes the vendor from other vendors of its kind, and financial solvency or stability. The RFP should ask for such information about each vendor that submits a proposal.

Competitive procurement process   An often state-mandated process that affords vendors an equal opportunity to submit a proposal or bid stating its ability to supply a good or service, for example, books and serials. In this process, the rules and requirements are the same for all vendors, with no vendor being given special advantage. Competitive procurement is most often accomplished via the RFP, RFQ, RFI, or bid process.

Comprehensive approval plan   An approval plan that provides materials in many formats from a variety of publishers in a large number of subjects. Such plans are very inclusive and are most appropriate for libraries with large budgets.

Computer-based services   Computerized services that the library requires or desires from the vendor. They may include various system interfaces and capabilities, as well as other electronic services such as electronic ordering, claiming, management reports, and vendor inventory.

Consolidated approval plan   A plan in which the library contracts for all book acquisition with one vendor. This has the advantage of requiring only one profile, one set of vendor procedures, and one systems configuration to consider. Generally, the discount offered is greater for larger accounts.

Consortia   Groups of libraries or other entities that work together for a common goal or interest. Many libraries are entering into consortial arrangements with other libraries to procure more advantageous pricing arrangements and other concessions.

Contract   A legal, written agreement between the library or institution and the vendor clearly stating the requirements and specifications of the agreement. Often the contract will consist of the library's RFP and the vendor's proposal, along with the award letter and conditions of the award.

Contract compliance   The specification that both the library and the vendor must act in accordance with the terms of the contract. Noncompliance is usually grounds for canceling the contract.

Conversion fee   The fee that some foreign vendors charge to libraries that pay in U.S. dollars to convert them into the currency of the vendor's country. Most vendors, however, have banks in the United States so that libraries can make payment in dollars without penalty.

Copublished materials   An item that is published jointly by more than one entity. Art exhibition catalogs are examples of materials that are often copublished. Many small museums and galleries copublish the catalogs of their exhibitions because they cannot bear the costs alone. Such copublishing can be a problem if the vendor does not have adequate ways of guarding against duplication.

Copyright holder   The individual publisher or developer who legally has the right to publish, reprint, or reproduce the copyrighted material. The holder may or may not be the vendor of the material. Most states allow for the purchase of materials from the copyright holder without bid, regardless of the cost of the item.

Copyright royalties   A sum paid to a copyright holder. Royalties must be paid to publishers for more than the minimal use of copyrighted material, regardless of format. Nonpayment can result in prosecution.

Cost projections   Forecasts, estimates, or best guesses made by vendors using information on current trends and gathered from publishers and other sources to determine the rate of inflation for various categories of materials. Libraries find cost projections supplied by vendors, particularly periodicals vendors, very useful because the projections help them allocate their budgets.

Country of origin   The country where an item is published. When determining if and how to divide its business, some libraries prefer to purchase materials from a vendor in the country of origin.

Cover letter   A letter (sometimes referred to as a *boilerplate*) consisting of standardized wording used by the library or purchasing office to provide the vendor with clear information regarding the type (subscriptions, standing orders/continuations, approval plans) and format (paper, electronic, CD-ROM) of materials that the RFP covers; the services the RFP seeks from the vendor; the estimated dollar value of the contract; the time frame in which the vendor has to respond; the format in which it should respond; a description of the library and its parent organization; the size and strength of the library collections; the state of library automation; contact names; and the criteria to be used to evaluate the vendor's proposal. Each RFP should have a cover letter.

Coverage   The publisher formats, subject areas, and amounts of titles covered by a vendor.

Credit   A surplus assigned to a library's account when a payment has been made and the item is not supplied, when the item was defective, or when a prepayment discount was given.

Critical thinking skills   Those skills necessary to interpret, understand, use, analyze, and evaluate information, answers, reports, articles, and books. They are highly desired for the RFP process.

Customer service   Assistance provided the library by the vendor. Such service includes a customer service representative(s) at the home office to answer detailed questions about orders, invoices, and computer-based services; a sales representative who visits the library; and any other service that will make for the efficient acquisition of materials.

Customized reports   Reports made to order or modified according to individual library requirements. They include reports about current expenditures, historical expenditures (e.g., the last three years), fulfillment time, and number of titles supplied in a given subject. Reports can often be generated on-site via access provided by the vendor.

Data integrity and privacy on the Net   *See* Authentication; Encryption.

Dealer   A vendor of library materials.

Debarment   The exclusion of a vendor from consideration for a contract for a valid reason.

Deposit accounts   A sum of money kept in an account with the vendor for the library. This practice may result in a larger discount or deposit credit to libraries.

Disclaimer   The exclusion of some part of an RFP, if certain conditions arise. For example, as used in an RFP, a disclaimer of an annual dollar value of the award would mean that, if the library does not have the funding available in a given year, it could spend less than was specified in the RFP without invalidating the contract.

Discounts /discount rates   Reductions in the list prices of materials. Most approval and many standing order vendors will offer libraries substantial discounts. Although these discounts depend on the discounts offered to the vendors by publishers, such discounts are often established at a set rate for the library's purchases if the range of materials to be bought is fairly broad.

Dispatch data   An electronic data interchange (EDI) message from the publisher. It verifies the date of shipment of materials from the publisher and serves as the manifest notice of the shipment of goods. Dispatch data are not specific to a library customer for order status, claims, or claims response. Libraries can, however, use dispatch data to determine if a title was recently shipped and thus prevent the library from claiming it prematurely.

Domain   An alphabetic representation of an Internet site's IP address number (e.g., www.ala.org).

Domestic approval plans   Approval plans for materials that are published in the United States. In some cases, Canadian materials may be covered by domestic approval plans.

Domestic serials   Serials that are published in the United States and, in some cases, in Canada.

Download   To transfer data from one system to another. For libraries, to download a record is to transfer that record from a bibliographic utility or other source to a local database or online catalog system. Often, integrated library systems offer the opportunity to download bibliographic information to which order information can then be attached so that an order can be placed with a vendor. Downloading a record or other information can also be accomplished from a vendor's online systems.

Duplication   The receipt of more copies of a title than the library ordered. Most academic libraries do not buy duplicates; however, public libraries frequently do. Approval plan vendors must be able to exclude a library's standing orders from titles supplied on the approval plan, as well as materials simultaneously published in the United States and England or The Netherlands.

EDI   *Electronic Data Interchange.* The computer-to-computer exchange of business messages in standard format transactions without the use of human intervention.

EDI translation software Commercially available software packages ranging from personal computer stand-alone versions to mainframe versions that allow coded EDI messages to be converted to and from a native system, on the library's, vendor's, or publisher's systems. These translation programs are used by some integrated library systems.

EDIFACT *See* UN-EDIFACT.

Electronic Data Interchange *See* EDI.

Electronic invoices Electronically generated invoices processed on the library's integrated library system. Vendor data used in the process can be received over the phone lines, from the Internet, on tape, or on diskette.

Electronic journals Journals that are published, distributed, and accessed electronically in addition to or instead of paper form.

Electronic ordering Requests for materials sent directly to the vendor's system via the Internet as e-mail, coded EDI messages, or FTP files. Electronic ordering eliminates the need for generating and sending paper purchase orders. Many integrated library systems provide electronic mail interchange for sending electronic orders.

E-mail Electronic mail messages distributed from one computer system to one or more persons using the Internet. Many vendors and libraries communicate via electronic mail; it is fast and convenient.

Encryption The process of encoding a bit stream before transmission to provide data security. Encryption files must be unencrypted before the receiver can read the message. Passwords/user IDs are required to access the information.

Ephemera Printed materials that are intended to have short-lived interest or usefulness. These materials may be collected to support a research library's comprehensive collection. Such items are not generally included in an RFP.

Evaluation criteria Standards for evaluating the vendor proposals to the RFP, reflecting the concerns and needs of the library. Each criterion should be assigned a weight and number of possible points so that the vendor will have a clear understanding of the factors by which its proposal will be judged.

Evaluation factors *See* Evaluation criteria.

Evaluation form A standardized form containing the various point-weighted criteria that each member of the RFP committee will use to evaluate each vendor proposal.

File Transfer Protocol *See* FTP.

Financial condition of the company The financial state of the vendor, indicating whether or not it is financially sound and stable. To ensure the vendor's financial solvency, the RFP should require the respondent to supply a statement of the financial health of the company.

Firewalls Single or multiple security devices that reside in computers or partitioned sections of a computer that deny access to unauthorized users. Firewalls are generally used to separate the public or external sections from the private or internal sections of a library's or company's computer. Users must have a password/user ID or IP address authentication to pass through the firewall(s) to reach the desired data.

Firm orders Books ordered on a title-by-title basis, whether from a publisher, book dealer, or vendor. They are normally not returnable nor are they supplied on approval plans.

Format The physical rendition of information (e.g., microfilm, book, videotape).

Format-based collections A library collection based on the physical rendition of information. Libraries will often award contracts on the basis of the format of needed items. For example, a library might write an RFP for North American and Canadian serials or for microfilm of newspapers.

Frequency change A change in the publication interval. A title, generally a serial title, is produced at certain intervals or frequencies (e.g., weekly, monthly, quarterly, annually); a frequency change means the title is now produced at an interval that is different from its previous interval.

FTP *File Transfer Protocol*. Allows the transfer of files from one computer to another. The user can either transfer files electronically from remote computers back to the user's computer or can transfer files from the user's computer to a remote computer. For example, the library can transfer files for its current shipment of approval books electronically from the vendor's remote computer back to the library's computer to create bibliographic and order records for those books in its integrated library system.

Fulfillment rate The time period that the vendor takes to fill orders and the number of orders filled. Many electronic systems will generate this information on a regular basis.

Fund codes Codes used in integrated library systems to represent accounts of money devoted to different purchasing areas (e.g., broad areas such as science or humanities or narrower areas such as psychology or dance). Fund codes define the specific budget line an item will be charged against in an integrated library system. They can also be supplied to a periodicals or approval plan vendor to add to the electronically downloaded or invoiced record. In addition, they are used to produce management reports by fund.

Gateway Used in different ways, such as a mail gateway or an IP gateway, but generally as a means to forward and route data between two or more networks of any size; a link between two different systems.

General terms and conditions Stipulations in a contract used to define those issues that affect the award, fulfillment, and possible longevity of the contract. These provisions may include, but are not limited to, information regarding acceptance and rejection of goods and services, addresses for notices, assignment of the contract, multiple awards, cancellation, changes and alterations after the award, conflict of interest clauses, discounts, requirement of financial statement, references required, governing law, indemnification and insurance, inspections, patent and copyright indemnity, penalties, proposed negotiation rules, termination and delays, warranties, and equal opportunity and affirmative action statements. These are usually found in the cover letter.

Gifts and exchange A department, section, or area in a library that is responsible for receiving (often unsolicited) gifts from a variety of sources and exchanging materials (usually periodicals) with other libraries both nationally and internationally.

Global change An operation in integrated library systems (generally requiring one or very few keystrokes) that affects a specified field in all records that contain that field, substituting one code for another.

Hot button issues Issues that are of immediate but perhaps fleeting interest.

HTML *Hypertext Markup Language*. HTML is the language that defines how to code a document for use in World Wide Web applications and is the programming source code behind the Web browser display of a document. HTML is a subset of SGML (Standard Generalized Markup Language). *See also* SGML.

Hypertext/Hyperlink Links between World Wide Web (hyperlinks) resources and the documents that contain the links (hypertext documents). World Wide Web documents have HTML commands embedded in them that connect the link with the text. Hyperlinks can be clicked on with a computer mouse and lead to other Web pages or to other sections of the same Web page.

Hypertext Markup Language *See* HTML.

ILS An acronym for Integrated Library System. An integrated library system is one in which components or modules work together to perform library functions, such as ordering, receiving, claiming, cataloging, online public catalog, circulation, reserves, interlibrary loan, and World Wide Web and database access, providing on-site as well as remote use to patrons and library staff. ILSs are also sometimes referred to as library management systems.

Information broker A person or company that sells information; a middleman.

Instructional programs Vendor-sponsored programs that provide instruction and information for new library customers to acquaint them with the vendor and its online system, and for new or existing customers regarding developments in the marketplace.

Information provider *See* Information broker.

Instructions to vendors Detailed directions to vendors centered on pragmatic matters relating to the RFP. These may include acknowledgment of addenda, alternative offers, cancellation, clarifications, copies of offer, failure to respond, late submissions, modifications, period of offer acceptance, public information, rejection of offers, telegraphic offers, taxes (materials vs. services), and withdrawal of offers. The instructions usually include a detailed statement of conflict of interest and debarment. These are usually found in the cover letter.

Integrated Library System *See* ILS.

Interdisciplinary materials Materials that address more than one branch or area of learning. These can be problematic when profiling subject headings for an approval plan.

Internal auditor's report A report prepared by an internal auditor of a business audit carried out by the vendor itself on a continuous basis, ensuring the accuracy and reliability of the vendor's accounting records. These reports can be supplied as part of the vendor's proposal to demonstrate the financial stability and solvency of the vendor.

International Standard Book Number   *See* ISBN.

International Standard Serial Number   *See* ISSN.

Internet   A global network of linked computer networks; the series of interconnected networks that include local area, regional, and national backbone networks. The Internet was created by the U.S. Department of Defense for military purposes. It now serves a broader global community, including educational institutions, government agencies, commercial organizations, and individuals.

Internet Protocol address   *See* IP address.

Invoice data element   A unit of information displayed on or pertaining to an invoice. These may include information displayed on the invoice such as library bill-to/ship-to addresses, title, library-generated purchase order number, ISBN/ISSN, fund code, and discount or service charge for books and serials. In addition, for serials, frequency of publication and notice of cessation or title change may also be displayed on the invoice. Elements pertaining to the invoice include format of the invoice or number of paper copies desired.

IP address   *Internet Protocol address.* A unique identifier composed of four sets of numbers separated by periods that indicate how to reach an Internet computer (e.g., IP number = 192.35.222.222). IP addresses are used to determine the path to a computer's physical location via interconnected wide area networks and local area networks.

ISBN   *International Standard Book Number.* Established in 1969, it is a unique 10-digit number assigned to a nonserial publication. It can be used for ordering, invoicing, and searching for a title in an electronic database.

ISSN   *International Standard Serial Number.* It is a unique number assigned to a serial publication. It can be used for ordering, invoicing, and searching for a title in an electronic database.

Java scripts   A scripting language for World Wide Web pages. Scripts written with java script can be embedded into HTML documents. Java script is intended to provide a quicker and simpler language for enhancing Web pages and servers. Java scripts can perform an action, such as play an audio file or execute a program displaying information, when a user opens or exits a page.

Jobber   Also referred to as a *wholesaler*, *middleman*, or *subcontractor* of a good or service, or one who deals with something for profit; may be used interchangeably with *vendor*.

Laser disk   A nonmagnetic disk possessing large storage capacity where data are recorded and read by a laser.

Levels of access   Password levels, determined by the system administrators, that can provide or deny access and show reduced or enhanced information to an individual user in an integrated library system or other electronic system. For example, although bibliographers may need to have access to order information, they probably do not need access to the program that actually places an order.

Library bill-to/ship-to address   *See* Bill-to/ship-to address.

Library contact   Name(s) provided to the vendor in the RFP of library personnel it can contact regarding questions or specific information it may require. The library contact is generally the chair of the RFP committee; a systems/technical staff member may also be a contact person.

Library generated purchase order number   A unique number (usually ending in a check digit—a randomly assigned number) generated by an integrated library system or other electronic ordering system.

Library management system   *See* ILS.

Licensing agreements   *See* Site licenses.

LISTSERV   A mailing list of e-mail addresses for individuals who have subscribed to it. LISTSERVs are generally devoted to a particular topic or subject area (e.g., ACQNET for Acquisitions, or SERIALST for serials), and are used to discuss information and problems. Any message sent to the list will be automatically, or through a moderator, sent to everyone in the group.

Long-range plan   A formulated, systematic plan for predicting future trends and directing future activities to achieve expected results for an organization for periods longer than one year.

Machine Readable Cataloging   *See* MARC.

Management reports   *See* Customized reports.

MARC   *Machine Readable Cataloging.* It provides a standard for file, record, and data structure for transfer of bibliographic information.

MARC Records *See* Bibliographic records in machine-readable form.

Medium   A term often used synonymously with *format*. As a fine arts term, it is the material or form used by an artist or composer, for example, painting, graphic art, sculpture, architecture, decorative arts, or photography. The library should clearly state in the RFP which media are included or requested.

Member   A person or institution belonging to an association, society, group, or organization. A library may become a member of an organization to receive the best prices available for its published materials; memberships may even be the only way to acquire these titles. The publications are generally billed at one membership price.

Method books   Progressive instructional materials used for the study and teaching of music and musical instruments.

Microform   The photographic images of a document reproduced on film or paper. Microfiche and microfilm are common types of microforms. Although some materials are produced only in these formats, they are also particularly popular and useful formats for materials no longer in print or materials that need to be preserved, such as periodicals or newspapers. They generally require far less storage space than paper documents.

Minority vendor   A business owned by a member of an ethnic minority. Some states have special regulations that must be followed to ensure minority businesses get equal treatment when competing for a contract for goods or services. The RFP committee needs to be aware of any such regulations that will apply in its state.

Mix   The percentage of titles that fall into a given subject category (e.g., science, humanities, social sciences, art). The vendor receives varying levels of discount or no discount at all from publishers, with some subject areas tending to generate higher discounts than others. The discount rate that the vendor receives from the publisher affects the discount the library receives from the vendor for books, or the service charge that the library pays to the vendor for serials.

Monograph   "A nonserial item (i.e., an item either complete in one part or complete, or intended to be completed, in a finite number of separate parts)." (Michael Gorman and Paul Winkler, editors. *Anglo-American Cataloging Rules, 2nd ed., 1988 revised.*)

Monographic series   "A group of separate items related to one another by the fact that each item bears, in addition to its own title proper, a collective title applying to the group as a whole. The individual items may or may not be numbered." (Michael Gorman and Paul Winkler, editors. *Anglo-American Cataloging Rules, 2nd ed., 1988 revised.*)

Monographs in publishers' series   Volumes published in a series that have only a very broad subject in common. Created as a marketing device by publishers.

Music score   "A series of staves on which all the different instrumental and/or vocal parts of a musical work are written, one under the other in vertical alignment, so that the parts may be read simultaneously." (Michael Gorman and Paul Winkler, editors. *Anglo-American Cataloging Rules, 2nd ed., 1988 revised.*)

News alerting services   *See* Push/pull WWW technologies.

NGO   *Nongovernmental organization.* NGOs include organizations that incorporate more than a single concern or country (e.g., the United Nations, UNESCO).

Nonprejudicial language   Language that is unbiased, impartial, and nondiscriminatory. The RFP committee must ensure that the cover letter, RFP document, reference questions, and evaluation forms are free from prejudicial language that unfairly favors one vendor over another.

Nonreturnable   Materials that cannot be sent back to the vendor or publisher from which they were obtained by the library for a refund, exchange, or credit. Some publishers, particularly small ones or professional organizations, will sell to a vendor only when there is an agreement that no titles can be returned.

Nonsubject parameters   Characteristics in a library's approval plan profile that do not relate to the subject of the books. They may include characteristics such as format, academic level, price, and publisher. Applied in combination with the subject parameters, they determine which books are to be sent to the library or which are to be excluded.

Numbered series   "A separately numbered sequence of volumes within a series or serial." (Michael Gorman and Paul Winkler, editors. *Anglo-American Cataloging Rules, 2nd ed., 1988 revised.*)

OCLC   *Online Computer Library Center, Inc.* OCLC is a bibliographic utility based in Dublin, Ohio. It provides bibliographic, database, and other library services to libraries throughout the world, often through regional intermediary vendors.

Online Computer Library Center, Inc.   *See* OCLC.

Online Public Access Catalog   *See* OPAC.

On-site visit   A situation in which a vendor representative gives a presentation to a library's staff at its location or site. This is generally done prior to submitting a response to the RFP, but it may be done by the finalists during the negotiation stage, or at any other time the library requests one.

OPAC   *Online Public Access Catalog.* A number of integrated library systems provide OPACs; many in-house systems provide them as well.

Out-of-print searching   A service in which a vendor attempts to locate and secure for the library a book or serial that is no longer in print.

Outsourcing   The contracting-out of certain library functions to a private enterprise. Using a vendor to obtain books via approval plans and serials is a form of outsourcing.

Passworded level of access   The extent to which a password can be used to gain access to various segments or levels (acquisitions, binding, circulation, fund accounting, serials control, the public catalog) of a library's integrated library system. Without an authorized password, access is denied, limiting access to the system.

Prepayment   A payment made for a specific book or serial prior to that title being supplied to the library. This practice is especially common for nonreturnable or expensive materials. Many publishers require prepayment for selected titles, while most vendors do not require prepayment.

Prepayment credit   A percentage of the total library-expenditure prepaid to periodicals vendors who offer libraries a prepayment discount for early payment of the annual renewal invoice.

Procurement code   A set of legal rules or statutes for acquiring goods or services.

Professional associations or societies   A group or body of individuals united by a common interest, principle, or purpose pertaining to a specific profession. These groups may publish important materials of special interest to their members. They often make their materials available to libraries only through institutional membership in their organization.

Profile   The document that tells a vendor what materials to supply or not to supply on an approval or blanket order plan. It contains instructions not only on what subjects are to be included and excluded, but also includes instructions on such nonsubject categories as format, cost, publisher, language, and country of origin. The library and the vendor must work together closely to create the profile, as it is the instrument that determines the success or failure of any plan. The profile must be monitored continuously and modified as needed for the plan to function optimally.

Property stamping   The act of stamping a book or serial (generally using a rubber stamp and ink pad) with the name of the library and other pertinent information to indicate the library's ownership of the material. This service can be provided as part of a vendor's shelf-ready materials service—as a value-added service—for an additional fee.

Publisher's status reports   Reports organized by vendors, based on information sent to them by publishers about the publication status of books and serials, and that provide libraries with details on the titles that they have ordered from the vendors.

Purchase order number   A unique number assigned by the library to identify an order. This number may be assigned automatically by the library's integrated library system or manually if the library's acquisition system is not electronic.

Purchasing department   The department in an institution charged with overseeing the purchase of materials. Such departments do not usually involve themselves in the purchase of specific books and serials for the library because of its highly specialized nature, but they will generally oversee the RFP process to ensure that all phases follow competitive procurement regulations and process the contract award documents.

Purchasing officer   The person assigned to the library to oversee and facilitate the RFP process.

Push/pull WWW technologies   Mechanisms that allow the user to either "receive" or "get" desired information. Push technology sends data from the World Wide Web to the user without further user intervention; the user requests this specified type of data once and updates are sent automatically as they become available. Pull technology is used by the user to access World Wide Web information directly. For example, a user signs up for a news alerting service and receives automatic messages on specific topics (push); a user goes to a company's World Wide Web site to find and read the press release section (pull).

Rapid update   A function, available on most integrated library systems, that allows the operator to quickly change a data element in fixed-length fields or an information string in variable-length fields, in one record after the other, making the same change to each record.

Recommendation document   A document provided by the RFP committee to the appropriate person in the library (e.g., dean, director, management group) and then to the purchasing officer when it has reached a purchasing decision. The recommendation document should open with a statement of all vendors submitting proposals and the criteria used for evaluating them. It should contain a clear and concise statement naming the vendors being recommended for the various contracts, the reasons for their recommendations, and the average evaluation score for each vendor along with the cost comparison. In addition, this document should discuss the considerations that led the committee members to their recommendations.

Recommendation form   A standardized form containing the types or categories of RFPs for which the library is soliciting vendor proposals (e.g., trade press approval plans, domestic periodicals). This form is used only when the library is producing more than one RFP. The form provides space for the evaluator to recommend a vendor for each RFP category (e.g., Vendor X for science and technology approval plans, and Vendor Y for European serials). This one-page recommendation form clearly states to the person tabulating the results which vendor is being recommended for each type of RFP by the evaluator. Used in addition to the evaluation form.

References   Libraries comparable in type and size to the library writing the RFP. A member of the RFP committee contacts or consults a person, cited as a reference by a vendor, for information about that vendor. All vendors submitting proposals to the library must provide the RFP committee with a list of references. If possible, one of these references should be a library that recently transferred its account to the vendor, and one of them should have the same Integrated Library System as the library writing the RFP.

Regional and local ephemera   *See* Ephemera.

Regional and local publications   Materials that are published by small local and regional publishers, which are often issued in very small print runs. Most large approval vendors are not able to supply such materials; libraries should arrange with local vendors to acquire these items.

Request for Information   *See* RFI.

Request for Proposal   *See* RFP.

Request for Quotation   *See* RFQ.

Research Libraries Group   *See* RLG.

Research Libraries Information Network   *See* RLIN.

RFI   *Request for Information.* The RFI asks for general information from the vendor regarding its available services. It does not state library requirements or desired elements. RFIs are often valuable tools for a library that is trying to determine what it requires prior to writing the RFP.

RFP   *Request for Proposal.* The RFP can be viewed as a process as well as a document. As a process, it provides a clear, impartial method for a library to state its needs, evaluate vendor proposals, and justify its vendor selection and contract award, based on objective decisions regarding those proposals rather than solely on emotional reactions either for or against a particular vendor. As a document, it serves to monitor vendor compliance and performance. In the document, the library's requirements and desired elements for vendor services are clearly articulated as are the steps to be followed for vendors that wish to submit proposals to handle the library's account(s).

RFQ   *Request for Quote or Quotation.* When using an RFQ, awards are based on the lowest price bid for a good or service. No other factors are taken into consideration in a true RFQ, although in some modified versions of the RFQ they may be considered to a lesser degree. This process is best suited to the purchase of goods rather than services.

Richard Abel   The bookseller usually credited with the development of approval plans.

RLG   Research Libraries Group. Established in 1974, it is an alliance of universities, libraries, societies, and other groups interested in the problems that research collections face in the acquisition, delivery, and preservation of information. RLG developed the RLIN (Research Libraries Information Network) database and other bibliographic files that include data describing books, periodicals, media, maps, posters, manuscripts, and other materials.

RLIN   *Research Libraries Information Network.* It is the cooperative database of the Research Libraries Group (RLG). This bibliographic utility is composed of large academic and research libraries.

Routing slips   Slips used to send/route specific publications to departments or groups of individuals upon arrival and processing in the library.

Rush orders   Orders placed with a vendor or publisher with the understanding that they will be supplied to the library on a priority basis.

Sales representative   An agent for the vendor, representing its products and services to libraries. The sales representative visits the library one or more times per year as needed to consult about the library's needs, check on the library's satisfaction with its service, discuss trends in the marketplace, and apprise the library of new developments or services available through the vendor.

Sample issue request   A request by the library to the publisher or vendor to supply a free issue of a periodical. These sample issues are generally used to make decisions regarding whether or not to add the title to the library's collection.

Sample list of serials titles   A representative list of serials titles that the library wishes to purchase from the vendor to whom the contract is awarded. Generally, the sample list should include approximately 10 percent of the library's serials titles, accurately reflecting the library's mix of titles. This list will help the vendor respond to the service charge portion of the RFP.

Scanner   A part of an optical character recognition device that systematically and rapidly reads and converts optical signals into electrical signals in a computer. It can then be read or modified.

Science/Technology approval plan   An approval plan that concentrates on providing materials for science, technology, and engineering. It can be very useful for some large research or academic libraries. Such a plan would probably include materials published by university presses, professional societies and associations, and trade publishers. It might also include foreign publications, especially those from Europe.

Scores and parts   The entire musical composition score and the portions for specific instruments parts. Music scores come in a variety of groupings. For example, a trio would include a score and three parts or a score and two parts enabling all performers in a trio to have the appropriate piece of music. *See also* Music scores.

Sealed bid sticker   An adhesive label placed on a vendor proposal by the vendor to seal it, ensuring that the information contained within is not tampered with until the bid is officially opened by the institution's purchasing officer designated to receive the bid.

Security strips   Magnetic strips placed in the spine of a book, between the pages of a serial, or affixed to nonprint media. These strips are then sensitized so that an alarm will sound if someone attempts to take the materials out of the building or area without checking them out and properly desensitizing them. The alarm system that reads the magnetic strip is located in detection panels that are positioned at exits.

Selectors or bibliographers   Generally found in academic or large public libraries, a librarian who is assigned to determine which materials to purchase for a particular subject area(s). This person is responsible for monitoring a budget allocation, approval plans, and periodical expenditures for the assigned area(s). A selector or bibliographer may also be responsible for working closely with academic departments or other constituents and for managing and evaluating the collections in his or her area(s).

Serial   "A publication in any medium issued in successive parts bearing numerical or chronological designations and intended to continue indefinitely. Serials include periodicals, newspapers, annuals (reports, yearbooks, etc.); the journals, memoirs, proceedings, transactions, etc. of societies; and numbered monographic series." (Michael Gorman and Paul Winkler, editors. *Anglo-American Cataloging Rules, 2nd ed., 1988 revised.*)

Serials check-in   A control system that records the receipt of serials (periodicals and other continuing publications). Serials check-in may be manual, using cards to record data, often housed in a Kardex file system; or automated, using a sophisticated database program in an in-house system or a serials control module in an integrated library system.

Serials holdings (statements or data) standard   The standard for serials holdings that sets the rules for creating consistent records of the serials located at a particular institution. It outlines the data elements, prescribed punctuation, and specification for displaying the data. According to the standard, serials holdings statements can be prepared at four levels of increasing specificity. The volumes or years of a serial a library owns are accessible to patrons and staff in the holdings data, which state volumes, issues, and years owned, as well as location.

Serials price increase   The amount or percentage that the price of a serial or category of serials has increased from one year or period to another. Because the cost of serials has grown at such a rapid rate, many libraries have experienced difficulty subscribing to all the titles needed by their patrons. Prices have increased faster than the Consumer Price Index for the last decade and a half with serials inflation generally topping 10 percent per year. Even with moderate serials cancellation projects, serials expenditures continue to erode materials budgets. Total annual serials expenditures vary with the type and size of the library, but generally range from a few hundred dollars for school and small public libraries to millions of dollars for medium to large academic and research libraries.

Serials vendor   A commercial agency that processes serials orders for all types of libraries. It provides a variety of services for the library, including placing orders with the publisher, processing renewals, consolidating many publisher invoices into one or several vendor-generated invoices, processing claims, and providing a variety of specialized customer and electronic services. Vendors maintain detailed records and management reports for titles that the library has on order with them.

SERIALST   The Serials in Libraries Discussion Forum. Started in October 1990, it is a moderated list that serves as an informal electronic forum for most aspects of serials processing in libraries. Topics include cataloging, acquisitions, collection management, serials budgets and pricing, binding, preservation, announcements, news, and job postings. (Definition taken from SERIALST's online welcome message: serialst@list.uvm.edu.)

Service charge   A charge above the cost of the titles managed by the vendor for the assistance or service provided to the library. The amount of the service charge will generally depend on the size and mix of the library's account. Service charges are usually associated with serials accounts due to limited or no publisher discounts, especially in the humanities and social sciences.

Service representative   The person at the vendor's office who is assigned to assist the library with all areas of its account, ranging from answering simple questions to solving complex problems.

Set   A group of materials expected to have a specific number of volumes usually determined in advance. The set may be published all at once or as a series of volumes over a period of years. Publication ceases when the set is complete or discontinued.

SGML   *Standard Generalized Markup Language.* An international set of rules for document tagging that indicate the nature of the content for electronic publications.

Shelf-ready materials   Journals and books that are supplied by a vendor, already processed and ready to be shelved by the library, for an added charge. They are cataloged, have spine labels with call numbers, are marked with the library's property stamp, and are ready for circulating. Various other services such as security striping and serials check-in from a remote site may be available; services offered vary by vendor.

Short shipments   The result of a vendor's not having enough stock on hand to supply all libraries at one time with an approval book. Those libraries not receiving the book in the first round of deliveries experience a short shipment. The vendor must then attempt to secure these books quickly to supply them to the remaining libraries.

SICI   *Serials Item Contribution Identifier.* Developed by SISAC, it includes the ISSN and other identifying information and can be used for interlibrary loan, serials check-in, and serials claiming as a unique identifier.

Simultaneous publications   Books that are published at the same time in two or more countries (e.g., the United States and the United Kingdom). Approval plan vendors providing both domestic and foreign publications need mechanisms to avoid supplying the book twice.

Single-purchase serial   A serial title purchased as a single issue or volume of a serial, often to fill in gaps in the library's collection.

SISAC   *Serials Industry Systems Advisory Committee.* SISAC consists of librarians, agents, vendors, publishers, information brokers, and others. It has used X12 to develop serials business standards and transactions sets for electronic data interchange; these are being incorporated into some integrated library systems. SISAC also developed the SICI and SISAC barcode symbols.

Site licenses   A written contract between the library and the entity authorizing access to certain digital information and electronic materials and setting forth specific terms, rules, and regulations for the use of the particular database or product.

Societies, associations, research institutes   *See* Professional associations or societies.

Split a contract   To award segments of a contract to two or more vendors.

Standard   A measure that serves as a nationally or internationally agreed upon basis or example to conform to, ensuring consistency. There are many such standards within the library field.

Standard Generalized Markup Language   *See* SGML.

Standing order   *See* STO.

Statement of financial solvency   A statement supplied on behalf of a vendor by a reputable financial institution or auditor attesting to its financial strength and indicating its capacity to meet its liabilities. This document provides important information to a library that is deciding which vendor to award its contract.

STM publishers   Companies that publish scientific, technical, and medical materials.

STO   *Standing order.* An instruction to a vendor to regularly supply a specified title. Standing orders are generally placed for nonperiodical serials such as annuals, yearbooks, and series. These titles are not generally paid for until they are received by the library. Some libraries, however, opt to prepay for them as part of their serials renewals, even though the price may only be a estimate.

Strategic planning   A formulated, detailed plan in which an organization identifies and develops its long-range goals and selects activities for achieving them.

SUB   An abbreviation for subscription. Subscriptions are a regular method of procurement for publications such as periodicals, journals, popular magazines, newspapers, abstracts, and indexes, generally issued more than once a year. These are generally paid for in advance of receipt by the library.

Subject parameters   The part of the approval plan profile that specifies which subjects should be sent to the library as books, which should be sent on bibliographic forms, and which should not be sent at all. They are used in combination with nonsubject parameters to form the library's total approval profile.

Subscription   *See* SUB.

Suspended publication   A publication that is temporarily not produced. Reasons for this vary but might involve financial exigency, natural disaster, war, or other similar difficulties.

Table of contents notes   The 505 field of the MARC record into which a cataloging agency can input table of contents information. Many approval vendors who provide cataloging as part of their service offer this valued-added service, for which there is often an additional fee. Libraries that acquire records with table of contents have the ability to index this field in their local online systems, thus enabling patrons to search for words appearing in the table of contents.

TCP/IP   *Transmission Control Protocol/Internet Protocol.* The set of protocols on the Internet that allows Telnet sessions, file transfer protocol, e-mail, and other services. These protocols are used to organize computers and communication devices into a network. Specifically, the IP transmits the data from one place to another, and the TCP manages the flow and ensures that the data are transmitted correctly.

Technical report literature   Documents issued by scientific laboratories, departments, or government agencies dealing with technical information. These are generally obtained from the issuing body or from the National Technical Information Service (NTIS). Many defense laboratories have electronic collections (some retroactive to the 1970s) obtainable free from their servers.

Telnet   The communications layer of the TCP/IP suite which allows users, programmers, and system administrators remote access to a server or computer, enabling a variety of communications to occur.

Timeline   A document displaying the projected activities involved in the RFP process, in order of their occurrence, with corresponding dates during which those activities will be accomplished. The RFP committee should prepare a timeline as one of its first actions. It should be a dynamic document, open to frequent modification, especially during initial meetings with the purchasing officer and the RFP committee.

Title-by-title selection   Book or serial titles that are selected one at a time instead of being received through approval plans, bibliographic forms, standing orders, or subscriptions. These titles may be ordered on the basis of selector/bibliographer decisions or patron requests.

Title change   The action of a publisher of a serial to change the title of that serial from one name to another. It is imperative that a vendor have mechanisms in place to notify libraries of these changes so that receipt can continue without interruption.

Trade publisher approval plan   An approval plan that supplies books, published by commercial publishers, generally intended for a nonspecialist audience. Trade publishers usually offer sizeable discounts to vendors who in turn offer discounts to libraries.

Transfer assistance allowance   A one-time allowance granted by the vendor to the library, usually in the form of a credit percentage or a reduced service charge, to defray the cost to the library of transferring its titles from one vendor to another.

Transfer process   The transfer of titles in a given category (e.g., domestic standing orders, European periodicals) from one or more vendors to one or more vendors, requiring careful planning. Also known as the transition process.

Translation software   *See* EDI Translation Software.

Transmission Control Protocol/Internet Protocol   *See* TCP/IP.

Types or categories of RFPs   Classes of materials that have common characteristics such as common subjects, formats of publications, publishers, or geographical considerations; specifically, university press approval plans, domestic subscriptions, European serials, art exhibition catalogs, and Latin American blanket orders. Separate RFPs can be written for each category.

UN-EDIFACT   *United Nations, Electronic Data Interchange for Administration, Commerce, and Transport.* It has developed into an international level of book and serial EDI messages for the entire business cycle. EDIFACT is being implemented in many integrated library systems in Europe and the United States.

University press approval plan   An approval plan featuring materials published only by university presses and generally intended for specialized, scholarly audiences.

University presses   Presses representing the publishing arm of the university to which they are attached. They range in size from large, publishing more than 200 books a year, to small and produce very small print runs. Supported and controlled by their universities, they are known for publishing scholarly research for specialized audiences, but they may publish some trade books intended for general readership, as well as scholarly journals. Their publishing programs often reflect local research specialties or regional interests. Although many presses, especially smaller ones, exist primarily on subsidies from their universities, others are making a profit.

UNM   *The University of New Mexico.* The main campus, founded in 1889, is located in Albuquerque, New Mexico.

URL   *Uniform Resource Locator.* It is the address that represents a Web server and its documents. It is usually preceded by *http://* for Web sites and often, but not always, includes *www*. For example, the URL for the American Library Association is *http://www.ala.org*.

Value Added Network   *See* VAN.

Value-added service   A service offered by a vendor that enhances a basic product, thus adding value to it (e.g., adding table of contents notes to a cataloging record).

VAN   *Value Added Network.* A a special network that provides a communications infrastructure through which messages travel to mailboxes for storage until they are picked up. VANs ensure the security of the communication and track the transmissions and receipt of the messages, as well as ensure that the messages meet standards such as X12, thus adding value to the network.

Vendor   The seller or provider of materials to libraries, regardless of format.

Vendor evaluation project   A plan designed to appraise or judge vendor performance—how well the vendor met the conditions of its contract with the library. Such factors as vendor turnaround time for orders, invoices, and claims as well as other performance data elements can be quantitatively measured. More subjective, qualitative measures regarding the vendor's service may also be considered in the evaluation.

Vendor performance data   Data used in vendor evaluation projects, including such elements as fulfillment rates or fulfillment times, rate of returns for approval plans, number of claims, and claims response time. Many integrated and other library systems can provide some of these data for the library.

Vendor's host system   A computer system used internally by the vendor. Customers may or may not have access directly into the system via Telnet or the World Wide Web. Generally, they are proprietary systems with interfaces to provide customer access via Z39.50 or a native mode.

Web browser technologies   Computer programs that allow users to access Web sites and Web pages by converting HTML into readable text, images, and sounds. Browsers can be graphical or text-based (e.g., Netscape Navigator, Internet Explorer, Mosaic, and Lynx).

Web page   Data (text, graphics, and audio) that are stored on a Web server as a file written in HTML and identified by a URL. The Web page may refer to other Web pages via hypertext links. A vendor's Web page outlines its services and other information about the company's background.

Web server   A service that makes a set of Web pages available to users.

Web site   A computer that is attached to the Internet, and runs a Web server.

Western Library Network   *See* WLN.

WLN   *Western Library Network.* Established in 1976 and formerly called the Washington Library Network, WLN is a nonprofit corporation providing a fully integrated online bibliographic database, database preparation and authority control services, and collection assessment services, primarily to libraries, government agencies, and other information provision services.

World Wide Web   *See* WWW.

WorldCat   An OCLC product, available for remote electronic searching, that is made up of international holdings cataloged by OCLC member libraries. It is a searchable bibliographic database of books, serials, recordings, manuscripts, and other materials.

WWW (W3 or The Web)   An acronym for the World Wide Web. Created in 1989, it is a global hypertext system that uses the Internet to access and retrieve information. The WWW is navigated by use of a Web browser to access HTML coded documents on Web servers around the world.

X12   *See* ANSI ASC X12.

Z39.50 1988 protocol   The name of the national standard developed by the National Information Standards Organization (NISO) entitled "Information Retrieval Service Definition and Protocol Specification for Library Applications." A search and retrieval protocol by which one computer can query another computer and transfer resulting records. This protocol provides the framework for online public access catalog users to search remote catalogs on the Internet using the commands of their own local systems, bringing a seamless interface between and among systems that would otherwise be incompatible.

Bibliography

ACQNET. acqnet-l@listserv.appstate.edu.

AcqWeb. URL: http://www.library.venderbilt.edu/law/acqs/acqs.html.

Alessi, Dana. "Vendor Selection, Vendor Collection, or Vendor Defection." *Journal of Library Administration* 16, no. 3 (1992): 117–30.

Alessi, Dana L., and Goforth, Kathleen. "Standing Orders and Approval Plans: Are They Compatible?" *Serials Librarian* 13, no. 2/3 (1987): 21–40.

Alley, Brian. "Reengineering, Outsourcing, Downsizing, and Perfect Timing." *Technicalities* 13, no. 11 (1993): 1, 8.

Anderson, Jan. "Order Consolidation: One Step in Containing Serials Prices." In *Vendors and Library Acquisitions*, edited by Bill Katz, 97–103. Binghamton, NY: Haworth Press, 1991.

Barber, David. "Electronic Commerce in Library Acquisitions with a Survey of Bookseller and Subscription Agency Services." *Library Technology Reports* 31, no. 5 (1995): 493–603.

Barker, Joseph W. "Vendor Studies Redux: Evaluating the Approval Plan Option From Within." *Library Acquisitions: Practice & Theory* 13, no. 2 (1989): 133–41.

Basch, N. Bernard, and McQueen, Judy. *Buying Serials: A How-to-Do-It Manual for Librarians.* New York: Neal-Schuman, 1990.

———. "Stretching the Acquisitions Budget by Negotiating Subscription Agency Service Charges." In *Legal and Ethical Issues in Acquisitions,* edited by Katina Strauch and Bruce Strauch, 129–133. Binghamton, NY: Haworth Press, 1990.

Bazirjian, Rosann. "ALCTS/Automated Acquisitions/In-Process Control Systems Discussion Group, American Library Association Conference, New Orleans, June 1993." *Technical Services Quarterly* 11, no. 4 (1994): 66–68.

———. "Integrating Vendor Products/Services into the Automated Acquisitions Environment: An Introduction." *Library Acquisitions: Practice & Theory* 18, no. 4 (1994): 417–18.

Biblarz, Dora. "Approval Plan." In *Encyclopedia of Library and Information Science* 56, suppl. 19, edited by Allen Kent, 21–28. New York: Marcel Dekker, 1995.

Bonk, Sharon C. "Towards a Methodology of Evaluating Serials Vendors." *Library Acquisitions: Practice & Theory* 9, no. 1 (1985): 51–60.

Born, Kathleen. "Strategies for Selecting Vendors and Evaluating Their Performance—From the Vendor's Perspective." *Journal of Library Administration* 16, no. 3 (1992): 111–16.

Boss, Richard. "Security Concerns Grow." *Library Systems Newsletter* 16, no. 6 (1996): 45–47.

Bostic, Mary J. "Approval Acquisitions and Vendor Relations: An Overview." In *Vendors and Library Acquisitions*, edited by Bill Katz, 129–44. Binghamton, NY: Haworth Press, 1991.

———. "Approval Acquisitions and Vendor Relations: An Overview." *The Acquisitions Librarian* 5, no. 3 (1991): 129–44.

Boyer, Calvin J. "State-Wide Contracts for Library Materials: An Analysis of the Attendant Dysfunctional Consequences." *College and Research Libraries* 35, no. 2 (1974): 86–94.

Brown, Lynne C. Branche. "An Expert System for Predicting Approval Plan Receipts." *Library Acquisitions: Practice & Theory* 17, no. 2 (1993): 155–64.

Brownson, Charles W. "A Method for Evaluating Vendor Performance." In *Vendors and Library Acquisitions*, edited by Bill Katz, 37–51. Binghamton, NY: Haworth Press, 1991.

Bryant, E. T. *Music Leadership: A Practical Guide*. London: James Clarke & Company, 1959.

Burton, Anthony. "Exhibition Catalogues," In *Art Library Manual: A Guide to Resources and Practice*, edited by Philip Pacey, 71–86. London and New York: Bowker, 1977.

Bush, Carmel C.; Sasse, Margo; and Smith, Patricia. "Toward a New World Order: A Survey of Outsourcing Capabilities of Vendors for Acquisitions, Cataloging, and Collection Development Services." *Library Acquisitions: Practice & Theory* 18, no. 4 (1994): 397–416.

Byrne, Nadene. "Selection and Acquisition in an Art School Library." *Library Acquisitions: Practice & Theory* 7, no. 1 (1983): 7–11

Calhoun, John C.; Bracken, James K.; and Firestein, Kenneth L. "Modeling an Academic Approval Program." *Library Resources and Technical Services* 34, no. 3 (1990): 367–79.

Cargill, Jennifer. "A Report on the Fourth International Conference on Approval Plans." *Library Acquisitions: Practice & Theory* 4, no. 2 (1980): 109–11.

Carpenter, Eric J. "Collection Development Policies Based on Approval Plans." *Library Acquisitions: Practice & Theory* 13, no. 1 (1989): 39–43.

Carpenter, Kathryn Hammell, and Alexander, Adrian. "U.S. Periodical Price Index for 1996." *American Libraries* 27, no. 5 (1996): 97–107.

Case, Beau David. "Approval Plan Evaluation Studies: A Selected Annotated Bibliography, 1969-1996." *Against the Grain* 8, no. 4 (1996): 18–21, 24.

Chalaron, Peggy, and Perrault, Anna. "Approval Plans: The Multi-Vendor Approach." In *Vendors and Library Acquisitions*, edited by Bill Katz, 145–59. Binghamton, NY: Haworth Press, 1991.

Chamberlain, Carol E. "Evaluating Library Acquisitions Service." In *Encyclopedia of Library and Information Science* 56, suppl. 19, edited by Allen Kent, 118–26. New York: Marcel Dekker, 1995.

Clark, Stephen D., and Winters, Barbara A. "Bidness as Usual: The Responsible Procurement of Library Materials." *Library Acquisitions: Practice & Theory* 14, no. 3 (1990): 265–74.

Coffey, James R. "Contracts and Ethics in Library Acquisitions: The Expressed and Implied." In *Legal and Ethical Issues in Acquisitions*, edited by Katina Strauch and Bruce Strauch, 95–110. Binghamton, NY: Haworth Press, 1990.

Compton, Bruce. "The ILS Vendor and EDI: A Perspective Library." *Library Administration & Management* 10, no. 3 (1996): 164–68.

Conference Call. "The Outsourcing Dilemma: Polar Opposites Bart Kane and Patricia Wallace Debate the Merits of the Hawaii Model." *American Libraries* 28, no. 5 (1997): 54–55.

Cramer, Michael D. "The Acquisitions Connection: Interfacing Library and Materials Vendors Systems: Report of the Program Sponsored by the LAMA SASS Acquisitions Systems Committee and the ALCTS RS Acquisitions Committee." *Library Acquisitions: Practice & Theory* 16, no. 3 (1992): 299–300.

Crotty, Anita. "Why Bother with Evaluation?" *Library Acquisitions: Practice & Theory* 18, no. 1 (1994): 51–56.

D'Andraia, Dana D. "Choosing a Vendor." In *Technical Services in Libraries: Systems and Applications*. Foundations in Library & Information Science, vol. 25, edited by Thomas W. Leonhardt, 257–72. Greenwich, CT: JAI Press, 1992.

Davi, Susan A. "Automatic Acquisition Plans for the Art Library." In *Current Issues in Fine Arts Collection Development*. Occasional Papers no. 3, edited by Janet Clarke-Hazlett, 29–34. Tucson, AZ: Art Libraries Society of North America, 1984.

Derthick, Jan, and Moran, Barbara B. "Serials Agent Selection in ARL Libraries." In *Advances in Serials Management* 1, 1–42. Greenwich, CT: JAI Press, 1986.

Dowd, Frank B. "Awarding Acquisitions Contracts by Bid or the Perils and Rewards of Shopping by Mail." *The Acquisitions Librarian* 5 (1991): 63–73.

Duranceau, Ellen (with contributions by Karen Wilhoit et al.). "Vendors and Librarians Speak on Outsourcing, Cataloging, and Acquisitions." *Serials Review* 20, no. 3 (1994): 69–83.

Eldredge, Mary. "The Exhibition Catalog: History, Curatorship, Publishing, Distribution, and Cataloging." *Art Documentation* 7, no. 2 (1988): 50–51.

———. "United Kingdom Approval Plans and United States Academic Libraries: Are They Necessary and Cost Effective?" *Library Acquisitions: Practice & Theory* 18, no. 2 (1994): 165–78.

Farries, Bob. "Developing a Request for Proposal for an Automated Library System." *Colorado Libraries* 19 (Spring 1993): 42–43.

Fisher, William. "A Brief History of Library–Vendor Relations Since 1950." *Library Acquisitions: Practice & Theory* 17, no. 1 (1993): 61–69.

Flood, Susan, comp. "Evolution & Status of Approval Plans." In *SPEC (Systems and Procedures Exchange Center) 221*, edited by Laura A. Rounds, 1–78. Washington, DC: Association of Research Libraries, Office of Management Services, 1997.

Franklin, Hugh L. "Sci/Tech Book Approval Plans Can Be Effective." *Collection Management* 19, no. 1/2 (1994): 135–45.

Freeman, Suzanne, and Winters, Barbara A. "Journeymen of the Printing Office." In *Legal and Ethical Issues in Acquisitions*, edited by Katina Strauch and Bruce Strauch, 83–93. Binghamton, NY: Haworth Press, 1990.

Gammon, Julia A. "EDI and Acquisitions: The Future Is Now!" *Library Acquisitions: Practice & Theory* 18, no. 1 (1994): 113–14.

Gibbs, Donald L. "The Acquisition of Current and Retrospective Latin American Materials." In *Acquisition of Foreign Materials for U.S. Libraries*, 2d ed., compiled and edited by Theodore Samore, 142–50. Metuchen, NJ: Scarecrow Press, 1982.

Glogoff, Stuart. "Reflections on Dealing with Vendors." *American Libraries* 25 no. 4 (1994): 313, 315.

Gold, Brian. "Acquisition Approaches to Exhibition Catalogues." *Library Acquisitions: Practice & Theory* 7, no. 1 (1983): 13–16.

Gorman, Michael, and Winkler, Paul eds. *Anglo-American Cataloging Rules, 2nd ed., 1988 revised.* Chicago: American Library Association, 1988.

Grahame, Vicki. "Approval Plan Processing: Integrating Acquisitions and Cataloging." *Technical Service Quarterly* 10, no. 1 (1992): 31–41.

———. *Guide to Performance Evaluation of Library Materials Vendors.* Chicago: American Library Association, 1988.

Gutierrez-Witt, Laura, and Gibbs, Donald L. "Acquiring Latin American Books." *Library Acquisitions: Practice & Theory* 6, no. 2 (1982): 167–75.

Harr, John M. "Paperbacks on Approval." *Against the Grain* 7, no. 3 (1995): 16.

Harri, Wilbert. "Implementing Electronic Data Interchange in the Library Acquisitions Environment." *Library Acquisitions: Practice & Theory* 18, no. 1 (1994): 115–17.

Hawks, Carol Pitts. "EDI, the Audit Trail and Automated Acquisitions: Report of a Presentation." *Library Acquisitions: Practice & Theory* 18, no. 3 (1994): 351–53.

Hazen, Dan. "Approval Plans for Latin American Acquisitions: Some Aspects of Theory, Strategy, and Cost." In *SALALM and the Area Studies Community: Papers of the Thirty Seventh Annual Meeting of the Seminar on the Acquisition of Latin American Library Materials*, edited by David Block, 169–75. Albuquerque, NM: SALALM Secretariat, University of New Mexico, 1994.

Hirshon, Arnold. "Beyond Our Walls: Academic Libraries, Technical Services, and the Information World." *Journal of Library Administration* 15, no. 1/2 (1991): 43–59.

Hirshon, Arnold, and Winters, Barbara A. *Outsourcing Library Technical Services: A How-to-Do-It Manual for Librarians.* New York: Neal-Schuman, 1996.

Hirshon, Arnold; Winters, Barbara A.; and Wilhoit, Karen. "A Response to 'Outsourcing Cataloging: The Wright State Experience.' " *ALCTS Newsletter* 6, no. 2 (1995): 26–28.

Hodge, Stanley P., and Hepfer, William. "Scientific and Technical Materials: A General Overview." In *Selection of Library Materials in the Humanities, Social Sciences, and Sciences*, edited by Patricia A. McClung, 229–49. Chicago: American Library Association, 1985.

Intner, Sheila S. "Outsourcing—What Does It Mean for Technical Services?" *Technicalities* 14, no. 3 (1994): 3–5.

Jasper, Richard P. "Academic Libraries and Firm Order Vendors: What They Want of Each Other." *Acquisitions Librarian* 3, no. 5 (1991): 83–95.

———. "Automating Acquisitions and Serials: Synthesis from Chaos." *Library Acquisitions: Practice & Theory* 17, no. 1 (1993): 79–84.

Jensen, Michael. (Johns Hopkins University Press). "Money Talks: Issues in Book and Serials Acquisitions Panel Discussion: Payment and Subscription Models for Online Publications." *College of Charleston Conference, Charleston, S.C.* (November 7, 1996): 3:30–5:00 p.m.

Johnson, Peggy, and Intner, Sheila S. *Guide to Technical Services Resources.* Chicago: American Library Association, 1994.

Jones, Lois Swan, and Gibson, Sarah Scott. *Art Libraries and Information Services: Development, Organization, and Management*. New York: Academic Press, 1986.

Kaatrude, Peter B. "Approval Plan Versus Conventional Selection: Determining the Overlap." *Collection Management* 11, no. 1/2 (1989): 145–50.

Keaveney, Sydney Starr. *Contemporary Art Documentation and Fine Arts Libraries*. Metuchen, NJ: Scarecrow Press, 1986.

Keeth, John Earl. "Approval Plan Rejects— To Keep or Not to Keep—Is That the Question?" *Library Acquisitions: Practice & Theory* 16, no. 2 (1992): 167–69.

Kusnerz, Peggy Ann. "Collection Evaluation Techniques in the Academic Art Library." *Drexel Library Quarterly* 19, no. 3 (1983): 38–51.

Lee, Lauren K. "Library/Vendor Cooperation in Collection Development." In *Vendors and Library Acquisitions*, edited by Bill Katz, 181–90. Binghamton, NY: Haworth Press, 1991.

Lynch, Clifford A. "Interoperability: The Standards Challenge for the 1990s." *Wilson Library Bulletin* 67, no. 7 (1993): 38–42.

———. "Serials Management in the Age of Electronic Access." *Serials Review* 17, no. 1 (1991): 7–12.

———. "The Transformation of Scholarly Communication and the Role of the Library in the Age of Networked Information." *The Serials Librarian* 23, no. 3/4 (1993): 5–20.

———. "Visions of Electronic Libraries." In *Bowker Annual Library and Book Trade Almanac*, 36th ed., edited by Filomena Simora, 75–82. New Providence, NJ: R. R. Bowker, 1991.

Magnuson, Barbara. "Science and Technology Book Reviews as Supplements to an Approval Program." *Science and Technology Libraries* 8 (Winter 1987/88): 75–94.

Magrill, Rose Mary, and Corbin, John. *Acquisitions Management and Collection Development in Libraries*, 2d ed. Chicago; London: American Library Association, 1989.

Matthews, Joseph R.; Salmon, Stephen R.; and Williams, Joan Frye. "The RFP—Request for Punishment: Or a Tool for Selecting an Automated Library System." *Library Hi Tech* 5, no. 1 (1987): 15–21.

McGee, Rob. "RFIs, RFPs, RFQs, Bid Analysis and Contracts. Part 1 & 2." In *Second National Conference on Integrated Online Library Systems Proceedings*, edited by David C. Genaway, 253–69. Canfield, OH: Genaway and Associates, 1984.

McKinley, Margaret. "Vendor Selection: Strategic Choices." *Serials Review* 16, no. 2 (1990): 49–53, 64.

Melcher, Daniel (with Margaret Saul). *Melcher on Acquisition*. Chicago: American Library Association, 1971.

Miller, Heather. "Ethics in Action: The Vendor's Perspective." *The Serials Librarian* 25, no. 3/4 (1995): 295–300.

Miller, Heather S. *Managing Acquisitions and Vendor Relations: A How to Do It Manual*. New York and London: Neal-Schuman, 1992.

Miller, Rachel. "The Impact of Automated Acquisitions on Collection Development: Report of the Program Sponsored by RASD Collection Development and Evaluation Section (CODES)." *Library Acquisitions: Practice & Theory* 16, no. 3 (1992): 300–301.

Miller, William. "Outsourcing: Academic Libraries Pioneer Contracting Out Services." *Library Issues* 16, no. 2 (1995): 1–4.

Montgomery, Jack G. "Outsourced Acquisitions?—Let's Meet the Challenge." *Against the Grain* 7, no. 2 (1995): 66–68.

Morris, Dilys E. "Electronic Information and Technology: Impact and Potential for Academic Libraries." *College & Research Libraries* 50, no. 1 (1989): 56–64.

Nardini, Robert F. "The Approval Plan Profiling Session." *Library Acquisitions: Practice & Theory* 18, no. 3 (1994): 289–95.

———. "Approval Plans: Politics and Performance." *College and Research Libraries* 54 (1993): 418–19.

New, Doris E. "Serials Agency Conversion in an Academic Library." *Serials Librarian* 2, no. 3 (1978): 277–85.

Nissley, Meta. "Rave New World: Librarians and Electronic Acquisitions." *Library Acquisitions: Practice & Theory* 17, no. 2 (1993): 165–73.

———. "Taking License: Librarians, Publishers, and the New Media." In *Legal and Ethical Issues in Acquisitions*, edited by Katina Strauch and Bruce Strauch, 71–82. Binghamton, NY: Haworth Press, 1990.

Ogburn, Joyce L. "An Introduction to Outsourcing." *Library Acquisitions: Practice & Theory* 18, no. 3 (1994): 363–66.

O'Neill, Ann L. "How the Richard Abel Co., Inc. Changed the Way We Work." *Library Acquisitions: Practice & Theory* 17, no. 1 (1993): 41–46.

———. "Outsourcing in Hawaii's PLs, Lessons, Unresolved Issues." *Library Hotline* 25, no. 44 (November 4, 1996): 1–2.

Pacey, Philip. *Art Library Manual: A Guide to Resources and Practice*. London; New York: R. R. Bowker, 1977.

Pasterczyk, Catherine E. "A Quantitative Methodology for Evaluating Approval Plan Performance." *Collection Management* 10, no. 1/2 (1988): 25–38.

Phillpot, Clive. "An ABC of Artists' Books Collections." *Art Documentation* 1, no. 6 (1982): cover, 169–82.

Pistorius, Nancy. "Drafting and Implementing Collection Development Policies in Academic Art Libraries." In *Current Issues in Fine Arts Collection Development*. Occasional Papers no. 3, edited by Janet Clark Hazlett, 16–21. Tucson, AZ: Art Libraries Society of North America, 1984.

Porter-Roth, Bud. "How to Write a Request for Proposal: A Step-by-Step Outline for Analyzing Your Needs and Soliciting Bids." *Inform* 5, no. 4 (1991): 26–30.

Posey, Edwin D. "Approval Plans: A Subject Specialist's View," In *Approval Plans and Academic Libraries; An Interpretive Survey*, edited by Kathleen McCullough et al., 132–36. Phoenix, AZ: Oryx Press, 1977.

Presley, Roger L. "Firing an Old Friend, Painful Decisions: The Ethics Between Librarians and Vendors." *Library Acquisitions: Practice & Theory* 17, no. 1 (1993): 53–59.

Price, Larry. "Book Wholesaling: Looking Toward the 21st Century." In *Vendors and Library Acquisitions*, edited by Bill Katz, 21–28. Binghamton, NY: Haworth Press, 1991:

Puccio, Joseph A. *Serials Reference Work*. Englewood, CO: Libraries Unlimited, 1989.

Putnam, Nancy J. "The Impact of Series Publishing on the Domestic Approval Plan." In *Shaping Library Collections for the 1980s*, edited by Peter Spyers-Duran and Thomas Mann, Jr., 115–19. Phoenix, AZ: Oryx Press, 1980.

Quinn, Cathy, and Millman, Sharon. "Love's Labor Lost or How Does an Exhibition Want to Be Remembered?" *Art Documentation* 13, no. 2 (1994): 81–82.

Quinn, Judy. "The New Approval Plan: Surrendering to the Vendor . . . Or in the Driver's Seat?" *Library Journal* 116, no. 15 (September 15, 1991): 38–41.

Racz, Twyla Mueller, and Root, Trudie A. "Trends Affecting Vendor Selection: One Academic Library's Experience." In *Vendors and Library Acquisitions*, edited by Bill Katz, 53–61. Binghamton, NY: Haworth Press, 1991.

Rebarcak, Pam Zager, and Morris, Dilys. "The Economics of Monographs Acquisitions: A Time/Cost Study Conducted at Iowa State University." *Library Acquisitions: Practice & Theory* 20, no. 1 (1996): 65–76.

Reidelbach, John H., and Shirk, Gary M. "Selecting an Approval Plan Vendor II: Comparative Vendor Data." *Library Acquisitions: Practice & Theory* 8, no. 3 (1984): 157–202.

———. "Selecting an Approval Plan Vendor III: Academic Librarians' Evaluation of Eight United States Approval Plan Vendors." *Library Acquisitions: Practice & Theory* 9, no. 3 (1985): 177–260.

Richards, Daniel T. "The Library/Dealer Relationship: Reflections on the Ideal." *Journal of Library Administration* 16, no. 3 (1992): 45–55.

Rossi, Gary J. "Library Approval Plans: A Selected, Annotated Bibliography." *Library Acquisitions: Practice & Theory* 11, no. 1 (1987): 3–34.

Ryland, John. "Collection Development and Selection: Who Should Do It?" *Library Acquisitions: Practice & Theory* 6, no. 1 (1982): 13–17.

SERIALST. serialst@list.uvm.edu.

Sasse, Margo, and Smith, Patricia A. "Automated Acquisitions: The Future of Collection Development." *Library Acquisitions: Practice & Theory* 16, no. 2 (1992): 135–43.

Schatz, Bob, and Graves, Diane J. "Request for Proposal or Run for Protection? Some Thoughts on RFPs from a Librarian and a Bookseller." *Library Acquisitions: Practice & Theory* 20, no. 4 (1996): 421–28.

Schmidt, Karen A. "Capturing the Mainstream: Publisher-Based and Subject-Based Approval Plans in Academic Libraries." *College and Research Libraries* 47, no. 4 (1986): 365–69.

———. "Choosing a Serials Vendor." *Serials Librarian* 14, no. 3/4 (1988): 11–16.

———. *Selection of Library Materials for Area Studies*, Part I: *Asia, Iberia, the Caribbean, and Latin America, Eastern Europe and the Soviet Union, and the South Pacific*, edited by Cecily Johns et al. Chicago: American Library Association, 1990.

Shearouse, Linda. "Museum Publications and Exchange." Conference Report, *Art Documentation* 3, no. 2 (1994): 40–41.

Shirk, Gary M. "Contract Acquisitions: Change, Technology, and the New Library/Vendor Partnership." *Library Acquisitions: Practice & Theory* 17, no. 2 (1993): 145–53.

———. "Outsourced Library Technical Services: The Bookseller's Perspective." *Library Acquisitions: Practice & Theory* 18, no. 4 (1994): 383–95.

———. "The Wondrous Web: Reflections on Library Acquisitions and Vendor Relationships." In *Vendors and Library Acquisitions*, edited by Bill Katz, 1–8. Binghamton, NY: Haworth Press, 1991.

Singer, Loren. "Collection Evaluation in Fine Arts Libraries." In *Current Issues in Fine Arts Collection Development.* Occasional Papers no. 3, edited by Janet Clark Hazlett, 7–15. Tucson, AZ: Art Libraries Society of North America, 1984.

Somers, Sally W. "A Comparison of Two Approval Plan Profiles: A Study in Success and Failure." In *Vendors and Library Acquisitions*, edited by Bill Katz, 161–69. Binghamton, NY: Haworth Press, 1991.

St. Clair, Gloriana, and Treadwell, Jane. "Science and Technology Approval Plans Compared." *Library Resources and Technical Services* 33, no. 4 (1989): 382–92.

Stanford University Libraries. "Redesign of Technical Services." URL: http://www-sul.stanford.edu/depts/diroff/ts/redesign/redesign.html.

Stave, Don. "Art Books on Approval: Why Not?" *Library Acquisitions: Practice & Theory* 7, no. 1 (1983): 5–6.

Subcommittee on Contract Negotiations for Commercial Reproduction of Library and Archival Materials. "Contract Negotiations for the Commercial Microform Publishing of Library and Archival Materials: Guidelines for Librarians and Archivists." *Library Resources and Technical Services* 38, no. 1 (1994): 72–85.

Thomas, Michael. "You Only Get What You Ask For: Tips on Writing an RFP." *Inform* 5, no. 3 (1991): 30–32.

Tuttle, Marcia. "Serials Control, from an Acquisitions Perspective." In *Advances in Serials Management* 2 (1988): 63–94.

Vertrees, Linda S. "Foreign Acquisitions: Frustration and Fun!" In *Vendors and Library Acquisitions*, edited by Bill Katz, 75–81. Binghamton, NY: Haworth Press, 1991.

Wanninger, Patricia Dwyer. "The Sound and Fury of RFP." *Library Journal* 115, no. 21 (1990): 87–89.

Warzala, Martin. "The Evolution of Approval Services." *Library Trends* 42, no. 3 (1994): 515–23.

Weigel, Friedemann. "EDI in the Library Market: How Close Are We?" *Library Administration & Management* 10, no. 3 (1996): 141–46.

Wilkinson, Frances C. "Electronic Products Access for Libraries: What Some Companies Are Doing to Help with Site Licenses." *Against the Grain* 8, no. 5 (1996): 20–23.

Wilkinson, Frances C., and Bordeianu, Sever. "In Search of the Perfect Cover: Using the RFP Process to Select a Commercial Binder." *Serials Review* 23, no. 3 (Fall 1997): 37–47.

Wilkinson, Frances C., and Dean, Barbara C. "Who's Buying, Who's Selling, and What Does the Future Hold: CEOs Speak Out." *Against the Grain* 7, no. 4 (1995): cover, 18–20.

Wilkinson, Frances C., and Thorson, Connie Capers. "The RFP Process: Rational, Educational, Necessary or There Ain't No Such Thing As a Free Lunch," *Library Acquisitions: Practice & Theory* 19, no. 2 (1995): 251–68.

Wilson, Karen A. "Vendor-Supplied Cataloging and Contract Cataloging Services: A Report of the ALCTS Creative Ideas in Technical Services Discussion Group. American Library Association. Midwinter Meeting. Los Angeles, February 1994." *Technical Services Quarterly* 12, no. 2 (1994): 60–63.

Winters, Barbara A. "Bids and Contracts: The State Environment." *Library Acquisitions: Practice & Theory* 15, no. 2 (1991): 231–35.

———. "Catalog Outsourcing at Wright State University: Implications for Acquisitions Managers." *Library Acquisitions: Practice & Theory* 18, no. 4 (1994): 367–73.

———. "NISO + BISAC + SISAC + Z39 + X12 = Chaos: An ALA Preconference on Standards for the Acquisition of Library Materials." *Library Acquisitions: Practice & Theory* 15, no. 1 (1991): 121–23.

Winters, Barbara A., and Flowers, Janet L. "Funding Future Acquisitions: Financial Resources for the 1990s." *Library Acquisitions: Practice & Theory* 15, no. 1 (1991): 125–27.

Wittenberg, R. Charles. "The Approval Plan: An Idea Whose Time Has Gone? And Come Again?" *Library Acquisitions: Practice & Theory* 12, no. 2 (1988): 239–42.

Womack, Kay et al. "An Approval Plan Vendor Review: The Organization and Process." *Library Acquisitions: Practice & Theory* 12, no. 3/4 (1988): 363–78.

List of Contributors

Co-Authors and Editors:

Russ Davidson
Curator of Latin American and Iberian Collections and Professor of Librarianship
University of New Mexico, Albuquerque, New Mexico

Joan C. Griffith
Manager, Electronic Products
Harrassowitz Booksellers & Subscription Agents, Wiesbaden, Germany

Ruth M. Haest
Paying Team Leader, Acquisitions and Serials Department
University of New Mexico, Albuquerque, New Mexico

Linda K. Lewis
Director, Collection Management Department and Associate Professor of
    Librarianship.
University of New Mexico, Albuquerque, New Mexico

Nancy Pistorius
Associate Director, Fine Arts Library
University of New Mexico, Albuquerque, New Mexico

Connie Capers Thorson
Director of the Library and Professor of Library Science
Allegheny College, Meadville, Pennsylvania.

Johann van Reenen
Director, Centennial Science and Engineering Library and Assistant Professor
    of Librarianship
University of New Mexico, Albuquerque, New Mexico

Frances C. Wilkinson
Director, Acquisitions and Serials Department and Associate Professor of
    Librarianship
University of New Mexico, Albuquerque, New Mexico.

INDEX

About the Authors

Frances C. Wilkinson

Professor Wilkinson is the Director of the Acquisitions and Serials Department and Associate Professor of Librarianship at the University of New Mexico, Albuquerque, New Mexico. She received her master of public administration from the University of New Mexico in 1987 and her master of library science from the University of Arizona in 1990. Her experience includes three years as director of the Acquisition and Serials Department, five years as head of the Serials Department, and more than twelve years in various technical and public services positions at the University of New Mexico General Library. She has published and presented workshops and poster sessions on various topics including computer ergonomics, publishing, binding, preservation, reference, acquisitions, and serials. She has served on numerous American Library Association and New Mexico Library Association committees and as a North American Serials Interest Group Executive Board member.

Connie Capers Thorson

Dr. Thorson is the Director of the Library and Professor of Library Science at Allegheny College, Meadville, Pennsylvania. She received her doctorate in English and American literature from the University of New Mexico in 1970 and her master of science in library science from the University of Illinois in Urbana in 1977. Her experience includes fifteen years as the head of the Acquisitions Department and two years as head of the Reference Department at the University of New Mexico General Library before joining the faculty at Allegheny College. She has published on faculty status for librarians, English drama of the Restoration and early eighteenth century, library technology, and the acquisition of library materials.